Minnesota Prehistoric
Archaeology Series No.

T0273178

Southwestern Minnesota Archaeology

12,000 Years in the Prairie Lake Region

Scott F. Anfinson

MINNESOTA HISTORICAL SOCIETY
ST. PAUL

MINNESOTA HISTORICAL SOCIETY PRESS
St. Paul 55102

© 1997 by Minnesota Historical Society. All rights reserved.
No part of this book may be used or reproduced in any manner
whatsoever without written permission, except in the case of
brief quotations embodied in critical articles and reviews. For
information, write to the Minnesota Historical Society Press,
345 Kellogg Boulevard West, St. Paul, Minnesota 55102.

Manufactured in the United States of America
10 9 8 7 6 5 4 3 2 1

International Standard Book Number 0-87351-355-X (paper)

♾ The paper used in this publication meets the minimum
requirements of the American National Standard for Information Sciences—Permanence for Printed Library Materials, ANSI
Z39.48-1984.

Library of Congress Cataloging-in-Publication Data

Anfinson, Scott F.
Southwestern Minnesota archaeology : 12, 000 years in the
Prairie Lake Region / Scott F. Anfinson.
        p. cm. — (Minnesota prehistoric archaeology series ;
no. 14)
        Includes bibliographical references.
        ISBN 0-87351-355-X (paperback)
        1. Indians of North America—Minnesota—Antiquities.
2. Indians of North America—Minnesota—Implements. 3. Stone
implements—Minnesota. 4. Excavations (Archaeology)—
Minnesota. 5. Minnesota—Antiquities. I. Title. II. Series.
        E78.M7A55 1997
        977.6'01—dc21   97-518
                                                          CIP

CREDITS: Maps and drawings, unless otherwise noted, are by
Scott Anfinson. Cover: prairie photograph, Bill Johnson; sherd,
Lee Radzak. Radzak drawings are reproduced courtesy of the
Minnesota Archaeological Society.

This publication is dedicated to
Elden Johnson, friend and teacher.

Contents

Figures and Tables

Acknowledgments

This publication is based on my 1987 doctoral dissertation at the University of Minnesota. Several sections have been deleted or significantly revised here, including the detailed analysis of the Fox Lake site, which appeared as Appendix 1, and the discussion of the early historic period of the Prairie Lake Region. Major additions include information on several important sites that have been investigated more recently, new radiocarbon dates, and the description of the Late Prehistoric Big Stone Phase.

Numerous individuals contributed to the completion of the dissertation and this publication. Excavations at the Fox Lake site were carried out with the help of Mike Michlovic, Donna McMaster, Bob Thompson, Les Peterson, Bill Yourd, Jon Hunn, and Pat Schissel-Anfinson. The Fox Lake Conservation Club, represented by Bob Roesler, generously allowed us to excavate on Weber Island and provided amenities to our field camp. Joe Hudak, Tim Ready, Larry Zimmerman, Signe Snortland-Coles, and Deb Zieglowsky provided essential unpublished data. Colleagues Mike Michlovic, Fred Schneider, Tom Shay, Craig Johnson, Clark Dobbs, Dale Henning, and Leigh Syms offered much needed information, advice, encouragement, or inspiration. The Institute for Minnesota Archaeology and the University of Minnesota Graduate School provided grants for the Fox Lake radiocarbon dates.

No student could ask for a more helpful and knowledgeable dissertation committee; Guy Gibbon, Elden Johnson, Orrin Shane, Herb Wright, and Fred Lukermann deserve special acknowledgment, particularly my advisor Guy Gibbon. Marilyn Holt and Minnesota Historical Society editors Jean Brookins, Ann Regan, Deborah Swanson, and Marilyn Ziebarth, as well as Chris Banks, have been very helpful in smoothing out the many rough edges.

Elden Johnson has been a major influence on my career as an archaeologist. He was my undergraduate advisor at the University of Minnesota; he recommended me for my job at the Minnesota Historical Society after I had completed my master's degree work at Nebraska; he served on my doctoral committee; and, as series editor, he was instrumental in revising this manuscript for publication. His friendship, insight, and advice are sorely missed.

Without the support of my family, none of this would have been possible. This support began very early in my life and was rooted in an intellectual tradition that questioned the world, yet taught that helping one another was the only truly worthwhile pursuit. This tradition was epitomized by my grandfather Ole Anfinson and my great-uncle Alfred I. Johnson. It was passed on to me by my father, nurtured by my mother, and accepted as gospel by my brothers and sister. They have all supported me in my work and they have my eternal gratitude.

My wife Patty and my children have borne the brunt of my archaeological affliction, and they deserve the most thanks. They have endured my selfish pursuit of the past and have lived with the promise that it would never end, only temporarily lessen in intensity with the completion of this publication.

Scott F. Anfinson

Chapter 1

Introduction

This study investigates the cultures of southwestern Minnesota before the inhabitants experienced contact with European explorers or the white settlers that followed. It provides a basic cultural history of the area and explores problems in classification and explanations of cultural change. Although the area is interesting for a variety of reasons, its principal archaeological value resides in the way its geography and past cultures interacted. Southwestern Minnesota was the southern margin of the last continental glaciation. It lies between the Great Plains and the Eastern Woodlands. Its rivers feed into the Mississippi, the Missouri, and the Red, thus connecting it with all three major midcontinental drainage systems.

Archaeological work has been going on in southwestern Minnesota for more than a century. Knowledge about most of this work, however, has not spread beyond a small group of archaeologists who are either intellectually interested in the area or have made environmental impact assessments there. Most of their archaeological reports are unpublished, making them difficult to review.

As this study illustrates, detailed archaeological work really has only begun in southwestern Minnesota and the larger region of which it is a part. While there have been many archaeological investigations, few have employed fine-scale recovery techniques; few have obtained radiocarbon dates; and few have undertaken comprehensive analyses of the recovered materials.

In any scientific inquiry, there are always more questions than answers, and this is especially true with regard to this area's archaeology. *Southwestern Minnesota Archaeology* provides some of the available answers, but also highlights important questions that still need answering. It is a starting place for research, not an ending place.

Defining the Prairie Lake Region

Most Minnesota archaeologists have discussed southwestern Minnesota as a region bounded by the Minnesota and Blue Earth Rivers and the western and southern state lines. While this definition may be useful in general discussions of the state's precontact history, it unsatisfactorily relies on modern political boundaries and convenient topographic features rather than archaeologically meaningful criteria.

Southwestern Minnesota is a part of many regions. To geographers it is the northwestern portion of the Midwest. To wildlife biologists it is the southern end of the Prairie Pothole Region. To botanists it is the northwestern corner of the Prairie Peninsula. None of these regions is especially useful in attempting to understand the prehistory of southwestern Minnesota, however, because none was defined to study early cultures. Even a cursory examination of the archaeological literature suggests that these regions do not reflect the behavioral patterns of the first inhabitants. These inadequacies suggest the need to define a new region, termed the Prairie Lake Region.

The Prairie Lake Region is in the center of the northeastern subarea of the Plains. It encompasses most of southwestern Minnesota, northeastern South Dakota, and north-central Iowa (Figure 1). The region is defined by the congruent distribution of tallgrass prairie vegetation and a concentration of lakes that are shallow, non-alkaline, and greatly varying in size. While the region's boundaries are delimited by distributions of natural elements, this study illustrates that important cultural elements also appear to be contained within the same boundaries. The region has proven to be archaeologically useful, especially for the period ca. 3000 B.C.–A.D. 900, classified by archaeologists as the Middle Prehistoric Period.

The Prairie Lake Region appears to be a useful archaeological region since it exhibits both properties of regions identified by Willey and Phillips (1958:19): archaeological and geographic cohesiveness. While the region's boundaries were established by natural forces, many archaeological factors investigated in this study coincide with the period 3000 B.C.–A.D. 900. The region featured a stable cultural tradition resistant to outside influences, especially during this period.

The Prairie Lake Region is not synonymous with the wildlife botanists' Prairie Pothole Region. The Prairie Pothole Region is a natural region defined by the co-occurrence of grassland and water-filled depressions; it encompasses a large portion of central North America (Figure 1). Its vegetation is mainly mixed-grass prairie, with tallgrass prairie on the eastern edge and fescue prairie at the western edge. Bodies of water in the glacially formed depressions are usually small sloughs rather than lakes. The purpose for its definition was not to study cultures but waterfowl. Because there are no well-defined archaeological complexes distributed throughout the entire Prairie Pothole Region, it is not an archaeologically useful region. The early history of southern Alberta is very different from that of central Iowa. Significant variations in climate, flora, and fauna within the Prairie Pothole Region would have had important adaptive implications for cultures inhabiting the region.

The Prairie Lake Region, on the other hand, has a relatively uniform natural environment and, as this study illustrates, a relatively cohesive cultural history. Its environment contrasts with adjacent regions in vegetation, surface water distribution, and topography. These differences were apparently significant to early cultural orientations.

The region does not extend to the southern limits of the Des Moines Lobe glaciation in central Iowa, because, while this area has extensive sloughs, it does not have large or mid-sized lakes. The drainage pattern in central Iowa also is better developed. Deeply cut river valleys, coupled with hilly topography, promoted extensive woodland development.

The upper James River–lower Sheyenne River region in eastern North Dakota has lakes of varying sizes and grassland vegetation. The lakes, however, tend to be alkaline and the grassland is a mixed-grass prairie. The lower James River region in eastern South Dakota has numerous sloughs but few freshwater lakes; it, too, is a mixed-grass prairie. The Red River Valley region in eastern North Dakota and northwestern Minnesota had extensive wet meadows and tall-grass vegetation, but it lacks lake basins in the flat topography of the Lake Agassiz plain.

Central Minnesota, just northeast of the Prairie Lake Region, has numerous lakes. It featured extensive tallgrass prairie areas at the time of white contact. However, many of the lakes are quite deep (> 10 m), and oak woods or maple-basswood-elm forest dominated the region. Southeastern Minnesota also had extensive tallgrass prairie areas, but the region lacked lakes (except in the Mississippi River bottoms). Too, the well-dissected topography of the Driftless Zone fostered extensive woodlands. The Big Sioux River region of northwestern Iowa, southeastern South Dakota, and extreme southwestern Minnesota was covered with tallgrass prairie. This region lacked lakes because of an absence of Wisconsin glaciation.

Problems of Cultural-Temporal Classification

Utilizing an appropriate cultural-temporal classification scheme is difficult throughout the northeastern Plains because of three major factors: 1) the characterization of the area as a periphery; 2) the inappropriate borrowing of cultural-temporal schemes from distant, dissimilar regions; and 3) a poorly developed absolute chronology.

The unfortunate but understandable characterization of the northeastern Plains as a periphery was made in 1961 by Waldo Wedel:

> In historic times, these prairies were controlled by the Dakotas and Assiniboines, who can be traced back into their Minnesota homeland of late prehistoric and early historic times. The principal archaeological remains now known from this region also resemble those of Minnesota and northern Iowa more closely than they do those of the Middle Missouri-Great Plains area; and their roots clearly lie toward the east rather than the west. In terms of Plains Indian culture, as well as geographically, the region is marginal to the greater culture area with which we are primarily concerned. Accordingly, its designation here as the Northeastern Periphery seems appropriate (W. Wedel 1961:210).

In 1961 relatively little was known about the early history of the northeastern Plains. The contact-period occupants of the region were viewed by many archaeologists as relatively recent immigrants. What was known of the precontact period largely was limited to Woodland mound and village sites, which were viewed as eastern derivations (e.g., Wilford 1955). Also

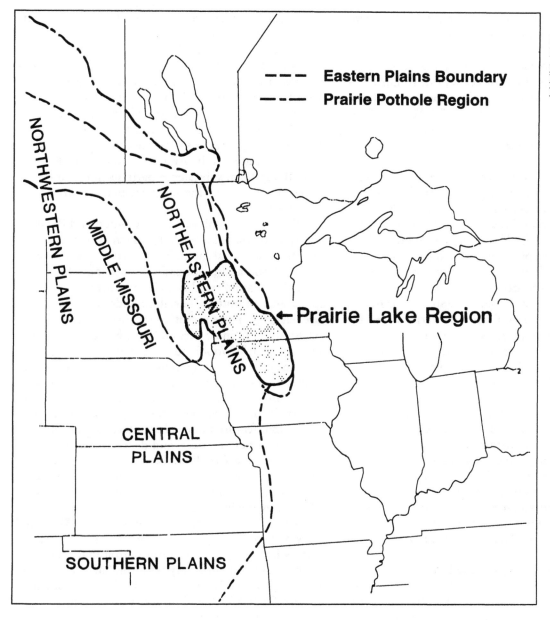

Figure 1. The Prairie Lake Region (stippled), sub-areas of the Plains, and the Prairie Pothole Region.

known were a few horticultural village complexes, such as Mill Creek and Cambria, which were characterized as Mississippian (e.g., Wilford 1945b). (In the public mind, the Mississippian culture that flourished along the Mississippi River often is associated with its temple mound building.)

Less than two decades after Waldo Wedel's overview of Plains archaeology, the implication of the term "periphery" was questioned:

> It has been customary to see the Plains in terms of its heartland (or heartlands) and its peripheries. The latter have been viewed as reflective and derivative of the more significant events in the central

areas. Only recently has it been possible to see that occupants of some of the peripheral regions had distinctive patterns of their own (Caldwell and Henning 1978:136).

Today, the northeastern Plains is known to have contained distinctive cultures of its own. The majority of these cultures are now better characterized as Plains-adapted. As time depth in the northeastern Plains has been extended back from the ceramic period, the inhabitants of the region have been found to resemble Plains bison hunters more than contemporaneous Archaic hunter-gatherer groups in the Eastern Woodlands (Agogino and Frankforter 1960; C. Shay

3

1971:66–73; D. C. Anderson and Semken 1980). Even the ethnographically known Dakota were not simply recent migrants into the Plains. They had occupied the eastern edge of the northeastern Plains (e.g., eastern North Dakota) for hundreds of years prior to European contact and before the Ojibwe settled in northern Minnesota (Michlovic 1980, 1983, 1985; White 1978; G. Anderson 1980). The same may be true for other ethnographically known Plains groups often characterized as recent arrivals.

The early cultures of the northeastern Plains have been oriented more toward the plains than the woodlands, and the area has been a grassland for 9,000 years. This refutes Waldo Wedel's contention that the area is "peripheral" to the Plains and has led to calls for the periphery concept to be dropped (Anfinson 1982b; Wood 1985). The implication of the term—that there are cultural heartlands more worthy of anthropological study (cf. Scaglion 1980:33)—is reason enough for its rejection. Even if the term is used in a purely ecological sense, suggesting that the northeastern Plains is an edge of a natural area, it would seem that a region several hundred kilometers across is more than an edge. It may indeed, however, be a region of transition.

A second problem in cultural-temporal classification in the northeastern Plains is that most frameworks were developed in distant, environmentally dissimilar regions. They have been applied to the northeastern Plains on the basis of similarities in a few artifacts, usually projectile points. This borrowing is often inappropriate, however, because artifact similarities do not mean that lifestyles were similar or that similar artifact forms were even contemporaneous.

For example, the lifeways of the Paleoindian complexes of the American Southwest have been extended intact to the northeastern Plains. (Paleoindian refers to the earliest human occupation in North America and is associated with projectile points that exhibit fluting, parallel flaking, narrow and tapering "lanceolate" forms, and basal grinding.) Yet, only a few fluted points (flattened by the removal of flakes from their faces) have been found in surface collections in the northeastern Plains. Also, no associations between extinct fauna and fluted points of the Southwest are known for the northeastern Plains. Similarly, the Besant complex of the northwestern Plains has been typified as the climax of intensive bison hunting (Frison 1978:223; Kehoe 1974), and Besant sites have been identified in the northeastern Plains based on the presence of Besant-like points (e.g., Nowak and Hannus 1982). However, no large-scale bison drives have

been recorded either ethnographically or archaeologically in the northeastern Plains.

Northeastern Plains Archaic Period components, referring to post-Paleoindian/pre-Woodland complexes, often are defined on the basis of a few ground stone tools or stemmed points recovered at sites lacking ceramics. Yet, there is little evidence for a shift to a more diffuse economic pattern in the northeastern Plains contemporaneous with the economic reorganization that initiated the Archaic Period in the Midwest. If anything, subsistence patterns in the northeastern Plains during the early Archaic period became more focal.

The three-part division of the Woodland Period, referring to first complexes that intensively used ceramics and burial mounds, was developed in the eastern Woodlands, especially Illinois and Ohio. The Early Woodland Period initially was defined by the appearance of pottery, burial mounds, and horticulture, elements more recently recognized to a limited extent in the Archaic Period. Now, however, most definitions of Early Woodland are based solely on the presence of pottery resembling early types previously defined in the eastern Midwest (e.g., *Marion Thick, Black Sand Incised*). The Middle Woodland Period is essentially an expression of the Hopewell Interaction Sphere that featured intensified interregional trade, elaborate burial practices, and distinctive artifact forms. The Late Woodland Period is a post-Hopewellian, pre-Mississippian period of localized developments featuring a complicated cord technology reflected by the impressions on ceramics.

While some ceramics resembling Early Woodland types have been found in the northeastern Plains, there is little radiometric confirmation that these ceramics are contemporary with the Early Woodland of the eastern Midwest or that other aspects of Midwestern Early Woodland lifestyles are present. Hopewellian influences in the northeastern Plains are scattered at best. There are almost no Hopewellian ceramics, few Hopewellian lithics (items made of stone), and relatively unelaborate initial Woodland mortuary expressions. Terminal Woodland ceramics in much of the northeastern Plains lack the complex cord technology found in the Late Woodland cultures farther to the east.

Archaeologists initially assigned the horticultural village cultures of the northeastern Plains to the Mississippian Tradition (e.g., Wilford 1945b). This cultural tradition originally was defined in the central Mississippi River Valley and associated with the extensive Cahokia, Illinois, site near modern-day St. Louis. Sites closely related to Cahokia often are referred to as

Middle Mississippian, while Oneota developments to the north are called Upper Mississippian. The Mississippian categorization has little meaning today in the Prairie Lake Region, where no Middle Mississippian sites are evident, although some interaction with Cahokia is indicated. The horticultural villagers of the northeastern Plains are associated more closely with either the Plains Village or Oneota traditions (Henning 1967).

The third problem in cultural-temporal classification is the lack of a well-developed absolute chronology. This makes it difficult to construct an accurate time framework on which to position the cultural complexes of the northeastern Plains. As of 1990, within the Prairie Lake Region there were less than 70 radiocarbon dates available (Table 1): 39 from Minnesota, 24 from South Dakota, and only 1 from Iowa. All but 11 have been published since 1980. In comparison, the Interstate-270 project in the American Bottoms near St. Louis has provided at least 162 dates (Bareis and Porter 1984:266–269).

Many of the dates from the Prairie Lake Region are either inaccurate (six deviate substantially from expectations and four others are less than 200 years old) or they have poor cultural associations. Most of the apparently accurate dates are associated with Plains Village or Oneota complexes. The dates from Archaic or Woodland sites have few direct relationships with available diagnostic materials. This is a result of the sites' intermixed soil horizons.

The temporal boundaries of the periods and phases used in this study are, for the most part, not firmly established by radiocarbon dating. With the exception of the Late Prehistoric horticultural village phases, only a few reliable dates are present for phase definition. Considering that the lowest standard deviations represent errors of at least +75 years, these few dates give only a rough idea of placement in time.

Keeping in mind the problems discussed above, a relatively simple cultural-temporal framework for the Prairie Lake Region has been developed to organize the cultural complexes herein. The precontact era has been divided into three periods separated by major changes in adaptive strategies. The first is the Early Prehistoric Period (10,000 B.C.–3000 B.C.), which began with the recession of the glaciers and ended with the establishment of the region's modern environment. The regional vegetation during the Early Prehistoric initially featured a series of forests. About 9,000 years ago, these forests were succeeded by prairie. Continued warming and drying desiccated most of the lakes, made woody vegetation scarce, and increased upland game species at the expense of aquatic and for-

est-edge species. The adaptive strategy for the early part of this period is poorly documented archaeologically, but the presence of an environment significantly different from later periods supports an argument for ways of life that were also significantly different. With the establishment of the prairie, focal bison hunting rapidly became the dominant way of life.

The Middle Prehistoric Period (3000 B.C.–A.D. 900) began with the establishment of the Prairie Lake Region environment, the same environment that was later observed by Europeans. Lake basins were filled with water most of the time, and patches of woodland were present in fire-protected areas near lakes and major rivers. This environment offered subsistence options other than bison hunting. While it was still important, a wide range of other animals and plants were also important, especially aquatic species. Major habitation sites were located on islands or peninsulas in the lakes. Variations in the availability of subsistence resources because of short-term climatic fluctuations such as drought may have caused some variations in subsistence-settlement patterns. Nevertheless, the period generally is characterized by long-term cultural stability.

The Late Prehistoric Period (A.D. 900–A.D. 1650) featured a number of horticultural village complexes that in part adapted or adopted the traditional lake-oriented Prairie Lake subsistence-settlement pattern developed in the Middle Prehistoric Period. Bison continued to be an important element in the diet. Dependence on horticultural products varied according to regional location, cultural orientation, wild-food availability, and climatic conditions. The period ended with the rapid cultural change brought on by European contact.

Within the Middle and Late periods, phases are used to depict discrete cultural units of limited durations, limited geographic areas, and distinct artifactual associations. These phases are, in accordance with the Willey and Phillips (1958:22) definition, "the practicable and intelligible units of archaeological study." A paucity of excavated sites in the region makes phase definition more tenuous prior to the Middle Prehistoric period. Therefore, no Early Prehistoric phases are defined formally here, although several are suggested. The terms Paleoindian, Archaic, and Woodland retain some usefulness as time designators with reference to specific traits.

SITE	SAMPLE #	MATERIAL	RCYBP	CORRECTED	ASSOCIATION	REFERENCE
Minnesota						
Cambria (21BE2)	GX-6778	charcoal	815±125	A.D. 1220	Cambria	O. Shane (1981)
Cambria (21BE2)	GX-6779	charcoal	775±130	A.D. 1260	Cambria	O. Shane (1981)
Price (21BE36)	I-8881	charcoal	845±80	A.D. 1210	Cambria	Lass (1980b)
Price (21BE36)	I-8882	charcoal	885±80	A.D. 1180	Cambria	Lass (1980b)
Price (21BE36)	I-8883	charcoal	1000±80	A.D. 1010	Cambria	Lass (1980b)
Mt. Lake (21CO1)	I-9611	bone	225±80	A.D. 1650	?	Lass (1980b)
Mt. Lake (21CO1)	I-9612	bone	185	Recent	?	Lass (1980b)
Hammit (21DL78)	Beta-35178	charcoal	260±50	A.D. 1650	?	Peterson (pc 1989)
Vosburg (21FA2)	I-795	charcoal	160±85	Recent	?	E. Johnson (1964b)
Vosburg (21FA2)	GX-6780	charcoal	670±140	A.D. 1280	Oneota	O. Shane (1981)
Vosburg (21FA2)	GX-6781	charcoal	675±140	A.D. 1260	Oneota	O. Shane (1981)
Vosburg (21FA2)	GX-6782	charcoal	345±140	A.D. 1510	Oneota	O. Shane (1981)
Vosburg (21FA2)	GX-7032	charcoal	585±105	A.D. 1355	Oneota	O. Shane (1981)
Vosburg (21FA2)	GX-7033	charcoal	525±125	A.D. 1410	Oneota	O. Shane (1981)
Vosburg (21FA2)	UGA-4123	charcoal	835±80	A.D. 1210	Oneota	Dobbs (1982)
Vosburg (21FA2)	UGA-4124	charcoal	1035±80	A.D. 1000	Oneota	Dobbs (1982)
Poole (21FA72)	Beta-15253	charcoal	490±140	A.D. 1410	Oneota	Anfinson (1987a)
Rynearson (21FA97)	Beta-15254	charcoal	350±140	A.D. 1490	Oneota	Anfinson (1987a)
Pedersen (21LN2)	I-8689	charcoal	<245	Recent	?	Lass (1980b)
Pedersen (21LN2)	I-8690	charcoal	3495±85	*1800 B.C.	Archaic	Lass (1980b)
Pedersen (21LN2)	I-8982	bone	705±80	A.D. 1280	Lake Benton	Hudak (1976)
Pedersen (21LN2)	I-8983	bone	1135±90	A.D. 920	Lake Benton	Lass (1980b)
Pedersen (21LN2)	I-8984	bone	2050±80	80 B.C.	Fox Lake	Hudak (1976)
Fox Lake (21MR2)	I-13067	bone	620±100	A.D. 1360	Late Prehistoric	Anfinson (1987b)
Fox Lake (21MR2)	I-13068	bone	1480±130	A.D. 580	Fox Lake	Anfinson (1987b)
Fox Lake (21MR2)	I-13069	bone	2500±130	660 B.C.	Archaic	Anfinson (1987b)
Fox Lake (21MR2)	Beta-6644	charcoal	790±70	A.D. 1260	Late Prehistoric	Anfinson (1987b)
Fox Lake (21MR2)	Beta-6645	charcoal	1210±70	A.D. 780	Woodland	Anfinson (1987b)
Fox Lake (21MR2)	Beta-6646	charcoal	1430±70	A.D. 640	Woodland	Anfinson (1987b)
Great Oasis (21MU2)	I-785	charcoal	2980±180	1240 B.C.	?	E. Johnson (1964b)
Great Oasis (21MU2)	WIS-522	charcoal	1050±180	A.D. 990	Great Oasis	Henning and Henning (1978)
Great Oasis (21MU2)	WIS-532	charcoal	975±65	A.D. 1020	Great Oasis	Henning and Henning (1978)
Jackpot Junct (21RW53)	Beta-35176	bone	4890±110	3700 B.C.	Archaic	Peterson (pc 1989)
Jackpot Junct (21RW53)	Beta-35177	charcoal	4730±110	3515 B.C.	Archaic	Peterson (pc 1989)
Round Mound (21TR1)	I-791	wood	1025±100	A.D. 1010	Woodland	E. Johnson (1964b)
Browns Valley (21TR5)	NZA-1102	bone	8790±110	*7824 B.C.	Paleoindian	O. Shane (1991)
Browns Valley (21TR5)	NZA-1808	bone	9049±82	8050 B.C.	Paleoindian	O. Shane (1991)
Alton Anderson (21WW4)	I-12880	bone	4760±100	*3560 B.C.	?	Lothson(1983)
Granite Falls (21YM47)	Beta-27883	bone	6390±100	*5380 B.C.	Archaic	Dobbs (pc 1990)
Granite Falls (21YM47)	Beta-30541	bone	7050±100	5970 B.C.	Archaic	Dobbs (pc 1990)

Table 1. Radiocarbon dates from the Prairie Lake Region as of 1990. Corrections based on Stuiver (1986). *Dates are averaged corrections.

SITE	SAMPLE #	MATERIAL	RCYBP	CORRECTED	ASSOCIATION	REFERENCE
South Dakota						
Oakwood Lakes (39BK7)	A-2222	bone(c)	1220±305	A.D. 785	Woodland	Hannus (1981)
Oakwood Lakes (39BK7)	A-2223	bone(c)	1380±290	A.D. 640	Woodland	Hannus (1981)
Oakwood Lakes (39BK7)	A-2224	bone(a)	1550±140	A.D. 545	Woodland	Hannus (1981)
Oakwood Lakes (39BK7)	A-2224	bone(c)	1580±140	A.D. 420	Woodland	Hannus (1981)
Oakwood Lakes (39BK7)	A-2226	bone(c)	2170±100	*260 B.C.	Woodland	Hannus (1981)
Oakwood Lakes (39BK7)	A-2227	bone(a)	1450±75	A.D. 610	Woodland	Hannus (1981)
Oakwood Lakes (39BK7)	A-2227	bone(c)	1700±95	A.D. 320	Woodland	Hannus (1981)
Oakwood Lakes (39BK7)	A-2228	bone(a)	1665±70	A.D. 395	Woodland	Hannus (1981)
Oakwood Lakes (39BK7)	A-2229	bone(a)	1750±80	*A.D. 280	Woodland	Hannus (1981)
Oakwood Lakes (39BK7)	A-2229	bone(c)	1700±90	A.D. 320	Woodland	Hannus (1981)
Oakwood Lakes (39BK7)	A-2230	bone(a)	1645±90	A.D. 410	Woodland	Hannus (1981)
Oakwood Lakes (39BK7)	A-2230	bone(c)	2230±245	*300 B.C.	Woodland	Hannus (1981)
Winter (39DE5)	WIS-1358	charcoal	400±70	A.D. 1465	Plains Village?	Haug (1983b)
Winter (39DE5)	WIS-1359	charcoal	1180±70	A.D. 860	Woodland	Haug (1983b)
Winter (39DE5)	WIS-1371	charcoal	1100±70	A.D. 940	Woodland/PV?	Haug (1983b)
Winter (39DE5)	WIS-1372	charcoal	1250±70	A.D. 770	Woodland	Haug (1983b)
Winter (39DE5)	WIS-1373	charcoal	1950±70	A.D. 50	Woodland	Haug (1983b)
Hilde (39LK7)	I-14246	charcoal	4040±100	2580 B.C.	Archaic	Lueck et al. (1987)
Hilde (39LK7)	I-12298	bone	3800±110	2240 B.C.	Archaic	Lueck et al. (1987)
Hartford Beach (39RO5)	WIS-1868	charcoal	830±70	A.D. 1220	Plains Village	Haug (1983b)
Hartford Beach (39RO5)	WIS-1370	charcoal	650±70	A.D. 1290	Plains Village	Haug (1983b)
DeSpiegler (39RO23)	I-779	bone	1350±110	A.D. 660	Woodland	E. Johnson (1964b)
DeSpiegler (39RO23)	I-792	bark	670±110	A.D. 1290	Woodland?	E. Johnson (1964b)
Sisseton Md (39RO26)	I-7186	charcoal	830±85	A.D. 1220	Woodland	Sigstad and Sigstad (1973b)
Iowa						
Caseys Mound (13WB6)	M-1343	bone	785±100	A.D. 1250	Great Oasis	Tiffany (1981)

Table 1 (continued). Radiocarbon dates from the Prairie Lake Region as of 1990. Corrections based on Stuiver (1986). Bone dates: a = appetate, c = collagen. *Dates are averaged corrections.

Explanations of Cultural Change

Archaeologists in the Plains and the Midwest often have used climatic change as an explanation for significant cultural changes (e.g., Griffin 1960; Baerreis et al. 1976). Most of these studies use a model of post-glacial climatic periods developed by Reid Bryson and various associates (e.g., Bryson and Wendland 1969; Bryson, Baerreis, and Wendland 1970). The Bryson model may be flawed, however, in that it depicted all climatic changes as being rapid and global (cf. Anfinson and Wright 1990). Furthermore, even the valid parts of the Bryson model often are misused by archaeologists who find climatic change a convenient method of explaining cultural change largely because the archaeological record is so incomplete.

Cultural changes can indeed be linked to climatic changes. However, reasons for the significant cultural changes that are evident in the Prairie Lake Region usually cannot be attributed to a single factor. Climatic change may have played a role in the alteration of subsistence-settlement systems, especially during the Pleistocene-Holocene transition or in horticulturally reliant societies. Nevertheless, many of the most important cultural changes were clearly a result of other factors. These include the diffusion of ideas, local innovations, the introduction of better varieties of maize, widespread population pressure, political dominance, and migration.

Even the effects of climatic change on precontact horticultural societies often are overstated. Plains archaeologists, in particular, are burdened with the image of the 1930s drought, a vivid picture of dust storms, dry stream beds, and withered crops. Many of the problems associated with the 1930s drought, however, are not applicable to precontact droughts or economies. Soil erosion and dust storms in the 1930s resulted largely from poor farming and grazing practices.

Early horticulturists only used a small amount of land for crops at any one time, and their crop lands were usually in river valleys where soil moisture was less affected by rainfall variations. Their crops were also less specialized, with a single village planting many varieties of maize with differential reactions to drought and temperature. Economic systems also were not as interdependent. An adverse year in one region may have had little effect on the people in a nearby region.

Drought is, and was, not uncommon in the western Midwest. In a normal human lifetime at least one severe drought probably occurred, even during favorable climatic episodes. However, alternative subsistence strategies were present in the cultural memories of horticultural societies, allowing them to survive without horticulture. Severe recurring droughts, such as those predicted by Bryson for the Pacific Climatic Episode (characterized by increased westerly winds which caused increased dryness in the period A.D. 1200–1500), would no doubt have required subsistence-settlement changes in drought-sensitive areas like the eastern Plains. The fact that some groups in southern Minnesota and the Dakotas continued to practice horticulture throughout the period, however, indicates that it was not necessary to abandon it completely. Cultural dislocations in the northeastern Plains therefore cannot be attributed to climatic reasons alone.

Ethnographic models of cultural changes also present difficulties in our attempts to understand the precontact cultures of the Prairie Lake Region. Drastic changes occurred in cultures in and around the region in the early nineteenth century. These changes limit our ability to accurately model precontact lifeways based on historically known cultures. This is especially true because the region's dominant groups at the time of contact, the Yankton and Yanktonai, are the least known of the Dakota. The best available ethnographic information is for the Eastern Dakota or Santee. They are relatively recent year-round inhabitants of the region who were undergoing rapid cultural changes during the period when most pre-reservation accounts of them were written.

Based on accounts of Eastern Dakota groups, the dominant lifeway in the Prairie Lake Region was one of feast or famine, with particular emphasis on famine after the advancing frontier of Euro-Americans reduced the numbers of wild game (e.g., Woolworth and Woolworth 1980:86; Pond 1986:31; Meyer 1967:23). Major villages were restricted to the Minnesota River Valley and the shores of Big Stone and Traverse Lakes. The time of feasting was in summer and fall when bison were plentiful in the region's western part and when certain wild plant foods such as prairie turnips and water lilies were abundant. Hard times came in winter and early spring when small bands of Dakota pursued deer and small game in or near the river valleys. When the bison began to disappear in the midnineteenth century, hard times ruled even in the summer.

What is known about the Dakota subsistence-settlement pattern may help us to understand some of the resources that were available, especially the plant foods and how to obtain them. What we do know, however, has limited usefulness in helping to construct a comprehensive subsistence-settlement model for a time before the fur trade. After the fur trade, native inhabitants experienced rapid acculturation and dependence on resources from outside the Prairie Lake Region. Movements of many different tribes throughout the Midwest led to constant conflict.

The Prairie Lake Region Perspective

In terms of vegetation and precontact cultures, the Prairie Lake Region is more a part of the Plains than a part of the Eastern Woodlands. It is, however, a region of transitions. It is intermediate to the hardwood forests and the shortgrass and midgrass prairies. It is often a region of plentiful water, but the numerous lakes are shallow and susceptible to drought. Its watersheds are linked to three major continental drainage systems, but water flows out of the region, not through it.

Because of its location at the edge of the two major midcontinent vegetational associations, prairie and woodland, most archaeologists have assumed that the cultures of the northeastern Plains were peripheral expressions of major cultural developments to the east or west. This conclusion was based not only on a poor understanding of the northeastern Plains cultures, but on an assumption that there were only a few cultural heartlands in the midcontinent.

This study illustrates that at least one region of the northeastern Plains featured cultural complexes that were more than diffuse reflections of cultural developments on the central Plains or in the Mississippi River Valley. During the Middle Prehistoric Period, the cultures of the Prairie Lake Region developed unique orientations. They resisted outside influences that had widespread success in adjacent regions. A regional perspective on northeastern Plains cultural development allows us not only to distinguish unique cultural expressions, but to examine cultural change within an appropriate spatial framework.

Chapter 2

Environment of the Prairie Lake Region

Although cultural systems emerge out of the complex interactions of many variables . . . technology and environment together have powerful effects. If cultural systems are to adapt and survive for a period of time, they must establish relatively stable relationships with their environment (Beals et al. 1977:219).

The only element of the Prairie Lake Region landscape that has remained relatively unchanged since the beginning of Euro-American settlement is landform. Vegetation, fauna, and surface water have changed greatly. Where prairie grasses once covered the ground as far as the eye could see, agricultural fields now form patchworks divided by towns, roads, fence lines, and farm groves. Cattle graze in pastures where bison once roamed. Many lakes have been drained. Rivers have been dammed or straightened. The landscapes known to early Prairie Lake Region inhabitants are now only memories. Even if accurate renditions of those landscapes can be constructed on the basis of early written accounts and paleoecological data, the tendency is to form falsely synchronic, static images. In reality the environmentally dynamic Prairie Lake Region experienced dramatic seasonal and long-term changes in its vegetation and surface hydrology over 12,000 years.

The Prairie Lake Region is a natural region defined by a congruent distribution of tallgrass prairie vegetation and numerous shallow lakes. Its landforms are the result of the most recent glaciation and the vegetation of a relatively stable climate over the last 5,000 years. It offered rich and varied resources for hunter-gatherer and early horticultural groups. Successful adaptation entailed understanding where and when to find the resources and how short- and long-term changes affected their availability.

Glacial Geology

Discussion of the Prairie Lake Region environment must begin with glacial geology. The area's topography and hydrology are products of glaciation, and its boundaries follow features of Late Glacial-era origin that delimit the distribution of lakes and, to some degree, vegetation. Bedrock geology is unimportant to this study because most of the bedrock is unsuitable for the manufacture of chipped stone tools and is deeply buried by till (unstratified glacial drift containing clay, sand, gravel, and boulders). The region's most extensive bedrock outcrops are granitic rocks along the deeply cut Minnesota River Valley near the river's headwaters. Small outcrops of Cretaceous rocks occur in the Prairie Lake interior, principally in northern Iowa. Sioux Quartzite outcrops are found in northeastern Cottonwood County and western Nicollet County in southwestern Minnesota (Morey 1981).

Two bedrock-based features, the Minnesota River Lowland and the Coteau des Prairies, shaped the Late Wisconsin glaciation of the Prairie Lake Region. The Coteau is a wedge-shaped highland with its point near the South Dakota-North Dakota state line about 65 km west of Minnesota. Its indistinct base extends for 240 km across southeastern South Dakota and southwestern Minnesota approximately even with the northern Iowa state line.

The Minnesota River Lowland is dominated by the broad, deeply entrenched Minnesota River Valley. The river is a classic underfit stream, whose discharge potential could not have carved the impressive valley through which it has flowed in the 12,000 years since the retreat of the glaciers. Instead, the valley was excavated largely by Glacial River Warren, which was Glacial Lake Agassiz's only outlet during its early history.

At least three layers of glacial drift underlie the Late Wisconsin drift in parts of the Prairie Lake Region. A pre-Wisconsin drift deposited by ice from southern Manitoba is the lowest and is often referred to as Old Gray Drift. It is exposed only in a few locations along the Minnesota and Big Sioux river valleys. The succeeding reddish-colored Hawk Creek Till is the only recognized drift of Lake Superior origin in the region. Of Early Wisconsin age, it is discontinuously distributed throughout the region's northern half. Overlying Hawk Creek Till in many areas is Granite Falls Till, exposures of which are found almost continuously along the Minnesota River Valley. The till probably was deposited by the Wadena Lobe, which subsequently built the massive Alexandria Moraine complex in west-central Minnesota between 20,000 and 35,000 years ago (Matsch 1972:553; Matsch et al. 1972:12; Wright 1972:524–25).

The final glacial advance through the Prairie Lake Region is the most important to this study, because it not only was responsible for most of the landforms, but it determined when the region became habitable for human groups. The last glaciation of the Prairie Lake Region was accomplished by a tongue of Laurentide ice that descended south along the Red River Lowlands about 17,000 years ago and split into eastern and western lobes when it encountered the head of the Coteau des Prairies. The western lobe followed the James River Lowland, and the eastern lobe moved southeast through the Minnesota River Lowland (Wright et al. 1973:170).

As the ice of the eastern lobe thickened, it advanced out, overriding the Alexandria Moraine to the north and the eastern flank of the Coteau des Prairies to the west. A southern extension of the lobe reached a maximum near Des Moines, Iowa, about 14,000 years ago. Thus, the parent lobe is referred to as the Des Moines Lobe (Ruhe 1969:61). The maximum is defined and delimited topographically by the Bemis Moraine which forms a great "V" between Roberts County, South Dakota, Des Moines, Iowa, and the Twin Cities area in eastern Minnesota (Figure 2).

The relatively rapid wastage of the Des Moines Lobe occurred in just 2,000 years. It took place in a series of recessional phases marked by the Altamont, Humboldt, Algona, and Big Stone moraines (Figure 2). By 13,000 years ago, the Des Moines Lobe had retreated from Iowa. By 12,500 years ago, the Mankato area in southern Minnesota was ice-free. By 12,000 years ago, the entire Prairie Lake Region was uncovered and Glacial Lake Agassiz was forming at the southern end of the Red River Lowland (Wright et al.

1973:181–82; Fenton et al. 1983:52; Clayton and Moran 1982). While the glacier itself was gone from the Prairie Lake Region by 10,000 B.C., stagnant ice remained buried in the drift for perhaps several thousand years. The gradual melting of this ice led to topographic instability and may have affected local climate (Wright et al. 1973:171; Steece 1972). The till deposited by the Des Moines Lobe is referred to as Cary Till in Iowa (Ruhe 1969) and New Ulm Till in Minnesota (Matsch 1972:554).

At the northern edge of the Prairie Lake Region, Glacial Lake Agassiz formed when the melt-water of the retreating glacier ponded behind the Big Stone Moraine. Earlier, a few smaller glacial lakes such as Minnesota and Benson formed in the region's interior during the retreat of the Des Moines Lobe (see Figure 6, Chapter 4), but these lakes were relatively short lived (Matsch and Wright 1969:125–26; Diedrick and Rust 1979). During the initial formation of Lake Agassiz, several outlets broached the Big Stone Moraine, but a single outlet near Browns Valley eventually captured the drainage. This outlet was paved with boulders, temporarily preventing erosion and allowing Lake Agassiz to expand to the Herman Beach about 11,700 years ago. With increased melt-water input as the lake followed the ice north, the boulder pavement finally eroded, and the lake rapidly drained, retreating to the Campbell Beach. About 11,000 years ago, an eastern outlet to Lake Superior opened, and the southern outlet was abandoned. Lake Agassiz temporarily stabilized at a series of lower beaches over the next 1,000 years (Fenton et al. 1983:68).

A readvance of the Rainy Lobe about 9,900 years ago closed the eastern outlet and caused Lake Agassiz to flood its more recent beaches. It stabilized once again at the Campbell Beach, and the River Warren (Minnesota River) spillway at the southern end once again opened. The Rainy Lobe retreated about 9,500 years ago, re-opening the eastern outlet and causing rapid drainage and the final abandonment of the southern outlet. By 9,000 years ago, Lake Agassiz had retreated north of the Canadian border (Fenton et al. 1983:71).

Hydrology

The distribution, structure, and form of the lakes of the Prairie Lake Region are the principal water features of interest to this study. Understanding the seasonal and yearly variations of the lakes is critical to understanding patterns of subsistence and settlement

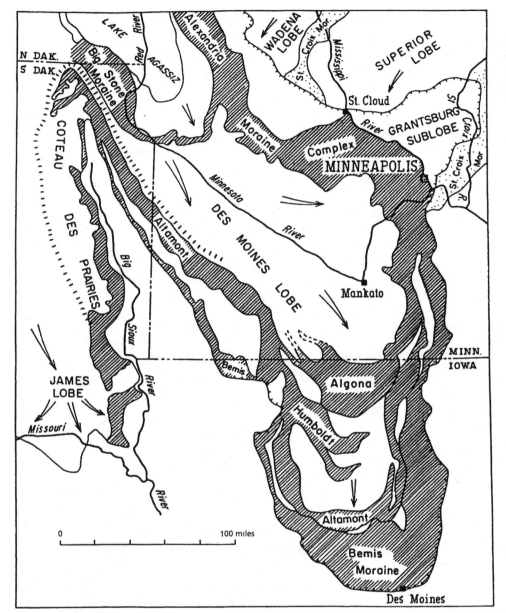

Figure 2. Glacial geology of the Prairie Lake Region showing terminal moraines (shaded) and direction of ice advances (arrows) (from Wright 1972).

in the region. These variations affected the availability of faunal and floral resources, as well as transportation, defense, and the availability of water for drinking and cooking.

A lake may be defined as a basin of at least 4 ha (10 acres) that is usually filled or partially filled with water. This definition does not focus on the water in the basin, but on the basin itself. In order to construct a model of the environment long ago, the natural cycle of significant lake-level fluctuation must be considered. The ephemeral nature of most of the Prairie Lake Region's lakes, in fact, is one of its distinguishing features.

The Prairie Lake Region of Minnesota contains the best readily available data regarding original lake distribution. At least 147,410 ha in 3,175 basins of at least 4 ha were present at the time of Euro-American settlement (Minnesota, Waters Section 1968). In South Dakota, there are currently 226 water-filled basins of at least 8 ha ([South Dakota] 1977). In Iowa, Harlan and Speaker (1969:2–5) listed 52 natural lakes, with the smallest 5.2 ha (13 acres).

There are 91 lake basins in the Prairie Lake Region more than 400 ha in area and 34 basins more than 800 ha. Table 2 lists the region's large and very large lakes. The two largest lakes are Traverse and Big

LAKE	AREA (acres/hect.)	LOCATION (county)
Traverse	11,600/4695	Traverse, MN; Roberts, SD
Big Stone	11,185/4527	Big Stone, MN; Roberts, SD
Swan	9246/2782	Nicollet, MN
Thompson	8870/3590	Kingsbury, SD
Lac qui Parle	8400/3400	Chippewa/Lac qui Parle, MN
Heron	8251/3339	Jackson, MN
Poinsett	7866/3183	Hamlin, SD
Marsh	6100/2469	Big Stone/Lac qui Parle, MN
Spirit	5684/2300	Dickinson, IA
Preston	5216/2111	Kingsbury, SD
Whitewood	4966/2009	Kingsbury, SD
Kampeska	4813/1948	Codington, SD
Waubay North	4769/1930	Day, SD
Bitter	4173/1689	Day, SD
West Okoboji	3939/1594	Dickinson, IA
Clear	3643/1474	Cerro Gordo, IA
Albert	3610/1461	Hamlin/Kingsbury, SD
Shetek	3596/1455	Murray, MN
Storm	3080/1247	Buena Vista, IA

LAKE	DEPTH(ft./m.)	LOCATION (county)
West Okoboji	132/40.5	Dickinson, IA
Ten Mile	50/15.2	Otter Tail, MN
Pickerel	43/13.2	Day, SD
Fish	32/9.8	Cottonwood, MN
Cochcrane	27/8.3	Dueul, SD
Enemy Swim	26/8	Day, SD
Spirit	25/7.7	Dickinson, IA
East Okoboji	24/7.4	Dickinson, IA
South Silver	22/6.7	Martin, MN

Table 2. Surface areas of the largest lakes in the Prairie Lake Region (top) and Prairie Lake Region lakes more than 6 m (20 feet) deep.

Stone along the Minnesota-South Dakota border. Both were formed when tributary streams dammed the outlet river valley of Lake Agassiz. The largest lake not in a river valley in the Prairie Lake Region is Swan Lake in Nicollet County, Minnesota; it is 3,765 ha in extent.

One of the most striking aspects of the lakes of the Prairie Lake Region is their shallowness. Most are not more than 3 m deep, and most have mean depths under 1.5 m. Only nine lakes are more than 6 m deep, and only three are more than 10 m deep (Table 2). Lake West Okoboji in northern Iowa is exceptionally deep for the region, with a maximum depth of 40.5 m. The second deepest lake is Ten Mile Lake at the extreme northern end of the region in Otter Tail County, Minnesota, with a maximum depth of 15.2 m.

Almost all of the natural lakes of the Prairie Lake Region are direct or indirect products of the last glaciation (Zumberge 1952). Most of the basins were formed by irregular depositions of till. The few deep lakes were formed by the melting of ice blocks buried in till or outwash. A number of lakes along the Bemis Moraine formed when sediment dammed melt-water channels. The only natural lakes in the region of non-glacial origin are oxbow lakes in the river bottoms, mainly found in the Minnesota River Valley.

Since their initial formation more than 11,000 years ago, the lakes of the Prairie Lake Region have undergone drastic water-level fluctuations. The gain and loss of water in the basins are principally a result of precipitation and evaporation (Manson et al.

1968:4). Most lake levels are affected very little by ground water interchange, except in areas where the lakes occupy basins in outwash aquifers such as on the Coteau in eastern South Dakota ([South Dakota] 1977). The shallowness of the basins and the lack of groundwater interchange make most of the region's lakes very susceptible to severe level reductions in times of drought.

Each lake is nevertheless unique. Variation in watershed size, type of drift basin occupied, and steepness of surrounding slopes are important factors in water-level fluctuation. The permeability of the adjacent soil is also important because it determines the amount of runoff. Permeability depends on the parent material of the soil, type of vegetational cover, existing degree of water saturation, rainfall intensity, and whether the soil is frozen during the spring snowmelt. Short-term droughts may lower some lake levels, while other lakes may experience a slight rise depending on local conditions. Long-term droughts, however, reduce lake levels throughout the region, and some basins completely dry up. Such droughts are not rare in the Prairie Lake Region. Fluctuations of 5 m or more in some lakes may be expected at least once during a human lifetime (Rothrock and Ullery 1938). Radle's (1981) study of Medicine Lake in northeastern South Dakota indicates that droughts were especially frequent and severe between 9,000 and 3,500 years ago.

Water quality in the Prairie Lake Region is highly variable, but most lakes are hard water with dissolved chemical concentrations of over 200 ppm. Salts are concentrated in lakes by evaporation, so the alkalinity tends to increase with the increased aridity from east to west. Prairie lakes become more alkaline in periods of low water (Wilson 1958; Radle 1981). True alkaline lakes are not common in the region and largely are limited to the Coteau in eastern South Dakota. These alkaline lakes contained freshwater until 9,000 years ago (Radle et al. 1989).

Although thousands of water-filled basins still exist in the Prairie Lake Region, at least half of the basins have been drained. In Minnesota 90 percent in some counties have been drained; 60 percent is perhaps an average figure for all of southwestern Minnesota (Borchert and Yaeger 1969:25). The total area drained is a lower percentage, however, because small basins tend to be drained more readily than large basins. The region's largest drained lake is probably Lake Great Oasis in northwestern Murray County, Minnesota, which has a basin of about 600 ha. Lakes in Iowa have suffered drainage at least as extensive as those in southwestern Minnesota. The eastern South Dakota and west-central Minnesota portions of the

region generally have less than 50 percent of their basins drained.

The Prairie Lake Region contains thousands of small potholes and seasonal ponds under 4 ha in size. These bodies of water represented significant resources to early inhabitants, especially for their waterfowl habitat. Stewart and Kantrud (1971) classified these small bodies of water on the basis of vegetational zones and permanency. Lensink (1984) studied use by early inhabitants of these small bodies of water in northern Iowa.

Numerous streams drain the Prairie Lake Region, as illustrated in Figure 3. Several major rivers have their headwaters there: the Minnesota, Red, Des Moines, and Big Sioux. The region is part of three major continental drainage systems: the Mississippi, the Missouri, and the Red (to Hudsons Bay).

The Minnesota River is the region's most distinctive river because of its impressive valley and extensive bottom lands. The valley is up to 8 km wide and has vertical drops through a series of terraces of up to 77 m. The valley's upper end features several large lakes formed by sediment dams built by tributary streams. Numerous small lakes are found throughout the remaining length of the river on both the floodplain and higher terraces. The river is 570 km long from Browns Valley in extreme western Minnesota to its junction with the Mississippi River at St. Paul in extreme eastern Minnesota. Its watershed includes 44,000 square km; all but 5,200 square km are in Minnesota. Only the river's upper half is in the Prairie Lake Region, but this segment contains almost all of the river's major tributaries.

The upper Minnesota River has three principal drainage areas: Northern, Western, and Southern (Waters 1977). The Northern area contains the Chippewa and Pomme de Terre rivers, which have their headwaters on the Alexandria Moraine. The Pomme de Terre flows through a well-defined glacial melt-water channel, intersecting several lakes within the valley. The Chippewa River follows a meandering path and has numerous small tributaries.

The Western drainage of the upper Minnesota River has four major tributaries: the Lac qui Parle, Yellow Medicine, Redwood, and Cottonwood. All of these rivers have their heads on the eastern edge of the Coteau des Prairies and are characterized by swift stretches near their headwaters as they descend the Coteau. Once on the till plain, they follow slow, meandering courses before culminating in brief, steep descents to the Minnesota River through deep gorges (Waters 1977:290).

Figure 3. Major rivers in and around the Prairie Lake Region.

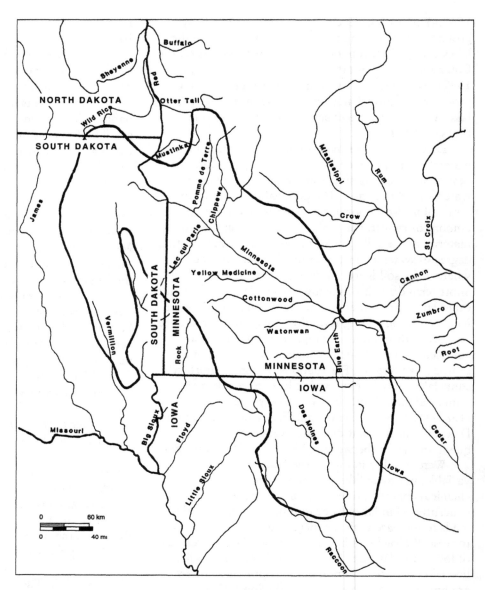

The Southern drainage of the upper Minnesota River is dominated by three rivers: the Blue Earth, Watonwan, and Le Sueur. Only the Blue Earth River actually enters the Minnesota; the other two intersect the Blue Earth a few miles above its mouth. The Watonwan flows from the west and the Le Sueur from the east. The Blue Earth flows north, with its headwaters near the Minnesota-Iowa state line. This drainage is flanked by drainages that flow south (Waters 1977:281). Two smaller streams of note that also flow into the Blue Earth River are Elm and Center creeks. Both enter the river from the west near its headwaters.

Because the region it drains is so susceptible to drought and because of the limited interaction with large groundwater reservoirs, the upper Minnesota River has a highly variable flow both seasonally and from year to year. At Montevideo, near the river's upper end, a flow of 680 cubic meters per second (cms) was measured on May 10, 1952, but the river did not flow at all there for a number of days during dry periods in 1933, 1934, and 1936 (Minnesota State Planning Agency 1970:98). Flooding is common in the spring and also during periods of heavy rainfall in the summer and fall. The extensive drainage of lake basins probably has led to higher and more frequent floods than in earlier times.

The Minnesota River is slightly alkaline (200 ppm) during most of the year, with the alkalinity increasing at times of low water. It is also a very turbid stream, except in the late fall. Much of the suspended sediment is caused by erosion of cultivated fields. It was no doubt less turbid prior to white settlement.

Another of the major river systems which drains the Prairie Lake Region is the Des Moines. Both major branches of the river head in southwestern Minnesota. The West Fork begins near Lake Shetek in Murray County and flows southeast along the base of the Coteau des Prairies. Unlike most other rivers in southwestern Minnesota, the West Fork of the Des Moines flows through a series of lakes and lacks the swift headwaters of the rivers that flow down the flanks of the Coteau (Waters 1977:297). The West Fork initially follows a shallow valley, but by the time it reaches the Iowa border it has cut an impressive gorge up to 46 m deep. It is joined by the shorter East Fork just north of Fort Dodge, Iowa. The East Fork headwaters are in eastern Jackson County. The Des Moines and its tributaries drain most of the Iowa portion of the Prairie Lake Region, although the headwaters of the Iowa and Cedar rivers in the east and the Little Sioux River in the west are also in the region. After the Des Moines leaves the Prairie Lake Region, it flows southeast for another 320 km to the Mississippi.

Besides the Des Moines and the Minnesota, the two other rivers of major importance to the Prairie Lake Region are the Big Sioux and the Red River of the North. Although the Big Sioux flows through only a small portion of the region and the Red is technically outside of the region, tributaries to these rivers link the region with two major continental drainage systems.

The Big Sioux has its headwaters on the top of the Coteau in northeastern South Dakota and bisects the Coteau in its path south. All but the headwaters of the Big Sioux drainage were unglaciated during the Late Wisconsin so, for the most part, the land surrounding the Big Sioux contains no lakes. The Big Sioux enters the Missouri River just above Sioux City, Iowa.

Because of an early cartographical irregularity, the Red River is called the Bois de Sioux as it leaves Lake Traverse. It officially becomes the Red at the mouth of the Otter Tail River. The Red River drains only a small portion of the Prairie Lake Region in the extreme north.

Climate

Climate was ultimately responsible for the creation of the Prairie Lake Region. It not only caused the glaciation which formed the lake basins, but it was the principal factor in the origin and maintenance of the tallgrass vegetation. Borchert (1950) illustrated the importance of "the master hand of climate" with regard to the distribution of the Prairie Peninsula earlier defined by Transeau (1935). Bryson (1966) provided additional detail regarding the climatic factors delimiting the tallgrass prairie.

The Prairie Lake Region, located at the northwestern edge of the Prairie Peninsula, has a continental climate characterized by marked seasonal variations in temperature and precipitation. In winter the flow of air is generally out of Canada, producing a cold, dry climate. Occasional bursts of Arctic air bring extreme cold, while moisture-laden southern or western air brings heavy snowfall. In summer, the predominant flow of air from the Gulf of Mexico results in a warm, moist climate, with summer-like weather occasionally extending into late fall. Hot, dry weather is not infrequent in the summer because of an air flow originating in the southwestern United States.

In the yearly cycle July is usually the hottest month, with mean highs varying from the low 80s (degrees Fahrenheit) at the north end of the Prairie Lake Region to the high 80s at the south end. There is a slight increase in summer temperatures from east to west, with maximums reaching more than 100° and as high as 115° (Kuehnast 1974; Waite 1974; Hodge 1974).

The coldest time of the year is January, when mean lows ranging from 0°F in the north to 10° in the south. Mean January highs are in the low 20s in the north and just below freezing in the south. There is also an east-west gradation in winter temperatures, with colder temperatures being found in the west, the opposite of summer. Low temperature extremes in winter can reach 50° below zero, excluding wind chill.

The first freezing temperatures occur in late September in the northern Prairie Lake Region and in early October in the southern part. The last freeze generally takes place in mid-May in the north and as early as late April in the south. The frost-free season, important to horticulture, varies from 130 to 150 days from north to south. Lakes freeze over by late November in the north and by mid-December in the south. Ice usually leaves northern lakes by mid-April and the southern lakes by late March.

Two-thirds of the region's annual precipitation falls between May and September, the effective growing season in the Prairie Lake Region. Rainfall amounts vary east to west, with the eastern edge of the region receiving 75 cm per year and the western edge 50 cm per year. June is usually the wettest month and January the driest. Over 50 cm of rain have been recorded in one 24-hour period. Snowfall ranges from 75–100 cm per year throughout the region; an average of at least 2.5 cm of snow is present in the region for 80 to 90 days.

Blizzards, thunderstorms, and tornadoes are common occurrences, causing extensive damage and even loss of life. Thunderstorms and tornadoes are most common in early summer. Thunderstorms are characterized by strong winds, frequent lightning, heavy rainfall, occasional hail, and significant drops in temperature. Blizzards can occur from early November to mid-April, featuring combinations of significant snowfall, temperatures of 20° or less, and winds more than 35 mph (Kuehnast 1974:707). Many blizzards last three or four days and are characterized by extremely low wind chills and poor visibility.

Drought is also a regular occurrence in the Prairie Lake Region. Moderate droughts occur once every few years and severe droughts perhaps several times in a human lifetime. Severe droughts can result from moderate droughts persisting several years in succession. The abnormally hot, dry weather of droughts causes a hydrological imbalance in the region that may not be corrected even by several heavy rains (Felch 1978:26). Occasional heavy rains do not necessarily ease crop stress during a drought, since much of the water rapidly runs off without replenishing soil moisture. Drought is a regional phenomenon; it is not unusual for one region to have adequate rainfall, while adjacent regions are dry.

Historic droughts in the Prairie Lake Region do not follow a regular cycle. In the last 150 years, there have been at least six major droughts, with a number of moderate ones irregularly spaced between. Severe droughts occurred in 1827–35, 1862–63, 1881–95, 1906–13, 1931–40, and 1952–57. The droughts of 1910 and 1936 were especially severe.

The effects of drought on the Prairie Lake Region vary according to local conditions. In general, moderate droughts cause a lowering of lake levels and some vegetational stress, especially to woody plants. Severe droughts cause many of the lakes to dry up completely and woody vegetation to die in particularly dry areas. More prairie fires occur during droughts, causing even more destruction of trees. Cultivated crops are particularly susceptible to the adverse effects of drought, because most are not adapted to severe water stress.

Paleoecology

Most lakes within the Prairie Lake Region are too shallow for reliable palynological analysis (the study of pollen and spores). Yet, studies of the region's deep lakes and of sites just outside the region provide enough data to reconstruct a general picture of paleoecological changes over the last 12,000 years. Van Zant's (1976, 1979) study of Lake West Okoboji in northern Iowa is particularly helpful, as are Watts and Bright's (1968) study of Pickerel Lake and Radle's (1981) study of Medicine Lake in northeastern South Dakota. The only published palynological study of the post-glacial period in the Minnesota portion of the Prairie Lake Region is Jelgersma's (1962) investigation of a bog near Madelia. However, studies of sites just east of the region by Wright et al. (1963) and Grimm (1984, 1985) help define climatic and vegetational trends.

During the Late Wisconsin maximum 14,000 years ago, the entire Prairie Lake Region was covered with ice. Along the glacial margin just south of the region, a cool climate favored the development of spruce parkland vegetationally similar to that found today in northern Manitoba where the tundra ends and forest begins (Jelgersma 1962; Wright et al. 1963; Van Zant 1976). This vegetation featured spruce (*Picea*) and some larch (*Larix*) in the lowlands and herbs such as sedges (*Cyperaceae*) in the uplands. The spruce parkland extended from north-central Nebraska to Ohio and as far south as Kansas.

When the climate began to warm and the ice began to retreat about 13,500 years ago, the openings of the spruce parkland filled with black ash (*Fraxinus nigra*), birch (*Betula*), and alder (*Alnus*). This closed boreal forest followed the retreat of the glacier north. Spruce began to decline at the southern edge of the Prairie Lake Region as the climate continued to warm. Higher percentages of black ash and lower percentages of spruce and larch were present in northern Iowa by 12,000 years ago (Van Zant 1976:54). In northeastern South Dakota, the spruce-larch-black ash forest remained until about 10,500 years ago (Watts and Bright 1968:863; Radle 1981:39). Just east of the Prairie Lake Region the boreal forest contained more deciduous trees, especially birch and willow (*Salix*), along with some oak (*Quercus*), elm (*Ulmus*), ironwood (*Ostrya/Carpinus*), and hazel (*Corylus*). A significant percentage of non-arboreal pollen (NAP, or pollen from non-tree vegetation) at Kirchner Marsh-Lake Carlson in southeastern Minnesota may indicate prairie openings in the area in early post-glacial times (Wright et al. 1963:1384).

The post-glacial period in the Upper Midwest is characterized by a rapid decline in spruce followed by a brief peak in birch, alder, black ash, and fir (*Abies*). Deciduous forests then became widespread. Oak and elm soon dominated. An oak-elm forest was present at Lake West Okoboji by 11,000 years ago, remaining there for 2,000 years. At Pickerel Lake and Medicine Lake this deciduous forest was apparent by 10,500 years ago and initially was dominated by birch. However, it lasted for only a thousand years and contained significant prairie openings for almost all its tenure in the area. In southeastern Minnesota the appearance of the oak-elm forest coincided with the timing in northeastern South Dakota, but it lasted until about 7,000 years ago. Other deciduous trees present in the oak-elm forest of the Upper Midwest with areal variations in density were green ash (*Fraxinus pennsylvanica*), ironwood, hazel, maple (*Acer*), black walnut (*Juglans nigra*), basswood (*Tilia*), and hickory (*Carya*).

The warming, drying trend that fostered the deciduous forest continued, eventually causing the demise of the forest in most of the Midwest. The decline is marked by a rapid increase in NAP about 9,000 years ago along the western edge of the Prairie Lake Region. At Lake West Okoboji, Pickerel Lake, and Medicine Lake, trees soon were restricted to a few patches of oak, elm, green ash, and willow near the water's edge. Prairie dominated the uplands. During the peak of the warming, drying trend about 6,000 years ago, deep lakes like Pickerel and West Okoboji were reduced drastically in depth and area. Shallower lakes dried up completely, containing a little water only in the early spring or after occasional heavy rains.

An increase in frequency of fires is indicated by the charred seeds in lake cores dating to the thermal maximum. Trees were rare in the Prairie Lake Region at this time, even along the edges of surviving lakes. The area was probably more a mixed-grass prairie than a tallgrass prairie. This period is usually referred to as the Hypsithermal or Altithermal, but it also is known as the "Prairie Period" in the Midwest because the prairie border was much farther north and east of its early historic limits (Bernabo and Webb 1977; Bartlein and Webb 1982).

The end of the Prairie Period in southeastern Minnesota is denoted by an increase in oak pollen about 5,500 years ago. This increase was brought on by a cooler, wetter climate. Oak soon dominated southeastern Minnesota, although significant prairie patches remained. The prairie border retreated from northeastern Minnesota into central and northwestern Minnesota. Tree pollen increased slightly in the Prairie Lake Region by 3,000 years ago, but prairie dominated the region until intensive farming began in the late nineteenth century. The climate of the last 5,000 years has remained relatively stable, although smaller scale changes have occurred. A warm, dry trend occurred between A.D. 1200–1400, and a cool period began about A.D. 1550 (Bryson et al. 1970).

Vegetation

Prior to intensive white settlement, the Prairie Lake Region formed the heart of the True Prairie, an ecosystem dominated by tallgrass vegetation of the *Andropogon-Panicum-Sorghastrum* type (Risser et al. 1981:12). The True Prairie was the most typical and maximally developed grassland of the various tallgrass prairies present in North America (Clements and Shelford 1939). It stretched from south-central Manitoba to northeastern Oklahoma in a narrow band, except for an eastern bulge along the Minnesota-Iowa border and a western extension into northern Nebraska. The Prairie Lake Region formed the core of the eastern bulge (Figure 4). In most areas the exact boundaries of the True Prairie are difficult to define; they not only fluctuated according to varying climate, but blended into the mixed-grass prairie on the west and the grassland-forest of the Prairie Peninsula on the east.

While the True Prairie was a true grassland, rather than the mixed grassland-forest of most of the Prairie Peninsula, it was not devoid of trees. Trees grew protected from the frequent prairie fires in limited areas where sufficient moisture was available during all but the most severe droughts. There were indeed places in the True Prairie where no trees could be seen from horizon to horizon, but the image of a "sea of grass" incorrectly implies botanical uniformity. The prairie was as varied in vegetation as the forest. While trees may have been scarce, non-woody vegetation was both abundant and diverse.

Upland and lowland varieties of grasses dominated the vegetation of the True Prairie, although upland grasses were found in the lowlands and vice-versa. Lowland grasses such as big bluestem (*Andropogon gerardi*) are generally taller than upland grasses such as little bluestem (*Schizochyrium scoparious*). Together these two grasses contributed up to 75 percent of the plant cover in some areas of the True Prairie (Risser et al. 1981:39). Big bluestem can reach heights of 3 m, making it one of the principal namesakes of the tallgrass prairie. It is a nutritious forage for grazing animals in the spring and early summer, but by late summer the plant loses much of its nutritional value because of its need for structural support. Little bluestem, which reaches a maximum height of 1 m, becomes more important under drier conditions, and its nutritional value remains more constant than that of big bluestem. Lowland prairie areas warm up more slowly than upland areas in the spring, so identical species can have different maturation rates depending on local conditions (Risser et al. 1981:51).

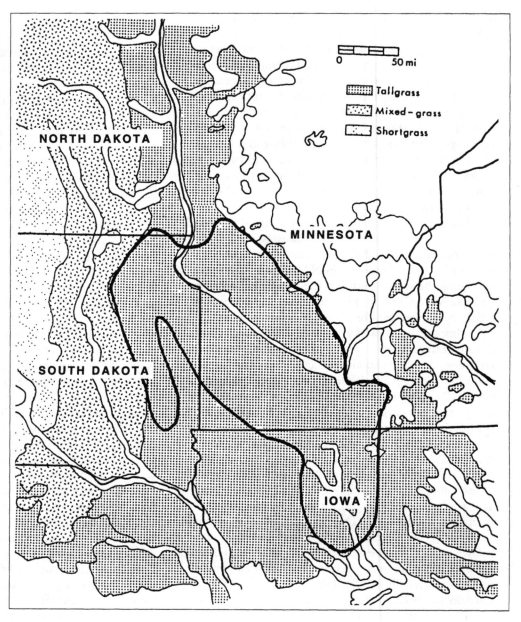

Figure 4. Presettlement vegetation of the Prairie Lake Region (from Küchler 1964). The unshaded areas are woodland.

Forbs, or plants not considered grasses, give the prairie much of its seasonal color and floristic variety (Moyer 1906–10a; Risser et al. 1981:51–53); some forbs are herbs, but commonly they are called "weeds." Prairie legumes, while not as abundant or visually apparent as the grasses and the forbs, offered humans nutritious food sources. Of particular importance in the early contact period was the prairie turnip (*Psoralea esculenta*). Usually found in the uplands, the prairie turnip has a large, oblong root that could be eaten raw or cooked. It had to be harvested in the early summer before the stalk broke off and was blown across the prairie, scattering seeds.

Another legume important to the historically known Native Americans in the Prairie Lake Region was the ground plum (*Astragalus caryocarpus*) (Moyer 1906–10b).

Woody vegetation in the Prairie Lake Region grew only on water margins and topographic breaks. The Minnesota River Valley and its major tributaries contained the most extensive wooded areas. River-bottom forests featured cottonwood (*Populus deltoides*), American elm (*Ulmus americana*), and green ash. Valley uplands had Big Woods species such as elm, sugar maple (*Acer saccarum*), and American basswood (*Tilia americana*). Another major river-valley forest intruded into the southern part of the region along the Des Moines River (Figure 4).

A few major wooded areas in the Prairie Lake interior were adjacent to major lakes and lake belts. A noteworthy example is the Great Oasis in northwestern Murray County, Minnesota, so named by early Euro-American explorers because they viewed it as an oasis of trees in a desert of grass. A floristic inventory of this area today includes green ash, American basswood, American elm, hawthorn (*Crataegus*), chokecherry (*Prunus virginiana*), wolfberry (*Symphoricarpos occidentalis*), prickly ash (*Zanthoxyllum americum*), and currant (*Ribes*). Such species are typical in the small woods on the islands and peninsulas in the region's shallow lakes.

The ravines and melt-water valleys on the slopes of the Coteau des Prairies and the Bemis Moraine also contained wooded areas. On the Coteau in South Dakota, these woods featured burr oak (*Quercus macrocarpa*), elm, green ash, basswood, box elder (*Acer nugundo*), and ironwood (*Ostrya virginiana*) (W. Johnson 1971). Lynd's Woods occupies a melt-water valley in central Lyon County, Minnesota, that contained species similar to those listed above.

An often overlooked aspect of the vegetation of the True Prairie is the wetland and aquatic vegetation of the sloughs and lakes. These plants provided important subsistence resources for humans in the Prairie Lake Region. Distribution of wetland plants varied according to water depth, permanency, and quality (Moyle 1945; R. Stewart and Kantrud 1971).

Many wetland plants adapted to survive fluctuating water levels. Cattail (*Tlypha latifolia*), arrowhead (*Sagittaria latifolia*), and bullrush (*Scirpus validus*) occupied lake margins and were utilized for food and raw materials by Native Americans. The cattail contained a succulent inner stem that was eaten, and the head was used for padding and dressings (Gilmore 1977:12–13; Angier 1974:50). The arrowhead's nutritious tuber was collected in the late autumn and stored for winter food (Gilmore 1977:17; Yarnell 1964:71; Angier 1974:26). The bullrush's inner stem was edible in the spring; its tuber was available in autumn and early spring; and its stems were used for weaving mats and baskets (Gilmore 1977:17; Wegner 1979:43; Yarnell 1964:50).

In deeper water were various species of water lilies, including the yellow pond lily (*Nuphar adrena*), the fragrant water lily (*Nymphaia odorata*), and the American lotus (*Nelumbo lutea*). All of these have nutritious tubers, which were gathered in the autumn or early spring by wading in the water and feeling for the tubers with bare feet (Yarnell 1964:50, 51, 56, 71;

Gilmore 1977:27). Dakota were reported by early Europeans to use water lily roots. This is well documented, although it is sometimes difficult to match Dakota plant names with modern scientific names (Nicollet 1976:44, 126; Geyer 1838:121; Pond 1986:28–29; Stevens 1890:61–63; Winchell 1911:496; Woolworth and Woolworth 1980:87).

Mention also should be made of wild rice (*Zinzania aquatica*) in the Prairie Lake Region, since the grain was important to many Upper Midwest tribes in the Late Prehistoric and early contact periods (Jenks 1897–98). An aquatic grass that grows in marshes, shallow lakes, and the margins of slow-moving streams throughout most of eastern North America, wild rice is concentrated in the western Great Lakes area, where Indians used it as a staple crop. It is one of those rare wild plant foods that provide an abundant, nutritious, and readily available crop without cultivation. Of the major cereal grains, only oats has a higher protein content (Edman 1969:7).

While wild rice is found throughout the entire Prairie Lake Region, it never was as abundant as it is in the Headwaters Lakes area of north-central Minnesota. In Minnesota the current principal range of stands of ten acres or more is limited to the woodlands of the central and northern parts (Edman 1969:30). In the period when native inhabitants first interacted with Europeans explorers, the only large stands of wild rice in the Prairie Lake Region appear to have been along the bottoms of the Minnesota River.

While Pierre Le Sueur in 1700, Peter Pond in 1773–74, and Thomas Anderson in 1806–10 did not mention finding wild rice in the Minnesota River Valley, Jonathan Carver in 1766, William Keating and Stephen Long in 1823, George Featherstonhaugh in 1835, and Joseph Nicollet and Karl Geyer in 1838 all described patches of wild rice in the river (Carver 1976:95; Keating 1959:372, 374; Long 1978:167; Featherstonhaugh 1970:1:311, 331, 335; Nicollet 1976:111; Geyer 1838:103). Nicollet's expedition also noticed wild rice in Swan and Middle lakes in central Nicollet County and in the Sakatah and Elysian lakes area in southern Le Sueur County (Nicollet 1976:125; Geyer 1838:25, 26). Government land surveyors in the 1850s noticed wild rice in some lakes in eastern Blue Earth County (Trygg 1964). Early exploration accounts mentioned no wild rice in lakes of southwestern Minnesota's interior.

Since Carver is the only pre-1820s explorer to mention actual stands of wild rice in the Prairie Lake Region, it is possible that the Santee Dakota planted the major stands of wild rice in the Minnesota River bottoms and perhaps a few of the eastern lakes beginning in the early nineteenth century. Prior to this, large stands of wild rice may not have been present in the region. The Dakota, Ojibwe, and Assiniboin are known to have sown wild rice in other regions to produce new stands (Landes 1968:199; Jenks 1897–98:1057).

Fauna

About 50 species of mammals were native to the Prairie Lake Region at the time of white contact (Ernst and French 1977). Most were also common in adjacent grassland regions, although the aquatic species were more numerous in the Prairie Lake Region. While the great majority of prairie mammals were small, burrowing animals of limited economic importance to early human inhabitants, most of the large upland mammals and many of the aquatic mammals were critical to successful cultural adaptations.

Immediately following the glacial retreat, the Prairie Lake Region was revegetated rapidly by a boreal forest, although the region may have briefly claimed a more open environment with mammals such as the woolly mammoth (*Mammuthus primigenius*) and the musk ox (*Ovibos moschatus*) roaming a tundra-like environment. When the boreal forest developed, now-extinct mammals such as the giant beaver (*Castoroides*) and the mastodon (*Mammut americanum*) may have been in the region. About 9,000 years ago, when the prairie became dominant, most of the historically known fauna were already present in the region. At this same time, many Pleistocene animal species became extinct throughout North America (P. Martin and Wright 1967).

The largest mammal of the Prairie Lake Region for the 10,000 years prior to white settlement was the bison. In the early Prairie Period, now-extinct varieties of bison (e.g., *Bison bison antiquus, Bison bison occidentalis*) provided important sources of food for early human groups. Modern bison (*Bison bison bison*) were distributed throughout most of North America by the time Europeans began to explore the New World (Roe 1970). Large herds, however, were common only on the Great Plains. Spread of the modern bison east of the Mississippi River largely may have been a phenomenon that occurred just prior to contact with Europeans (C. Shay 1978).

At the time of contact, bison were found throughout the Prairie Lake Region, although numbers and herd sizes dramatically increased as one moved westward through the region. In the early nineteenth cen-

tury, bison were rare east of the region, but large herds were still common in its western part. These herds may have moved seasonally into the Prairie Lake Region, arriving in summer and leaving in the fall (Long 1978:175, 292; Van der Zee 1913:80; Keating 1959:302, 350, 371; Nicollet 1976:57–59). Bison disappeared from the region in the mid-nineteenth century, with the last bison reported in southwestern Minnesota in 1879 (Moyle 1965:172) and in northwestern Iowa in 1870 (Bennett 1934:65).

Elk (*Cervus canadensis*) were the second largest mammal found in the Prairie Lake Region in precontact and early contact times. The Long Expedition of 1823 reported a herd of at least 100 at the region's north end (Long 1978:176). In 1844 the Allen Dragoon Expedition saw hundreds of elk in the southern part of the region (Van der Zee 1913:79–80).

Two species of deer were present in the Prairie Lake Region: mule deer (*Odocoileus hemionus*) in the west and white-tailed deer (*Odocoileus virginiana*) in the east. Large numbers of deer were not common in the south and west. Deer were probably most prevalent in the Minnesota River Valley and woodland border areas to the north. Some pronghorn antelope (*Antilocarpa americana*) occasionally were found in the region.

A small but important mammal of the Prairie Lake Region was the muskrat (*Ondontra zibethicus*). Large numbers in the shallow lakes offered a ready source of food, clothing, and, eventually, furs for trade. In the fall of 1866, a single Indian hunter took 1,800 muskrats in the region's eastern part in only two months (Sibley 1950:195). Other mammals of potential economic importance were the white-tailed jackrabbit (*Lepus townsendii*), cottontail rabbit (*Sylvilagus floridanus*), woodchuck (*Marmota monax*), beaver (*Castor canadensis*), raccoon (*Procyon lotor*), and grizzly bear (*Ursus arctos*).

Most North American grasslands are characterized by a simple and meager collection of regional birds because of limited habitat variability (Risser et al. 1981:74). This was not true of the Prairie Lake Region because innumerable wetlands fostered huge waterfowl populations. Most birds of the Prairie Lake Region were warm-season inhabitants only, however, migrating south for the winter. Ducks, geese, cranes, and other waterfowl were present in large numbers during the spring breeding season. Many remained all summer, but in the fall, enormous flocks would literally darken the sky as they migrated south.

Few upland game birds were present in the region prior to white settlement; the principal exception was the sharp-tailed grouse (*Pedioecetes phasianellus*). The greater prairie chicken (*Tympanuchus cupido*) was not present, and early recorded references to prairie chickens usually meant sharp-tailed grouse (Green and Janssen 1975:72).

Fish were an abundant food resource, and in the spring, the grassy margins of the sloughs undulated with breeding fish, especially northern pike (*Esox lucius*). The shallow lakes often have severe winter kills because of oxygen depletion, and bullheads (*Ameirus*) are probably best adapted to the shallow lakes and the last to survive in times of low water or low oxygen. Other fish common to the region are gars (*Lepisosteus*), suckers (*Carpiodes*), buffalofish (*Ictiobus*), sunfish (*Lepomis*), and perch (*Perca flavens*) (Eddy and Surber 1947).

Amphibian and reptile species were not numerous in the Prairie Lake Region, although a few species were present in relatively large numbers (Breckenridge 1944). Probably most important to early humans were turtles, especially the painted turtle (*Chrysemys picta belli*) and the snapping turtle (*Chrysemys serpentina*). Two other species were probably also present, the ornate box (*Terrapene ornata*) and spiny softshell (*Trionys ferox*) turtles. The region's numerous sloughs provided excellent habitats for frogs and other amphibians. Mussels and crayfish were locally available in the lakes and sloughs, with mussels being especially abundant in the Minnesota River.

The Prairie Lake Region has been a dynamic environment over the last 12,000 years, experiencing both long term trends and short term changes. Human reactions to these changes helped define the cultural divisions of the region but did not determine them. The intermingling of environmental restrictions and opportunities, along with the invention and the diffusion of ideas, ultimately led to a unique cultural expression.

Chapter 3

History of Archaeological Research

Extensive archaeological work has been done in the Prairie Lake Region for more than 100 years. The initial assessment of the area's precontact history was based largely on the mid-twentieth century work of Lloyd Wilford of the University of Minnesota. While Wilford's vision of southwestern Minnesota was somewhat sketchy, it provided a sound basis for future work. Working without the benefit of radiocarbon dates or fine-scale recovery methods, Wilford constructed his overview largely on analysis of ceramics and paid little attention to subsistence and settlement patterns.

As of 1990, more than 50 precontact archaeological sites had been excavated in the Prairie Lake Region, about equal numbers being burial and habitation sites. Almost all the Minnesota sites are along or south of the Minnesota River. This leaves the west-central Minnesota portion of the Prairie Lake Region virtually unknown archaeologically.

While recent investigations have increased dramatically our knowledge of eastern South Dakota, the paucity of diagnostic ceramics from most of these investigations limits our ability to relate the South Dakota sites to the Minnesota and Iowa sites. Radiocarbon dates were one of the most important contributions of archaeological work in South Dakota in the 1980s.

Excavations in the Iowa Prairie Lake Region, especially those at the Arthur site (13DK27), have demonstrated the similarities and differences between the southern end of the region and areas to the north. The lack of radiocarbon dates and published site reports from Iowa especially hampers a better understanding of regional interrelationships.

Demonstrated academic interest in the Prairie Lake Region has been limited, and Wilford's work remains the most sustained scientific examination. Cultural Resource Management (CRM) projects have increased knowledge of the region, but most of these reports are not readily available. Many of these unpublished CRM documents were obtained from various agencies for use in this study.

Minnesota

Archaeological research in southwestern and west-central Minnesota began in the late nineteenth century with the Northwestern Archaeological Survey directed by Alfred Hill and carried out largely by Theodore Lewis (Keyes 1928). Lewis visited most of the Minnesota counties in the region to map mound groups and other earthworks. He worked primarily south of the Minnesota River in the 1880s and north of the river in the 1890s. Some archaeological data also were recorded by Newton Winchell and Warren Upham for the Geological and Natural History Survey of Minnesota (Winchell and Upham 1884–88). Most of the archaeological data from the Hill-Lewis surveys and Winchell-Upham were published in Winchell's *The Aborigines of Minnesota* (1911).

The first scientific excavations in the Minnesota Prairie Lake Region were undertaken by William Nickerson for the Minnesota Historical Society at the Cambria site (21BE2) in 1913 and 1916. Nickerson also excavated the Judson Mound (21BE148) in 1916. Nickerson's 1917 site report on the Cambria excavations was published in the *Minnesota Archaeologist* (Nickerson 1988). It is surprisingly comprehensive, considering he was a self-trained archaeologist working in the early twentieth century.

The University of Minnesota began archaeological work in the region in 1934. Albert Jenks and his assistant, Lloyd Wilford, excavated several mounds (21TR1, 21TR2, 21TR3, 21TR4) and a possible Paleoindian site (21TR5) in the Lake Traverse vicinity (Jenks 1937; Wilford 1970). They tested the Fox Lake site (21MR2) in southwestern Minnesota a year later. Wilford's doctoral dissertation presented the first detailed overview of Minnesota's precontact history, including discussions of the Browns Valley Man (21TR5) and Round Mound (21TR1) sites, with a brief mention of the Fox Lake site (Wilford 1937).

Following Jenks's retirement in 1938, Wilford directed the University of Minnesota's archaeological program for the next 21 years. Wilford not only catalogued the state's known sites, but he excavated 18 mound and 16 habitation sites in the Minnesota portion of the Prairie Lake Region (E. Johnson 1974:6–7). Wilford wrote detailed site reports for all of these excavations, but only the mound reports were published after his retirement (Wilford 1970; Wilford et al. 1969; E. Johnson 1973). Synopses of the Humphrey (21FA1), Cambria (21BE2), and Great Oasis (21MU2) village investigations were published in an article on Mississippian villages in *American Antiquity* (Wilford 1945b).

Wilford's view of southwestern Minnesota was included in several overviews of the state's precontact history (Wilford 1941, 1955, 1960a), and it prevailed largely unaltered into the 1970s as the basis for the region's cultural history. He did not recognize any Paleoindian or Archaic complexes in southwestern Minnesota, although Browns Valley was noted as a Paleoindian site. The lack of an Archaic horizon presents an especially large gap in the region's cultural history, considering that it spanned a period of more than 5,000 years. Wilford defined only a single Woodland complex, Southern Minnesota Woodland, that existed in both southeastern and southwestern Minnesota. In Wilford's view, Mississippian intrusions into southwestern Minnesota ended the Woodland Period.

Several excavations funded by the Works Progress Administration and Civilian Conservation Corps and directed by the Minnesota Historical Society in the 1930s and 1940s were the only other investigations in Minnesota's Prairie Lake Region in the mid-twentieth century. These excavations focused on historic sites along the Minnesota River (Smith 1938; Nystuen and Lindeman 1969; Minnesota Historical Records Survey Project 1941). The one exception was G. Hubert Smith's excavation at Schoen Mound #1(21BS2) overlooking Big Stone Lake (Smith 1941).

The 1960s witnessed sporadic precontact archaeological research in the Minnesota Prairie Lake Region.

Usually, projects were associated with emergency salvage excavations of burial sites encountered during construction (e.g., Valentine 1969; Norquist 1967a, 1967b). During this period, the University of Minnesota concentrated its archaeological research in the north-central and east-central wild rice areas of Minnesota, and the Minnesota Historical Society dealt almost exclusively with historic sites.

The 1970s saw a resurgence of archaeological work in southwestern Minnesota because of new federal preservation laws, and academic interest as well. In 1971 a joint University of Minnesota-University of Nebraska expedition, led by Dale Henning, excavated at the Big Slough (21MU1) and Great Oasis (21MU2) sites (Anfinson 1977; Hudak 1972b; Henning and Henning 1978). Additional attempts were made to locate unrecorded sites through interviews with local informants and field survey (Hudak 1971). Also in 1971, Gordon Lothson of the Minnesota Historical Society undertook a detailed study of the petroglyphs at the Jeffers site (21CO3) in Cottonwood County (Lothson 1976). At least 10 other precontact sites were investigated by scientific institutions in southwestern Minnesota in the 1970s. These included the Science Museum of Minnesota's excavations of the Pedersen (21LN2) and Mountain Lake (21CO1) sites (Hudak 1974; O. Shane 1978, 1982), Mankato State University's excavations at the Price (21BE36) and Nelson (21BE24) sites (Scullin 1979, 1981), and the University of Minnesota's excavation of the Vosburg site (21FA2) (Dobbs 1984).

Numerous federally required CRM studies also were completed in the Prairie Lake Region of Minnesota in the 1970s (Minnesota Historical Society 1979:157–72). Several resulted in extensive archaeological excavations to mitigate the adverse effects of construction. Of particular note is the Hildahl complex (21YM33-35) investigations for the Trunk Highway 23 project, which encountered Early Prehistoric, Woodland, and Cambria components (Hudak 1978; Dobbs 1979). A major survey effort by the Minnesota Historical Society's Statewide Archaeological Survey (SAS) investigated six Prairie Lake Region counties (Blue Earth, Brown, Douglas, Faribault, Kandiyohi, and Redwood) from 1978 to 1981 (Figure 5), but no detailed reports have been published (Minnesota Historical Society 1981).

Academic interest in the Prairie Lake Region of Minnesota waned in the 1980s. The limited Fox Lake site excavations carried out for the author's dissertation (Anfinson 1987b), the Oneota investigations of Clark Dobbs and Orrin Shane along the Blue Earth River in the eastern portion of the region (Dobbs and

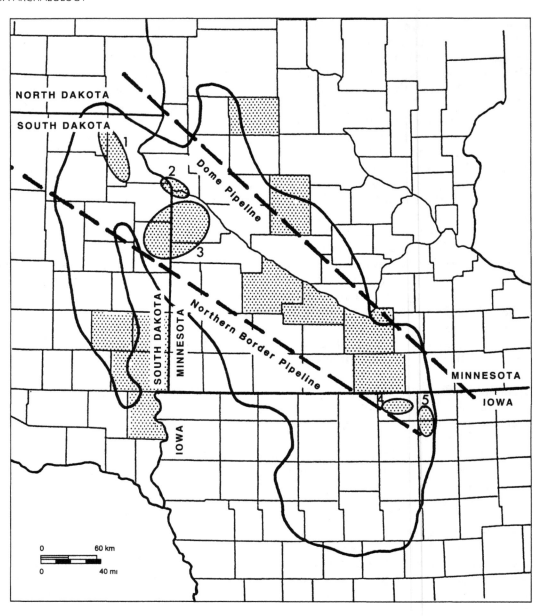

Figure 5. Major recent archaeological reconnaissance surveys in the Prairie Lake Region. Stippled Minnesota counties were included in the Minnesota Historical Society's Statewide Archaeological Survey. Shaded South Dakota counties include surveys reported by Winham et al. (1985), Hannus et al. (1986), and Lueck et al. (1987). Stippled ovals are surveys by: 1—Rood and Rood (1984–85), 2—Eggers (1985), 3—Beissel et al. (1984), 4—Lensink (1981a), and 5—Mallam and Bettis ([1979?]).

Shane 1982), and the recent Granite Falls Bison site excavations (see Chapter 4) were the only major non-CRM research efforts.

CRM projects continued at a steady pace in the 1980s, but most of these consist of limited reconnaissance surveys. Examples are the Northern Border Pipeline survey (Hudak 1983), the Upper Minnesota River Project of the Army Corps of Engineers (Beissel et al. 1984; Dobbs 1989), the Big Stone Wildlife Refuge Survey of the U.S. Fish and Wildlife Service (Eggers 1985), and the Bureau of Land Management's testing at the Lura Lake site (21BE44) at the region's eastern edge (Harrison 1985). Most of the surveys

have involved areas south of the Minnesota River. Major archaeological surveys in west-central Minnesota are unpublished (e.g., SAS surveys of Kandiyohi and Douglas Counties) and/or contain little useful data (e.g., Lane 1974).

Highway reconnaissance surveys have been responsible for most of the archaeological work done in the Prairie Lake Region in the 1980s. The Municipal-County Highway Archaeological Survey examined a number of locales at the eastern end of the region (Anfinson and Peterson 1988, 1989). In the Center Creek area, two Oneota sites were investigated intensively in the mid-1980s. This resulted in significant recovery of artifacts and two radiocarbon dates (Anfinson 1987a).

The Trunk Highway Archaeological Survey has been responsible for major archaeological undertakings on State Highway 27 west of Alexandria, on U.S. Highway 212 east of Granite Falls, on State Highway 59 south of Marshall, and on State Highway 14 east of New Ulm. Detailed reports on these projects are not yet available, although a few preliminary reports have been produced (e.g., Skaar 1991; Justin 1991). Radiocarbon dates have been obtained for several of the trunk highway projects (see Table 1, Chapter 1).

In 1991 the Minnesota State Historic Preservation Office (SHPO) sponsored an archaeological survey in Traverse County at the north end of the Prairie Lake Region. Completed by the Institute for Minnesota Archaeology (IMA), the Traverse County survey recorded 35 new sites, examined previously recorded sites, and inventoried local collections (C. Johnson 1991).

South Dakota

The earliest archaeological work in the Prairie Lake Region was done in eastern South Dakota by an army surgeon, Aaron Comfort. In 1869 he mapped site locations, excavated several mounds, and tested a Great Oasis habitation site in the vicinity of Fort Wadsworth (Fort Sisseton) at the north end of the Coteau des Prairies (Comfort 1978). In the 1880s and 1890s, Theodore Lewis mapped mound groups, enclosures, boulder outlines, and petroglyphs in eastern South Dakota (T. Lewis 1886, 1889, 1890, 1891).

Little additional archaeological work was done until William Over of the University of South Dakota Museum investigated the area in the 1910s and 1920s. He mapped 29 mound groups and 1 habitation site in the Prairie Lake Region of South Dakota (Sigstad and Sigstad 1973a). Over tested the Hartford Beach habitation site on Big Stone Lake and excavated mounds in 10 of the groups.

Only sporadic archaeological investigation followed. In 1935 Wilford and Jenks excavated the Kallstrom Mound (39RO301) on the west side of Lake Traverse (Wilford 1970:22–24). In 1953 Wilford returned to the Lake Traverse area to salvage the DeSpiegler burial (39RO23) encountered in a gravel pit for a road project (E. Johnson 1973:44–52). Wilford also tested the Zacharias site on the west side of Lake Traverse in 1953 (Wilford [ca. 1958]b).

The Prairie Lake Region in South Dakota largely was ignored in the 1940s, 1950s, and 1960s, as archaeological interest centered on reservoir salvage work in the Missouri River trench. An exception was James Howard's 1966 excavation of the Spawn Mound (21LK201) for the Over Museum (Howard 1968).

In the 1970s CRM studies, the establishment of the South Dakota Archaeological Research Center, and the founding of the South Dakota Archaeological Society sharply increased archaeological work in eastern South Dakota. Work was limited initially to surface surveys of known sites (e.g., McNerney 1970; Nelson 1973; Lass 1980a); exceptions were the 1973 excavation of the Sisseton Mound (39RO26) in Roberts County (Sigstad and Sigstad 1973b) and limited testing of several habitation sites (Haug 1977, 1979; Haug and Sterner 1978).

In the 1980s a number of important excavations took place in South Dakota's Prairie Lake Region. Included were investigations at the Oakwood Lakes site (39BK7) in Brookings County (Hannus 1981), the Winter site (39DE5) in Deuel County (Haug 1982), the Hartford Beach site (39RO5) in Roberts County (Haug 1982), and the Waubay Lakes site (39DA7) in Day County (Bradley and Ranney 1985).

Major 1980 reconnaissance surveys included the Northern Border Pipeline survey (Hannus 1985) and the eastern Coteau survey (Rood and Rood 1984–85). The South Dakota State Historic Preservation Office sponsored several major reconnaissance surveys in the eastern part of the state, including a survey of Minnehaha County (Winham et al. 1985), a survey of Moody, Lincoln, and Union counties (Hannus et al. 1986), and a survey of Lake County (Lueck et al. 1987).

Iowa

The north-central Iowa area of the Prairie Lake Region was poorly understood until the 1970s because of the small amount of archaeological work. In the mid- and late-nineteenth century several local amateurs conducted surveys in a few eastern counties (W. Williams 1869; Aldrich 1884; Webster 1887), but the Hill-Lewis surveys largely ignored the area. The only early excavations in the area were Duren Ward's excavation of a mound on West Okoboji Lake in 1904 (Ward 1905) and Mildred Mott Wedel's excavation of two mounds near Webster City in 1938 (Keyes 1940). In the mid-twentieth century, salvage excavations at the Gypsum Quarry site (13WB1) in 1960 yielded Great Oasis and Woodland ceramics (Flanders and Hansman 1961); excavations at the Soldow site

(13HB1) in 1961 produced pre-Woodland lithics (Flanders 1977); and the 1971 excavations at the Crim site (13ET403) yielded Woodland, Great Oasis, and Mill Creek ceramics (D. C. Anderson 1977).

More recently, several sites were excavated on East Okoboji Lake in conjunction with a sewer project. Limited testing at two sites (13DK7, 13DK30) produced some Woodland artifacts, while extensive excavations at the Arthur site (13DK27) revealed a multicomponent Woodland site with minor Archaic, Oneota, and Plains Village components (Tiffany 1982b). The Iowa Northern Tier Archaeological Project undertook an extensive survey in eastern north-central Iowa focusing on Winnebago, Worth, and Cerro Gordo counties (Mallam and Bettis [1979?]). Its principal results include a major study of settlement patterns (Lensink 1981a, 1981b, 1984) and the excavation of the E. B. Stillman site (13CG23), a Late Woodland site on an alluvial fan (Mallam and Bettis 1981). The Northern Border Pipeline survey in Kossuth, Winnebago, and Hancock counties located only a few isolated artifacts and produced very little information about the area's past (Hudak 1983).

In 1988 the University of Iowa undertook archaeological work in Dickson County (Lynch 1988:629). An intensive survey of drained Sylvan Lake was completed, along with test excavations at the Frerichs site (13DK12) on Stony Lake. The results of these investigations have yet to be published.

Considering the amount of archaeological investigation done in the Prairie Lake Region, its precontact cultures should be well known. The fact that very little of this work has been publicly presented, however, helps explain why the region's ancient history remains poorly understood, especially by the general public. If the motto of the "new" archaeology of the 1970s was "Archaeology is anthropology or it is nothing," archaeology's motto in the twenty-first century should be: "Archaeology must be public or it will be nothing."

Chapter 4

Early Prehistoric Period (10,000–3000 B.C.)

The Early Prehistoric Period in the Prairie Lake Region is poorly understood because there are few excavated archaeological sites. Surface finds of projectile points suggest that certain Paleoindian and early Archaic technological complexes were present in the region. Archaeologists are unable, however, to describe regional cultural phases for the Early Prehistoric Period, with firm chronologies and well-described subsistence-settlement patterns, material cultures, and mortuary treatments.

We do know that the initial Early Prehistoric environment of the Prairie Lake Region differed greatly from that of later periods. The post-glacial environment present during Clovis times (ca. 9500–9000 B.C.), for example, was in especially sharp contrast to that of later times. Vegetation featured boreal forest dominated by spruce but containing significant amounts of larch and black ash. The climate was slightly cooler and wetter than today, although seasonal changes probably were less pronounced because of the influence of the still-extensive ice sheet to the north. The gradual melting of large blocks of ice buried in the till resulted in a constantly changing landscape. Glacial melt-water filled innumerable surface depressions, and several large but relatively short-lived glacial lakes formed in southern Minnesota. To the north, Glacial Lake Agassiz grew with the increasing melt-water, and its southern outlet, Glacial River Warren, began to rapidly carve the Minnesota River Valley.

The post-glacial boreal forest of the Prairie Lake Region has no modern vegetational parallel, so it is difficult to determine the full range of subsistence resources that were available there to the first human occupants. The forest was apparently more open than modern spruce taiga (subarctic forest), so there would have been more browse and habitat diversity. The initial mammalian inventory of the Prairie Lake Region probably included mastodon, woodland musk-ox, giant beaver, bear, moose, elk, and deer (J. Brown and Cleland 1968; L. Martin et al. 1985). Some cold-water fish (e.g., northern pike) could have been present in the rivers, glacial lakes, and melt-water ponds relatively soon after deglaciation (K. Stewart and Lindsay 1983). Plant foods available for human consumption were also probably more common than in the taiga of today and would have included nuts, berries, and perhaps water plants.

As the glacial ice continued its retreat into Canada and the climate continued to warm, the coniferous forest of the Prairie Lake Region gave way to a deciduous forest initially dominated by birch and alder but soon succeeded by elm and oak. This forest was present in the southwestern part of the region by 9000 B.C. and covered the entire region by 8000 B.C. The landscape stabilized as the last remnants of stagnant ice melted and the southern outlet of Lake Agassiz outlet was temporarily abandoned. Seasonality became increasingly pronounced with warmer summers and cooler winters.

The environment of the Prairie Lake Region during Folsom times (ca. 9000–8000 B.C.) would have featured dramatic changes in the climate, vegetation, and fauna. At the beginning, much of the Prairie Lake Region still was covered with a spruce-dominated coniferous forest, but it rapidly became more deciduous and open. By mid-Folsom times, the coniferous forest was restricted to the region's far northern part, and by late Folsom, the entire region was covered with an oak-elm forest.

Elk and deer became more common as the forest opened. Musk-ox, mastodon, and giant beaver disappeared. Small mammal populations expanded. Some bison were no doubt also present, although they were not numerous until the prairie began to dominate a thousand years later. Fish numbers increased as warm-water species invaded the region through the extensive streams and interconnected lake basins. Waterfowl also may have begun to appear in large numbers, establishing migratory patterns that would last for thousands of years. Plant-food availability also changed; in particular, acorns were more abundant.

Shortly after 10,000 years ago, at the beginning of Plano (Late Paleoindian) times, increased warming and drying began to thin the region's oak-elm forest. Many Ice Age mammals, especially the larger ones, became extinct in the Upper Midwest. This extinction may have been a result of overhunting by humans and the climatic shift that dramatically changed midcontinental vegetation and brought a seasonal weather cycle resembling that of modern times (Wright 1987:486–87). The southern outlet to Lake Agassiz was reactivated about 9,900 years ago and remained open for about 400 years.

By 9,000 years ago, the continued warming and drying brought widespread prairie vegetation to the region. Soon, deciduous woods were restricted to major river valleys, edges of major lakes, and other fire-protected areas. By 8,000 years ago, flora and fauna similar to that known in the early contact history recorded by white explorers was established temporarily. This environment, however, was short-lived, as prairie continued to expand to the east.

During the prairie peak between 7,000 to 6,000 years ago, the environment of the Prairie Lake Region featured less woody vegetation and fewer tallgrass plant species than present in early contact times. Upland animals, especially bison, increased in number. Meanwhile, forest-edge species (e.g., deer) and aquatic species (e.g., fish, muskrat) must have suffered significant population declines. Summer droughts would have been more frequent and severe, causing many lakes to dry up and remain so for long periods. Lakes that did not completely dry up experienced increased infilling with soil and higher salinity (Haworth 1972; Walker 1966). Often, prairie fires must have swept through large areas. Refuges for many species were not far to the east, however, and within the Prairie Lake Region, the Minnesota River Valley no doubt served as an oasis of woody vegetation and wetland even during the prairie maximum.

Paleoindian Tradition
(10,000–6000 B.C.)

Fluted-Point Complexes

Archaeologists use the artifacts left by a culture as a blueprint to distinguish individual groups. Among the most common artifacts found and used as clues today are weapon points and tool pieces. Partly through the presence of tools found at investigated sites, archaeologists have been able to trace human occupation of midcontinental North America to about 12,000 years ago. This occupation is associated with the Clovis fluted-point complex first identified in the southwestern United States and now recognized as existing throughout most of the lower 48-states, southeastern Canada, and Mexico. Although there are a few New World archaeological sites that may be older than 12,000 years, evidences for pre-Clovis peoples in the New World have yet to be well substantiated (Meltzer 1989; Lynch 1990).

Clovis dates in western North America generally fall between 9500 and 9000 B.C. In eastern North America, the fluted-point complex (often called Eastern Fluted) dates somewhat later to 9000–8000 B.C. Clovis points are well-made lanceolate points. They are fluted, or flattened by removal of large flakes, on both faces of the lower half and show grinding on the lateral edges and base. The Clovis tool kit also included triangular end scrapers, triangular bifaces with convex bases, and bone foreshafts (Bonnichsen et al. 1987:408). Clovis toolmakers often used colorful, high-quality raw materials; most tools were more formalized than the irregular flake tools common in many Archaic and Woodland sites.

Prairie Lake Region Fluted-Point Sites

A few Clovis points have been found in the Prairie Lake Region (Figure 6), but none has been recovered through excavation. In Minnesota, Clovis finds are reported from Waseca County (Michael Scullin, personal communication 1985), the southwestern corner of the state (point, accession no. 547-1, Lloyd A. Wilford Archaeology Laboratory collection, University of Minnesota; there is some disagreement as to whether or not the point is a true Clovis point or even from Minnesota), Blue Earth County (drawing, *Minnesota Archaeologist,* vol. 25, no. 4 [October 1963]:155), and Yellow Medicine County (point, accession no. 49.1/68.182, Archaeological Collections, Minnesota Historical Society). In Iowa's Prairie Lake Region, Clovis points have been reported from Webster (L. Alex

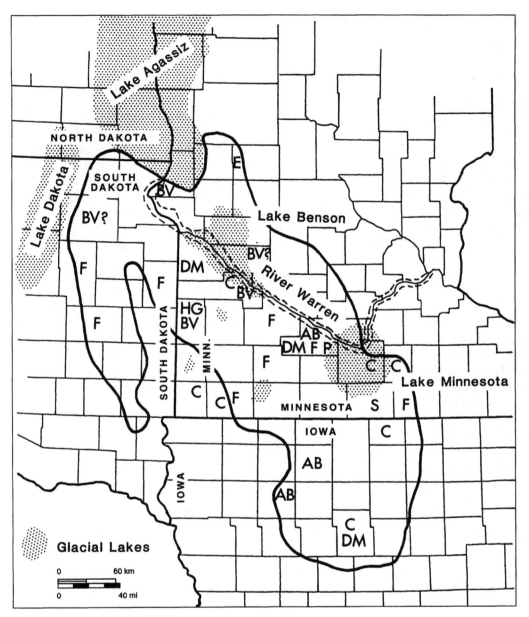

Figure 6. Glacial lakes (stippled), Glacial River Warren (dashed lines), and Early Prehistoric finds by county in the Prairie Lake Region. Abbreviations: C=Clovis, F=Folsom, AB=Agate Basin, E=Eden, P=Plainview, DM=Dalton/Meserve, SB=Scottsbluff, HG=Hells Gap, S=Scottsbluff, and BV=Browns Valley.

1980:65) and Winnebago counties (Lensink 1981a:41). No Clovis finds have been reported from eastern South Dakota.

West of the Mississippi River, Clovis was succeeded by Folsom about 11,000 years ago. The Folsom complex lasted for about 1,000 years. Folsom points are well-made lanceolate points. They have fluting over much of both faces. The chipped-stone inventory of the Folsom tool kit was dominated by unifacial, flaked tools including knives, scrapers, tools shaped with a beveled point called burins, gravers, and perforators. Abraders, large choppers, and an assortment of bone tools (e.g., projectile points, fleshers, notched disks, eyed needles) also are known (Bonnichsen et al. 1987:413).

Information regarding the Folsom occupation of the Prairie Lake Region is little better than that for Clovis. In the Minnesota portion of the region, Folsom points have been found on the surface in Nobles (Lew Hudson, personal communication 1978), Cottonwood (O. Shane 1989), Brown (Trow 1979), and Freeborn (O. Shane 1989) counties. The Brown and Freeborn county finds include at least three examples from each county. In South Dakota, Folsom points are reported from Clark (Keller 1982:5.4), Deuel (Haug 1982:52), and Kingsbury (K. Brown et al. 1982:12) counties. No

Folsom points have been reported from the Iowa portion of the Prairie Lake Region.

Plano Complexes

Archaeologists have grouped the post-Folsom Paleoindian complexes of midcontinental North America under the term Plano (Sellards 1952). These complexes exhibit well-made, lanceolate projectile points that lack fluting. Plano point types can be differentiated from each other by shape. Narrow leaf shapes with constricted bases include Agate Basin and Hell Gap points. Stemmed (shouldered) shapes include Scottsbluff, Eden, and Alberta points, along with Cody knives. Broad, concave base shapes include Browns Valley, Plainview, and Dalton (Meserve) points. The Plano point types most commonly found in the Prairie Lake Region are Agate Basin, Eden, Scottsbluff, Dalton (Meserve), and Browns Valley.

In the northwestern Plains, Agate Basin points date from 8500 to 7500 B.C., but in the eastern Plains similar points date from 8000 to 6000 B.C. (Bonnichsen et al. 1987:415). Agate Basin points are slender. They have slightly convex edges exhibiting horizontal flaking and basal grinding. Lengths range from 7 cm to about 15 cm.

Eden and Scottsbluff points are part of what has been called the Cody complex in the northwestern Plains. Originally dated to 6800 to 6400 B.C. (Irwin-Williams et al. 1973), Cody may begin several hundred years earlier (Greiser 1985). Eden points are long and slender with parallel sides and shallow basal stemming. Flaking can be collateral or random, and basal edges are usually ground. Lengths range from 5.5 cm to 18 cm. Scottsbluff points resemble Eden points, except they are more triangular in outline, have broader bases, and have more pronounced shoulders. Lengths range from 5 cm to 15 cm.

Dalton points may represent the transition from fluted point technology in the midcontinent. (Such points are termed Dalton in the Midwest and Meserve in the Plains). This type dates from 8500 to 7900 B.C. (Bonnichsen et al. 1987:418). Dalton points are triangular in outline on the upper body; the lower edges become almost parallel. Bases are deeply concave and thinned to the extent of resembling fluting. Long, parallel flake scars on the blade extend from the midline to the edges, producing a serrated appearance. Lengths range from 5 cm to 18 cm.

Prairie Lake Region Plano Sites

Browns Valley Site The Browns Valley site (21TR5), typesite for Browns Valley points, is the region's most renowned Paleoindian site. It is at the southeast end of Lake Traverse in extreme western Minnesota at the northwestern edge of the Prairie Lake Region (Figure 7). In October 1933, William Jensen, a local collector, found five lanceolate bifaces (lance heads having opposite sides alike) at the site. He also found two small abraders (used to wear away wood or stone by rubbing) and fragments of a human skeleton apparently associated with the bifaces in a gravel pit in Browns Valley. He then contacted Albert Jenks at the University of Minnesota, who brought his 1934 field school to the gravel-pit site for four days of excavation. While the burial pit was no longer visible, Jenks recovered a sixth biface and more bone fragments from the loose gravel in the general vicinity of Jensen's finds.

The University of Minnesota returned to the site in the summer of 1936, excavating along the gravel-pit wall for three months under the direction of a Jenks-trained graduate student, James West. Excavations continued into December under local supervision, but no additional skeletal remains or lanceolate bifaces were recovered.

Jenks considered the bifaces to be structurally and temporally related to Folsom and Yuma (Scottsbluff) points (Jenks 1937). Lloyd Wilford, Jenks' assistant, restored much of a single human cranium, along with the femora, humeri, clavicle, and left tibia. The bones appeared stained with red ochre. Jenks and Wilford concluded that the skeleton was that of a middle-aged male (Jenks 1937:18).

Following the analysis, Jenks returned five bifaces and the skeleton to Jensen. The University of Minnesota retained the single biface recovered by the 1934 field school. For the next half century, the Browns Valley skeleton remained somewhat of an enigma, initially attracting considerable nationwide attention and then gradually fading from view. The skeleton was considered lost following Jensen's death in 1960.

The bifaces from the site, however, retained their importance as examples of post-Folsom Paleoindian technology. Browns Valley points formally were defined by H. M. Wormington (1957:144), who likened them to Frederick points from the Jimmy Allen site in Wyoming. The Frederick complex dates from about 6400 B.C. to 6000 B.C. (Irwin-Williams et al. 1973:52).

Browns Valley points (Figure 8) are thin, broad, lanceolate points widest in the midsection. The four type specimens (two of the six bifaces from the type site are asymmetrical and considered to be knives) range in length from 3.6 cm to 8 cm, in maximum width from 2.2 cm to 3.4 cm, in basal width from 2.1

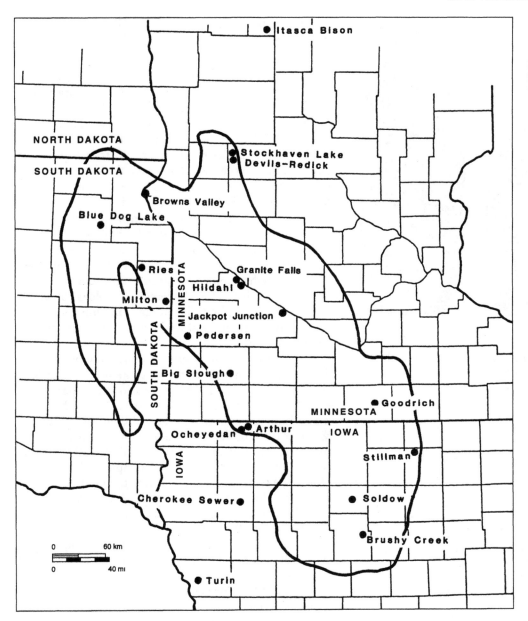

Figure 7. Locations of sites in and around the Prairie Lake Region with Early Prehistoric components.

cm to 2.5 cm, and in thickness from .5 cm to .65 cm. Their bases are slightly concave, and basal edges usually are ground. Flaking is oblique parallel. They are lenticular (like a biconvex lens) in cross-section with some thinning at the base. The type specimens are made of a kind of quartz known as chalcedony, brown in color.

While Browns Valley points clearly date to the Early Prehistoric, there remained some question about whether the skeleton from the site was of the same age. No points were recovered by the University of Minnesota excavations in direct association with the skeleton, although Jensen claimed to have dug one out

of the burial pit. A Late Prehistoric Plains Village component is also known from the site, as documented by Theodore Lewis' 1887 map of a fortification ditch only 50 m west of the 1933–34 finds (Figure 9). It is apparent from Jenks' report that the 1936 excavations encountered numerous features associated with the Plains Village component:

No additional traces of the Browns Valley Man culture were found, but we did find many evidences of later Indian habitation as expressed in fire hearths, artifacts and caches. Numerous small fire hearths were excavated. We inspected about fourteen of the larger hearths, sixty artifacts and four caches.

31

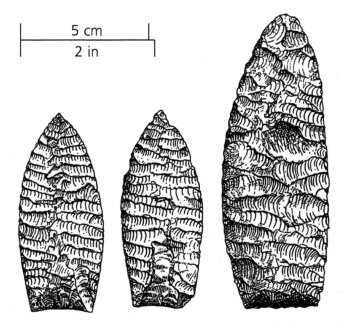

Figure 8. Two Browns Valley points and a knife from the 21TR5 type site (from Jenks 1937).

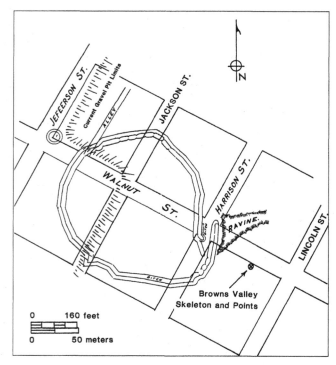

Figure 9. Map of the Browns Valley site (21TR5) showing the location of the skeleton and points with respect to the enclosure mapped by Lewis in 1887 (base map from Winchell 1911:309).

Animal bones were present in abundance . . . (Jenks 1937:11).

It was possible that the Browns Valley burial was of Late Prehistoric age, having been placed into a pit that intruded into an earlier cache of lanceolate points. The only way to directly associate the skeleton with the bifaces was to radiometrically date the bone.

In 1987 Jensen's two daughters found the missing Browns Valley skeleton and the artifacts in a basement closet in their old house. They gave the skeleton, five bifaces, and two abraders to the Science Museum of Minnesota. In 1990 a radiocarbon date for the Browns Valley skeleton was obtained using the accelerator mass-spectrometry method (O. Shane 1991). This process requires only a small quantity of bone. A 10 gm sample of cortical bone was removed from the skeleton's right femur. Four grams were sent to Thomas Stafford at the University of Colorado, who found the bone to be collagenous (containing an insoluble fibrous protein) and well preserved. It was thus suitable for dating.

The remaining six grams of bone were purified by Stafford and then sent to the Institute for Nuclear Science in New Zealand. The first radiocarbon date (Lab #NZA-1102) for the bone was determined to be 8790 ± 110 Radiocarbon Years Before Present (RCYBP). When corrected, the true age of the bone (and therefore the bifaces) is thought to be 9160 ± 110 years old (O. Shane 1991). An additional sample (NZA-1808) of a single isolated amino acid was then dated in 1991; it yielded an uncorrected date of 9049 ± 82 RCYBP. These dates confirm that the Browns Valley skeleton is 9,000 years old and, therefore, one of the few confirmed Paleoindian skeletons in the New World. It also may be the best preserved and most complete.

Hildahl Site Browns Valley points have been reported from one professionally excavated Prairie Lake Region site. The Hildahl #3 site (21YM35) on an intermediate terrace of the Minnesota River Valley near Granite Falls (see Figure 11) was excavated in 1977 by the Science Museum of Minnesota. The site contained Early Archaic, Middle Woodland, and Late Woodland components (Hudak 1978). Earlier surface collections also indicated a Cambria component.

The remains from the earliest Hildahl level are suggested to date between 4,500 to 8,500 years ago based on projectile-point styles (Dobbs 1979:64). Only 13 projectile points were recovered by the excavations, of which Hudak (1978:75) attributed 4 to the Late Woodland component, 6 to the Middle Woodland component, and 3 to the preceramic component.

Dobbs, on the other hand, attributed 8 points to the preceramic component and noted that 2 of these points closely resembled the smallest Browns Valley point (Dobbs 1979:61). Both were made of brown chalcedony.

The Hildahl #3 site had extensively mixed soil horizons because of recent agricultural activity, rodent burrowing, and slope wash. Therefore, associating the projectile points with other items is somewhat speculative. Only 37 identifiable bones and no floral remains appeared to be associated with the preceramic component. Fauna included bison, raccoon, muskrat, turtle, fish, and bird.

Other Plano Sites Browns Valley points also are reported from 21CP35 near the Spring Creek-Chippewa River junction near Montevideo, Minnesota. Extensive exposures of bison bone also have been found in the stream cuts nearby (E. Johnson 1964a:15). This site is near the Watson Sag, a broad valley carved by an early auxiliary channel of Glacial River Warren. The lower Chippewa River flows through the Watson Sag to its junction with the Minnesota River at Montevideo. This locality may offer good potential for discovering early sites in Minnesota. Browns Valley points also are reported in the landowner's collection from the Pedersen site (21LN2) on an island in Lake Benton (G. Joseph Hudak, personal communication 1986).

Brown County, Minnesota, seems especially rich in Plano-complex stone tool work (Figure 10). Surface collections have yielded three Agate Basin points, a Cody-like biface, a Plainview point, and a Dalton point (Trow 1979). These finds were concentrated in a few areas within the county. The Agate Basin points, the Dalton point, and the Plainview point are all from Leavenworth Township, southwest of the town of Sleepy Eye. The Plainview point and the Dalton point are from the Treml site (21BW29) on a peninsula in Alternat Lake. Two of the Agate Basin points are from the Cottonwood site (21BW6) on a bluff overlooking the Cottonwood River. The third is from a nearby field.

Other finds of Minnesota Prairie Lake Region Plano points include two Scottsbluff points and several lanceolate point bases from the Goodrich site (21FA36) in Faribault County (Lofstrom 1988). Eden points have been recorded at the Devils-Redick (21DL8) and Stockhaven Lake (21DL54) sites in northwestern Douglas County (Thomas L. Trow, personal communication 1981). A Hell Gap point is reported from Lincoln County (O. Shane 1989), and a Dalton point from Lac qui Parle County is in the Minnesota Historical Society collections.

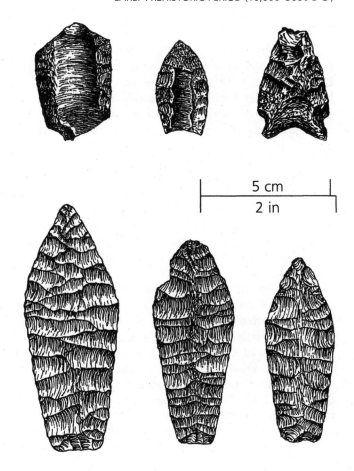

Figure 10. Early Prehistoric artifacts from Brown County, Minnesota (from Trow 1979).

In the Prairie Lake Region of South Dakota, Alberta points have been reported at the Milton site (39DE9) and the Ries site (39DE7) (Haug 1982:52; Haug and Sterner 1978). In Iowa, Agate Basin points have been found in Palo Alto and Buena Vista counties (L. Alex 1980:67), and a Meserve point was found in Webster County (L. Alex 1980:68). Three Scottsbluff points were found on the surface at the Soldow site (13HB1) in Humboldt County (Flanders 1977). Additional late Early Prehistoric artifacts from Iowa include two Cherokee (Hell Gap) points reported from Webster County sites 13WB49 and 13WB73 (Morrow 1984:32) and an Eden-like point found at the Stillman site (13CG23) in Cerro Gordo County (Mallam and Bettis 1981).

Paleoindian Overview

All of the currently known Clovis and Folsom points and most of the Plano points from the Prairie Lake Region are surface finds; provenience is largely by county. Therefore, it is impossible to document settlement patterns for the earliest human inhabitants of the region or to reconstruct their subsistence patterns or other cultural activities. The lack of excavated fluted-point sites immediately adjacent to the region further complicates attempts to understand these earliest cultures. Speculation can be made about Paleoindian lifestyles in the Prairie Lake Region, however. This is especially true when environmental reconstructions and, at least with regard to the Plano complexes, similarities to better-documented sites in adjacent regions are considered.

It should not be assumed that the earliest inhabitants of the Prairie Lake Region were simply big game hunters, as often is suggested for the Paleoindians of the southwestern United States. The environment of the Prairie Lake Region in Paleoindian times was very different from that of the American Southwest. Although large mammals may have been more abundant in the Early Prehistoric boreal forest than in modern boreal forests, such animals were still not present in large numbers or in large groups. Important subsistence resources no doubt included smaller mammals, fish, and vegetal foods. Diverse economic strategies are known to have been used in ice-age Europe 30,000 years ago (Stanley 1980:666).

While Clovis kill sites tend to be associated with mammoths, Folsom and Plano kill sites are associated with bison as well as a variety of small- and medium-sized animals. The late Plano occupation represents the first fully grassland adaption to the Prairie Lake Region. Bison hunting was probably the predominant subsistence activity, but the location of a number of possible Plano sites on lakes indicates that subsistence also depended upon the use of aquatic and forest-edge animals.

Humans grouped in small bands of perhaps 20 to 40 individuals may have been most common in Paleoindian times. The bands would have been highly mobile. The use of "exotic" lithic raw material also suggests that bands may have traveled great distances. They may have moved often, rarely reusing previous campsites. Thus, today we find habitation sites with low artifact densities—when sites are found at all.

During Clovis times, open upland locations may have been favored for campsites to escape the cool, wet lowlands and to provide views of the adjacent landscape. The edges of large lakes and rivers may not have been favored because they were exposed to the weather, topographically unstable, and had limited subsistence resources. Additionally, lacustrine, or lake-related, sites were not as desirable in the time of the early Paleoindian forest as they would be in later times when wood was more scarce.

Lacustrine and riverine habitation sites may have become more desirable during Folsom times as fish and aquatic mammal populations expanded. The Minnesota River Valley may have been especially favored. It would have been abandoned recently by Glacial River Warren, and the broad alluvial terraces may have had a relatively open terrain attractive to large grazing animals. Most sites in the Minnesota River trench subsequently would have been destroyed by the reactivation of Glacial River Warren in post-Folsom times.

Just west of the Prairie Lake Region in northwestern Iowa, the Cherokee Sewer site (13CK405) has yielded the best information on the late Early Prehistoric Period in the northeastern Plains (D. C. Anderson and Semken 1980). Located on an alluvial fan in the floodplain of the Little Sioux River near Cherokee, it was excavated in 1973 and 1976. Three major cultural horizons were defined at the site; the earliest (Horizon III) dated to 6400 B.C.; the intermediate (Horizon II) dated to 5200 B.C.; and the youngest (Horizon I) dated to 4400 B.C. Each horizon appears to represent a late winter bison processing site.

Horizon III of the late Paleoindian Period featured bison bone, bone tools, and lithics clustered around three hearth areas. A minimum number of 8 individual bison were present. Small amounts of deer and beaver remains also were recovered. A human group size of about 15 to 30 individuals is believed to have been at the site (Tatum and Shutler 1980:247). The lithic raw materials in Horizon III came primarily from local till sources. Pink quartzite (27 percent), Tongue River Silica (19.5 percent), and variously colored cherts and chalcedonies were the predominant types of raw material. The only non-local material was a chert (5 percent) that came from from southwestern Iowa (D. C. Anderson 1980:201).

Projectile points from Horizon III were mainly shallow stemmed varieties, with a few lanceolate points. The stemmed points have been called Cherokee points (Morrow 1984:32); they resemble Hell Gap points. The one complete lanceolate point was from the lowest cultural level at the site. It somewhat resembles Agate Basin points, although the Cherokee Sewer specimen has more rounded edges and a narrower base. Horizon III also contained choppers, large ovate bifaces, end scrapers, hammer-stones, and a burin (D. C. Anderson 1980).

The environment of the Prairie Lake Region 8,400 years ago would have been somewhat similar to that of nearby northwest Iowa where the Cherokee Sewer site is located; prairie vegetation had taken over both regions. Bison numbers would have been increasing as the prairie continued to expand to the east, and bison hunting was the principal subsistence activity.

The major difference between the two regions at this time was the presence of extensive lakes in the Prairie Lake Region. This may have led to some subsistence-settlement differences, although some of the shallow lakes may have begun to dry up. The location of the Goodrich site on the bottom of a now-drained lake basin and evidence for other sites in lake basins found by the Northern Border Pipeline Survey (Hudak 1983) indicate low water levels for some lakes. Small watering holes in the deepest parts of these basins would have attracted both humans and animals. The wood and water resources of the Minnesota River Valley were also no doubt extensively utilized during Plano times, although in early Plano times Glacial River Warren would have inundated the valley's lower terraces.

Mortuary patterns and physical characteristics for Paleoindians are largely unknown even outside of the Prairie Lake Region. There are perhaps six sites in the New World that have yielded human skeletal materials dating to earlier than 8,000 years ago.

Browns Valley is one of these sites (Young et al. 1987). The Browns Valley skeleton was apparently a semi-flexed pit burial, meaning that the body was slightly bent with the knees towards the torso before it was lowered into a pit for burial. Remains of red ochre indicate that the body was stained with the substance. It was accompanied by grave goods. The skeleton is that of a male in his mid-twenties to early forties. Physical characteristics include a long skull, short face, prominent brow ridges, and a wide lower jaw.

The skeleton of a young woman found near Pelican Rapids, Minnesota (originally known as Minnesota Man), also is considered to be of Paleoindian age. This site (21OT3) is located just north of the Prairie Lake Region. The skeleton was exposed in 1931 during road construction (Jenks 1936; E. Johnson 1988:7), and it reportedly was found in a stratum of glacial lake clay almost 10 feet below the modern surface. The skeleton was removed by the road crew before archaeologists visited the site. Therefore, the stratigraphy of the soil layers was disturbed, and the context in which the skeleton was found is open to dispute. A perforated elk antler thought to be a flaking tool and a marine shell pendant were found with the skeleton. The Pelican Rapids site is not considered to be a burial, but an accidental death.

Prairie Archaic Tradition
(5500–3000 B.C.)

In the Midwest the Archaic Tradition usually is considered to encompass complexes that have broader based economies than those of the Paleoindian Tradition but generally lack the ceramics, mound burials, and horticulture present in the Woodland Tradition. The boundaries between the Archaic Tradition and the traditions temporally on either side, however, are not as clear-cut as once thought. Evidence has been found for small-game hunting and gathering in the Paleoindian Tradition and for ceramics, mound burial, and horticulture in the Archaic (cf. Phillips and Brown 1983). There do, however, appear to be technological and economic changes associated with a more foraging-oriented way of life that differentiate Archaic complexes from those of the Paleoindian Tradition. Too, the appearance of ceramics is still a useful marker, signaling the end of the Archaic and the beginning of the Woodland Tradition in much of the Midwest.

The Archaic Tradition in the northeastern Plains seems to have begun about 7,500 years ago, although it may have begun as early as 10,000 years ago in the eastern Midwest. Evidence for the initial Archaic complexes of the northeastern Plains are seen in the use of side-notched projectile points, ground stone tools, and local, focused bison hunting. The widespread use of a variety of side-notched points throughout much of the Middle Prehistoric, however, makes it difficult to assign any site to the Archaic solely on the basis of the presence of points similar to the ones found at early Archaic sites. Conversely, Reeves (1973) believed that side-notched points from the early Archaic often are ascribed incorrectly to later periods.

The Archaic of the western Midwest often is referred to as the Prairie Archaic, since most of this area was covered by grassland after 8,000 years ago. Intensive bison hunting dominated the lives of Prairie Archaic people, although there is evidence for other economic activities as well. The Prairie Archaic upland hunting-gathering lifeway appears to have continued in lakeless regions north and south of the Prairie Lake Region after 3000 B.C. (Michlovic and Schneider 1988; Benn 1988). Meanwhile, a more lacustrine-oriented way of life was established in the Prairie Lake Region 2,500 years before the beginning of the Woodland Tradition.

It is likely that the technology and economic orientation of many of the early Archaic sites throughout the northeastern Plains will resemble Horizons I and II of the Cherokee Sewer site of northwestern Iowa where side-notched projectile points were found in association with bison bone. Horizon II at the Cherokee Sewer has been dated to 5200 B.C. and Horizon I dated to 4400 B.C.

Prairie Archaic Sites

Granite Falls Bison Site

There is only one well-dated early Archaic site in the Prairie Lake Region, the Granite Falls Bison site (21YM47). It is in the upper Minnesota River Valley about 2 km northwest of the Hildahl site (Figure 11) and about 1.2 km southwest of the Minnesota River, on a narrow terrace 5 m above the river level. Just west, the steep walls of the river valley ascend 30 m to the upland. Only preliminary reports are available for archaeological explorations.

The Granite Falls Bison site was uncovered in 1988 by the landowner while digging a trash pit with a backhoe. The trench penetrated alluvial and colluvial deposits to a depth of 2.8 m. A layer of bison bone was noticed at the bottom of the pit. The landowner-backhoe operator found a large ovate biface *in situ* with the bone.

The site was examined by the author of this study in August 1988 soon after its discovery. Much of the bone and the ovate biface were still in place. A pie-slice trench was present with dimensions of 5 m on the sides and 3 m and 1 m on the ends. The pit was flanked by an outcropping of granite on the west. Much bone was present in the backdirt pile. The site appeared to have multiple individual bison remains, some of which were immature. The biface had been removed briefly from the bone bed by the landowner and then replaced. The biface, made of yellow-gray Tongue River Silica, is 66 mm long, 38 mm wide, and 7 mm thick.

Subsequent excavations were undertaken at the Granite Falls Bison site by the Institute for Minnesota Archaeology (IMA) in 1988, 1989, and 1990. In late 1988, IMA investigations did not expand the original excavation but examined the already exposed remains in the pit bottom and screened the backdirt pile. A small, side-notched projectile point made of chert was found in the backdirt. The point is 3.7 cm long and 2 cm wide.

Standley Lewis of St. Cloud State University obtained radiocarbon dates on the bone of 6390 ± 110 RCYBP (Beta 27883) and 6840 ± 120 RCYBP (Beta 30541). Lewis documented that at least five bison were present at the site—four adults and one immature animal 1.6 years old. The site's seasonality was suggested to be late fall or early winter. Butchering

marks were evident on the limbs and neural spine (S. Lewis and Heikes 1990).

The IMA excavations in 1989 consisted of a 1 x 4 m unit just east of the original pit. Three of the 1 x 1 m squares were taken to within 15 cm of the bone bed; the fourth square was taken into the bone bed. This excavation found a concentration of lithic debris and fire-cracked rock; this indicated an additional cultural horizon at a depth of about 1.8 m (Pratt 1989).

The upper 1.3 m of sediment appeared to be largely colluvial. Below 1.3 m, alluvial sediments extended to bedrock, which varied in depth from 2 to 7 m. Deep coring in 1989 suggested the presence of several basins in the granite bedrock, one of which contained the exposed bison-bone bed. About 10 m west of the bison bone, coring indicated a buried soil horizon at 3.65 m in the deepest basin. This horizon has not been investigated archaeologically (Dobbs 1990).

In 1990, IMA expanded the formal excavation with a 3 x 3 m unit on the west side of the original pit. The younger cultural horizon at 1.8 m below the surface was indicated by a layer of weathered gneiss rock and a few pieces of lithic debris. The 3 x 3 m unit and the 1989 1 x 4 m unit were then excavated through the bison-bone bed. Examination of the deeper horizon documented that it was located on what had been a slight slope between 2.57 and 3 m (Christiansen [1990]).

Three projectile points were recovered from the bone bed, along with a hammer-stone and at least two basaltic chopping tools. A lithic reduction area and a possible hearth also were found. The points are all side-notched and made of chert. The largest point is made of blue-gray fossiliferous chert. It is 4.5 cm in length and 2 cm in width. The other two points are basal fragments about the same size as the 1988 point from the backdirt (George W. Christiansen III, personal communication 1992).

Horn cores from Granite Falls indicate that the bison were *Bison occidentalis*. It has been suggested that the bison were driven into the bedrock basins by early Archaic people 7,500 to 7,000 years ago. The bison were then trapped against the bedrock wall. Hunters would have been able to dispatch the bison while protected by bedrock pillars (Lewis and Heikes 1990).

Other Possible Prairie Archaic Sites

The Goodrich site (21FA36) is located in the middle of a drained lake in south-central Minnesota (Lofstrom 1988). The lake was probably dry for much of the late Early Prehistoric, although small

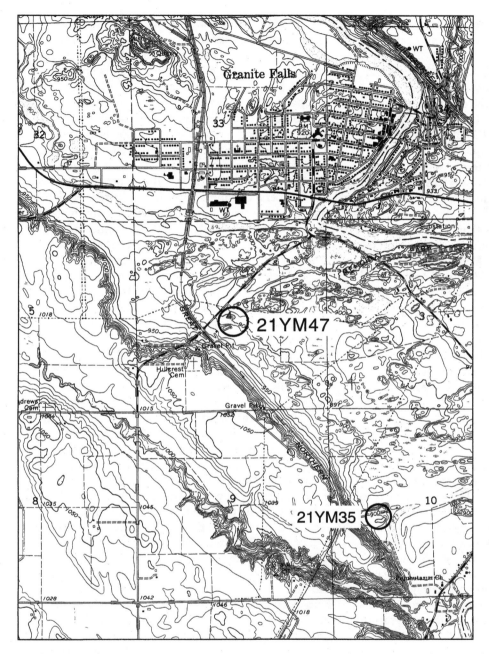

Figure 11. Locations of the Hildahl (21YM35) and Granite Falls Bison (21YM47) sites on the "Granite Falls" United States Geological Survey (USGS) 7.5' map.

watering holes often may have been present or water could have been near the surface and obtained through shallow wells. Side-notched and stemmed points from the lake bed indicate smoothing and polishing probably through post-depositional wave action, although several Scottsbluff points from the site are not polished, suggesting deep burial prior to lake refilling.

The side-notched points from the Goodrich site resemble points from Cherokee Sewer Horizons II and I, as well as concave-base early Middle Prehistoric

points from the Mountain Lake site (see Figure 14, Chapter 5). The Goodrich site has also yielded ground stone axes and mauls, scrapers, and bison bone.

The Soldow site (13HB1) is perhaps the best-documented late Early Prehistoric site in the Prairie Lake Region of Iowa. Located 32 km north of Fort Dodge on a knoll above the Des Moines River, it was excavated in 1961 (Flanders 1977). Three Scottsbluff points were recovered from the surface, but excavated points are mostly side-notched forms with ground, concave bases resembling points from Cherokee Sewer

Horizons II and I. The site may be a lithic workshop, but the presence of scrapers and a grinding stone indicates other pursuits as well.

Similar side-notched points also have been found at the Ocheyedan (13OA401) and Arthur (13DK27) sites in north-central Iowa, where such points have been called Little Sioux points (Morrow 1984:61). The Blue Dog Lake site (39DA201) in northeastern South Dakota has yielded similar points (cf. McNerney 1970). In southwestern Minnesota, side-notched points like Cherokee Sewer Horizon II forms are evident at the Pedersen (21LN2) and Hildahl #3 (21YM35) sites.

Another contemporaneous site may be the Jackpot Junction site (21RW53) in the Minnesota River Valley east of Redwood Falls (Peterson [1990]). Preliminary testing by the Minnesota Trunk Highway Archaeological Survey recovered stone flakes as well as bison, turtle, small mammal, and fish bone from depths of 1.5 m to 3 m. No projectile points have been recovered. Two radiocarbon dates have been obtained from the site. One (Beta 35176) from bone is 4890 ± 100 RCYBP (corrected to 3600 B.C.) and one (Beta 35177) from charcoal is 4730 ± 100 RCYBP (corrected to 3515 B.C.).

Prairie Archaic Overview

At the beginning of the Archaic Period about 7,000 years ago, the warming, drying trend was peaking. The prairie border was about 120 km northeast of its modern position. During the prairie peak between 7,000 to 6,000 years ago, woody vegetation would have been rare in the Prairie Lake Region. The prairie became mixed-grass rather than tallgrass. Summer droughts would have been more frequent and severe, causing many lakes to dry up and remain dry for long periods. Lakes that did not completely dry up experienced increased infilling with soil and increased salinity (Haworth 1972; Walker 1966; Radle et al. 1989). Prairie fires often must have swept through large areas of the region. Beginning about 6,000 years ago, a cooler, wetter climate was established. The prairie began a gradual retreat to the southwest, reaching its modern borders about 5,000 years ago.

To understand the Prairie Archaic, archaeologists have also studied artifacts from the Cherokee Sewer site in northwestern Iowa. Horizon II artifacts include side-notched and triangular, unnotched projectile points with straight or concave bases. There are also ovate and triangular bifaces, choppers, end scrapers, hammer-stones, a milling stone, and bone tools such as choppers and awls. Hideworking implements were

found in Horizon II. Subsistence remains are dominated by bison, but also include rabbit and skunk. The bison bone in Horizon II was very fragmented, indicating use of all the available meat. This is consistent with archaeologists' expectations for a late winter occupation (D. C. Anderson and Semken 1980).

Horizon I at Cherokee Sewer contained side-notched projectile points ranging in length from 2.8 to 6.2 cm. In general, the points from Horizon I are more isoceles in shape in contrast to the more equilateral Horizon II points. Horizon I also contained bifaces, end scrapers, choppers, a burin, and a few bone tools such as choppers and awls. Bison bone dominates the subsistence remains. Canid remains found in Horizon I suggest the earliest known evidence for the use of domestic dogs in the northeastern Plains.

Lithic debris distribution indicates three activity areas for Horizon II and four for Horizon I. Tongue River Silica dominates the lithic raw material (90 percent). Local cherts, quartzites, and chalcedonies make up most of the remainder, with a small percentage of fusulinid chert (D. C. Anderson 1980:201). All three horizons at Cherokee Sewer appear to be late winter bison kills occupied by family groups of 15 to 30 individuals.

Many of the projectile points from the early horizon at the Itasca Bison site (21CE1) in north-central Minnesota closely resemble side-notched forms from Horizon II at Cherokee Sewer and the side-notched points from Granite Falls Bison sites. The Itasca area, now a pine forest, was prairie during the initial Archaic Period. Thus, this site too may offer information regarding lifestyles in the Prairie Lake Region at the end of the Early Prehistoric. The Itasca Bison site, on Nicollet Creek immediately adjacent to Lake Itasca, is about 100 km north of the Prairie Lake Region and 50 km east of the modern prairie border. The site was excavated in 1937, 1963, 1964, and 1965 by the University of Minnesota (C. Shay 1971). C. Thomas Shay's site report is recognized widely as an excellent example of an interdisciplinary study in environmental archaeology.

The Itasca Bison site contains two loci 150 m apart. One is in the Nicollet Creek Valley, extending from the toe of the valley slope into a peat bog. The other is on a hill overlooking the valley about 15 m higher than the bog. The lower site is interpreted as a lakeshore habitation on a former extension of Lake Itasca. The lower site has been radiocarbon dated to between 6000 to 5000 B.C. Shay (1971:47) believed the hill and bog locations to be of the same age because of the similarities in raw materials and some projectile points. Yet, the upper site also appears to contain a Woodland occupation, based on the presence of corner-notched points.

The lower site area at Itasca yielded numerous bison bones from at least 16 individuals; some resemble extinct species. Other faunal remains from the bog include 22 mammal species besides bison, of which muskrat was the most numerous. There are also 11 species of bird, 3 of turtle, and 7 of fish, dominated by sucker, northern pike, and large-mouth bass. The sexes and ages of the bison suggest a fall occupation, but the turtle and fish bone may indicate a spring habitation (C. Shay 1971:65).

Associated with the bones from the bog are 6 projectile points, 7 knives, 3 choppers, 1 end scraper, 1 perforator, 2 cores, and 57 flakes. The projectile points (Figure 12) are small side-notched forms with concave bases somewhat resembling the side-notched points from the upper horizons at the Cherokee Sewer site. This suggests that the Itasca bison kill may be closer to 7,000 years old rather than 8,000 years old.

Based on the evidence from the Granite Falls, Cherokee Sewer, and Itasca sites, the initial Archaic occupation of the Prairie Lake Region may represent a climax of pedestrian bison hunting in the northeastern Plains. This subsistence focus was encouraged by the expansion eastward of large bison herds during the post-glacial thermal maximum. The warm, dry climate also limited other subsistence options, namely aquatic and forest-edge species. While bison hunting remained important in all regions of the northeastern Plains, other subsistence options were more viable when the climate became gradually wetter and cooler after 6,000 years ago.

Although focal bison hunting dominated the way of life of early Archaic peoples in the northeastern Plains, it was during this time that a number of technological innovations appeared that suggest foraging was also important to the economy. The appearance of milling stones, domestic dogs, and new projectile-point hafting techniques indicate shifts in the subsistence pattern. Seed gathering may have been used to fulfill dietary needs formerly satisfied by aquatic tubers and legumes. Dogs could be used not only for more effective hunting, but for transporting supplies between frequently shifting base camps and even for food. New hafting techniques may indicate more efficient methods of dispatching bison. This subsistence pattern could be termed "primary grasslands efficiency," as economic attention was focused on upland resources.

Sites of this time period reflect the small group sizes. Locations were no doubt sought that provided proximity to game (especially bison), shelter, wood, and water. With many of the smaller lakes dry, larger lake basins and rivers probably were preferred campsite locations. The scarcity of imported raw materials indicates an intensified use of local resources.

Mortuary treatments for the early Archaic of the Prairie Lake Region are not known but probably resemble burials at the Turin site (13MN2) in western Iowa, which is believed to represent a Prairie Archaic mortuary site (Fisher et al. 1985). It contained the remains of four individuals who were buried in flexed position in separate shallow pits. One of the burials had associated red ochre and grave goods. Among the grave goods was a side-notched projectile point similar to the Cherokee Sewer Horizon I type and a necklace of *Anculusa* shell beads.

Perspective on the Early Prehistoric Period

It may be premature to define Early Prehistoric phases for the Prairie Lake Region based on current knowledge. However, some distributional patterns are evident, and chronological parameters have been defined. It was suggested previously (Anfinson 1987b) that two late Early Prehistoric phases could be defined, a late Paleoindian Cherokee Phase (7000–5500 B.C.), based on Horizon III at the Cherokee Sewer site, and an early Archaic Itasca Phase (5500–3000 B.C.), based on the early horizon at the Itasca Bison site and Horizons I and II at Cherokee Sewer. With the discovery and examination of the Granite Falls Bison site, there is temptation to develop these phases further and perhaps rename the Itasca Phase for Granite Falls since the Itasca site is outside of the northeastern Plains.

While such phases may hold some usefulness for organizing the Prairie Lake Region's early occupation history, and probably that of the northeastern Plains as a whole, they will not be defined here. The reason is simple. We are only beginning to understand subsistence-settlement patterns, technology, mortuary techniques, and chronological limits for late Early Prehistoric cultures. When the Granite Falls site is better described and additional Early Prehistoric radiocarbon dates have been obtained from other regional sites, these phases may be resurrected.

As for the distribution of fluted-point complexes in the Prairie Lake Region, there appears to be a scarcity of Clovis points in the western half and a lack of fluted points in general from the northern part (see Figure 6). The latter may reflect west-central Minneso-

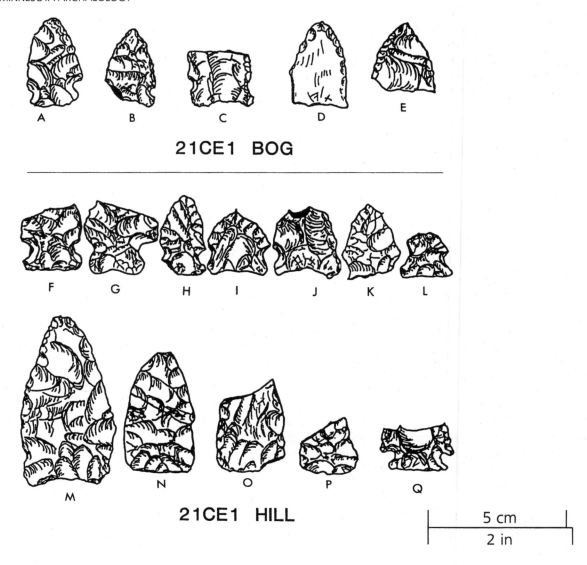

Figure 12. Projectile points from the Itasca Bison site divided by the hill or the bog loci (from Shay 1971).

ta's initial isolation by formidable barriers: Lake Agassiz, Glacial River Warren, and the melt-water engorged Mississippi River. The late survival of a relatively resource-poor boreal forest in this area also may have discouraged early settlement.

Plano-point distributions seem to reflect more localized traditions than are evident immediately following the Plano horizon. Agate Basin and Dalton (Meserve) points are found in the eastern part of the region in south-central Minnesota and Iowa, while Browns Valley points are found in the western part in northeastern South Dakota and southwestern Minnesota. This may result from the difference in available resources attributable to the gradual displacement of the forest by grassland, with large wooded areas remaining longer in eastern and northern areas.

While many Early Prehistoric artifact finds may be from upland or riverine terrace locations, most of the Folsom points, plus the Brown County, Minnesota, Dalton and Plainview points, are from water-related locations. This indicates some dependence on water resources following the disappearance of the boreal forest and prior to the Prairie Period. No fluted-point or Plano components have been documented, however, in excavated contexts from the island-peninsula sites containing multicomponent Middle and Late Prehistoric levels. This suggests a different Early Prehistoric subsistence-settlement pattern. Unlike during the late

Early Prehistoric, the lake basins would have been full of water during much of the Paleoindian times.

Initial human occupation of the Prairie Lake Region could not have been very dense, as indicated by the relatively sparse artifact finds. Deeply buried sites exist in the major river valleys and are difficult to find, but the region does have fewer deep-soil horizon localities than adjacent regions to the west, south, and east. This is because of limited loess or clay deposition and the lack of extensive river-bottom environments, with the exception of the Minnesota River Valley.

As the woodlands thinned with the warming, drying climate, bison played an increasingly important subsistence role during the Early Prehistoric. Prior to this, a more diverse economy utilizing a variety of mammals, fish, and even plant foods may have been present.

The region's environment was in a state of flux during the Early Prehistoric Period; no doubt, subsistence-settlement patterns were as well. Climatic stress on the environment as a whole may have been greatest during initial Archaic times in the second half of the Early Prehistoric Period, but one critical resource, bison, would have been more abundant. Focal bison hunting can be a very successful economic activity, as demonstrated by numerous Plains cultures in recorded, historic times. Successful bison hunting, coupled with technological innovations that offered significant subsistence from foraging, resulted in gradual human population increases in the northeastern Plains throughout the later half of the Early Prehistoric.

Continual environmental change required the peoples of the Prairie Lake Region to alter their lifestyles. These alterations climaxed during the Middle Prehistoric Period in a way of life uniquely suited to a region of both prairie and lakes.

Chapter 5

Middle Prehistoric Period (3000 B.C.–A.D. 900)

Mountain Lake Phase
(3000–200 B.C.)

With the return of a cooler, moister climate by 3000 B.C., the Prairie Lake Region took on an appearance that was to last into the contact period. The large bison herds shifted west, woody vegetation expanded slightly, and the shallow lakes were full of water most of the time. The region became environmentally and culturally distinct from adjacent regions, and the subsistence-settlement pattern that was to characterize the remainder of the Middle Prehistoric developed.

While bison hunting remained important to late Archaic peoples in the region, extensive aquatic resources, which had not been available to early Archaic peoples, became equally essential. In areas north and south of the Prairie Lake Region that lacked lake basins, focal bison hunting continued throughout the Archaic and Woodland traditions.

The Mountain Lake Phase is the terminal Archaic phase for the Prairie Lake Region. It could be called "Prairie Lake Archaic," for it was during this phase that human occupation focused on lacustrine island and peninsula sites and that the economy featured a blend of upland and aquatic resources.

Mountain Lake Site

The Mountain Lake site (21CO1) in southwestern Minnesota is the type site for the initial Middle Prehistoric phase. The site is on a prominent, wooded hill that was an island in a now-drained lake south of the town of Mountain Lake (Figure 13). Lloyd Wilford of the University of Minnesota first excavated at the site in 1957 and five years later produced an unpublished site report (Wilford 1962). G. Joseph Hudak of the

Science Museum of Minnesota excavated at the site in 1976. No comprehensive report is available for this later excavation, although Orrin Shane (1978) has discussed the faunal remains.

The 1957 Mountain Lake excavations opened three 10-foot squares and two 5-foot squares near the eastern edge of the site. Six-inch (15 cm) levels were used, and the soil may have been screened through 3/8-inch (1 cm) mesh. Four levels were completed in one of the 10-foot squares and three levels in the other two 10-foot squares. Heavy rains allowed only the first level to be excavated in the two 5-foot squares. Wilford (1962) identified a Woodland and an Oneota component based on the ceramics.

While Wilford stated in his site report that there were only two cultural horizons at the site, he had noted earlier, however, a type of projectile point he called "non-stemmed, non-triangular" which appeared to "apparently represent a somewhat older horizon" (Wilford 1962:19). An examination of the projectile points in the University of Minnesota collections indicates they are small lanceolate points, with straight to concave bases and contracting lower edges resembling incipient stemming. All five points of this type came from Wilford's lower levels. At least five more of these points are apparent in the Science Museum of Minnesota collections from 1976 (Figure 14, bottom row).

The 1976 museum investigation excavated 48 square meters in two contiguous units near the southeastern end of the island. The soil was removed in 5-cm levels and screened through 1/2-inch (1.3 cm) mesh. Besides the Middle Woodland and Oneota horizons noted by Wilford, the 1976 excavations determined there also was an Archaic horizon at the site (O. Shane 1978:3).

The 1976 excavations found evidence of an oval-shaped dwelling that initially was ascribed to the

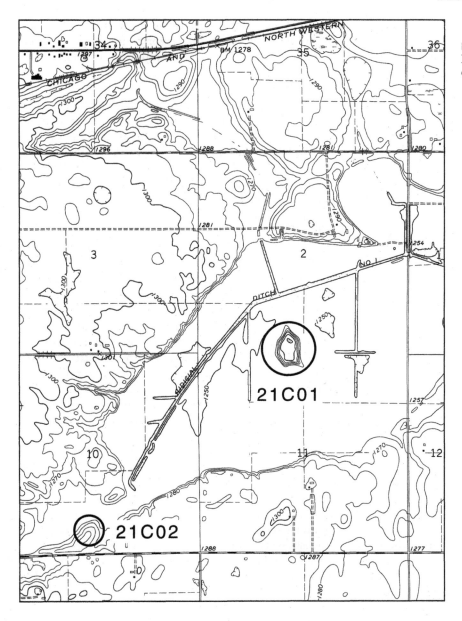

Figure 13. Locations of the Mountain Lake (21CO1) and Franz (21CO2) sites on the Mountain Lake USGS 7.5' map.

Archaic occupation (P. Miller 1980; Hudson 1979). A later examination of the artifact distribution indicated that the house was associated more likely with a later horizon (Timothy L. Ready, personal communication 1985). Two radiocarbon dates on bone from the site yielded dates around A.D. 1800 and were assumed to be in error (Lass 1980b:32).

Other Mountain Lake Phase Sites

Most of the major Middle Prehistoric habitation sites in the Prairie Lake Region have some evidence for a late Archaic horizon, but the evidence is usually not stratigraphically distinct. All the horizons in these sites are somewhat mixed in the dark, deep prairie soil because of rodent activity and other disturbances. Excavated habitation sites with apparent Mountain Lake Phase occupations include Pedersen (21LN2), Fox Lake (21MR2), Big Slough (21MU1), and Arthur (13DK27), based on radiocarbon dates and stratigraphic associations.

In 1958, while digging at Mountain Lake, Wilford also tested the nearby Franz site (21CO2) located 2 km southwest of the Mountain Lake site on an intermittent creek near the lake's southwest shore (Figure 13). The landowner of the Franz site had found a

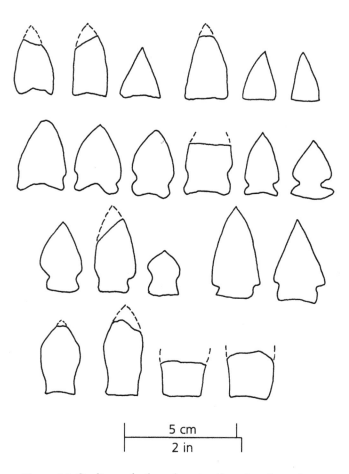

| 5 cm |
| 2 in |

Figure 14. Outlines of selected projectile points from the 1976 excavations at the Mountain Lake site (21CO1).

cache of 48 large ovate bifaces made of white chert. Wilford excavated a 10 x 10-foot unit adjacent to the cache, but the unit yielded only 2 more bifaces and a broken side-notched point. The site was attributed to the Archaic based upon the similarity of the bifaces to Archaic sites in Illinois (E. Johnson 1959). Caches of ovate bifaces have been found at several other Prairie Lake Region sites including Pomme de Terre River (21SW5), Seim-Livingood (21CP29), and Hilde (39LK7).

The Jeffers Petroglyph site (21CO3) in southwestern Minnesota is the most extensive petroglyph site in the northeastern Plains. Most of the petroglyphs have been attributed to the period between 1500 B.C. and 500 B.C. by Lothson (1976:31), based on numerous representations of atlatls, stemmed points, and tanged (or socketed) "Old Copper" points. Other glyphs appear to date from the Late Prehistoric. If some of the glyphs indeed date to the late preceramic era, many insights into the technology and ideology of the Mountain Lake Phase may be available. Lothson

believed the Jeffers petroglyphs are related to the practice of hunting magic, the performance of sacred ceremonies, and the recording of important events.

Technology

Lanceolate points similar to the Mountain Lake examples are evident in collections from the Pedersen site (21LN2) in southwestern Minnesota (Hudak 1976:Plate 9) and the Arthur site (13DK27) in northern Iowa (D. C. Anderson and Spriesterbach 1982: Figure 37). The Stillman site (13CG23) near the eastern edge of the Prairie Lake Region in northern Iowa also may have points of this type (Mallam and Bettis 1981: Figure 26).

The lanceolate points of the Mountain Lake Phase (Figure 14, bottom) somewhat resemble Plano points in outline, but the workmanship on the Mountain Lake examples is poorer. They are smaller, and the use of non-local materials is rare. Lanceolate points are found in Late Archaic horizons in west-central Illinois (J. Brown and Vierra 1983) and northwestern Missouri (Reeder 1980) associated with the Titterington and Nebo Hill phases; these points are generally longer than the Mountain Lake points.

The stemmed points of the Mountain Lake Phase can have expanding, straight, or contracting stems. They resemble Archaic types found throughout the Prairie Peninsula (cf. Cook 1976; P. A. Miller 1980; Montet-White 1968). Some of the lanceolate points of the Mountain Lake Phase may be preforms (preliminarily sized and shaped) for stemmed points.

Short lanceolate points are not the only projectile points associated with the Mountain Lake Phase. The lowest levels at most of the major multicomponent sites in the Prairie Lake Region also produce stemmed and side-notched points; not all produce the lanceolate type. The stemmed and side-notched forms vary widely in outline and size, making it is difficult to define clearly a Mountain Lake horizon at many sites. Similar points often are found in excavation levels associated with initial Woodland ceramics, and soil disturbance is extensive at most of these sites. Typically, when such a horizon is apparent, it is narrow and blends into the Woodland horizon above.

There appear to be no clearly defined side-notched types associated with the Mountain Lake Phase. At the Fox Lake site, the stratigraphically lowest side-notched points feature moderate sizes, shallow notches, and straight or slightly concave bases (Anfinson 1987b:297). At most major multicomponent sites in the Prairie Lake Region, side-notched points are found in all stratigraphic levels and vary widely. The preceramic levels, however, usually lack the deeply basallynotched lanceolate (McKean), stemmed (Hanna, Duncan), and side-notched (Mallory) points of the contemporaneous McKean complex of the High Plains (cf. Greiser 1985:91–92). However, side-notched points with deep concave bases are evident in initial Woodland levels at the Mountain Lake and Pedersen sites.

Because of horizon mixing, it is also difficult to define other aspects of Mountain Lake Phase technology. At the Fox Lake site, quartzite was used more commonly, and chalcedony was used as a raw material in the lowest levels. Chert was the most common material (Anfinson 1987b:293). Raw material types are generally from local till sources. Ground stone tools are found in low numbers at Prairie Lake Region Middle Prehistoric sites, but no firm associations have been made with the late Archaic.

The ovate bifaces from the Franz site may or may not be associated with the Mountain Lake Phase. Ovate bifaces classed as preform reduction blanks were found associated with the Hilde site (39LK7) burials dated to around 2500 B.C. (Lueck et al. 1987). Caches of similar bifaces have been found at several other Prairie Lake Region sites including 21SW5, 21CP29, and 21KH47. Caches of ovate bifaces are associated with the Early Woodland in New York (R. Mason 1981:211–13) and the Late Prehistoric in the northwestern Plains (M. Miller et al. 1991).

In the Prairie Lake Region copper tools are very rare, especially those with Archaic affiliations. A large copper spear point has been reported from 13DK7 on Lake West Okoboji ("Finds of the Year," *Iowa Archaeological Society Newsletter*, vol. 40, no. 2[1990]:4). A small conoidal (cone-shaped) copper point supposedly was found associated with bison bone in the bottom of the Minnesota River Valley near Franklin, Minnesota (Fryklund 1941:9). No precontact copper artifacts have been recovered from any of the excavated sites in the Prairie Lake Region.

Subsistence

While the projectile points of the Mountain Lake Phase may resemble more closely contemporaneous complexes to the east rather than the west, the subsistence pattern shows no evidence of early horticulture or even intensive use of seeds or nuts, hallmarks of the Midwestern Late Archaic period. Although Mountain Lake Phase subsistence studies are few and uncomprehensive, most multicomponent sites in the Prairie Lake Region yield few milling stones. The ones that are found appear to date to Woodland horizons. No remnants of cultivated plants have been found in Middle Prehistoric cultural levels at any Prairie Lake Region site.

Orrin Shane (1978:6) described only 17 identifiable bones from the preceramic horizon at the Mountain Lake site. All of the bones are either from bison or *Canis* sp. At the Fox Lake site, the lowest levels (which appear to be preceramic/initial Woodland) were dominated by bison, muskrat, and fish remains, but they included remains of several other small mammals, turtle, and waterfowl (Anfinson 1987b:283). The lower levels at the Arthur site in northern Iowa contained faunal remains similar to the Fox Lake site (Tiffany 1982b: Appendix E).

Dobbs's 1979 study of the early horizon at the Hildahl #3 site (21YM35) is entitled "Archaic Subsistence in Southwestern Minnesota," but it is of limited use in defining the subsistence patterns of the Mountain Lake Phase. As previously discussed, the Hildahl site is multicomponent and stratigraphically complex. Only 37 identifiable bones and no floral remains were associated with the preceramic component. Minimum numbers (1 bison, 1 raccoon, 1 muskrat, 2 turtles, 1 fish, and 1 bird) were determined. No milling stones were recovered.

Settlement Pattern

While there is some indication for Early Prehistoric occupation of some of the island/peninsula sites in the Prairie Lake Region, Mountain Lake Phase occupations appear to be the first clear evidence for a lake-oriented habitation pattern. These occupations predate Woodland use of the same settlement pattern by perhaps 2,500 years, although terminal Archaic and initial Woodland horizons are often stratigraphically blended at the sites (Figure 15).

Island and peninsula sites offered protection from prairie fires and perhaps enemy groups, provided easy access to water and aquatic resources, and, most of all, offered wood for fires and shelter. Island sites would have been difficult to occupy for brief periods in the early winter and early spring when ice was forming or breaking up; otherwise, they could have been used throughout the year. Large wooded areas, especially in river valleys, may have been preferred winter habitations, providing wind breaks, wood for fires, and material for houses. House forms for the Mountain Lake Phase are not known. As previously stated, the apparent house feature found by the 1976 excavations at the Mountain Lake site is associated with the Late Prehistoric horizon.

Mortuary Treatment

The best candidate for a Mountain Lake Phase burial is the Hilde site (39LK7) in the Prairie Lake Region of South Dakota. The Hilde site is on a hill

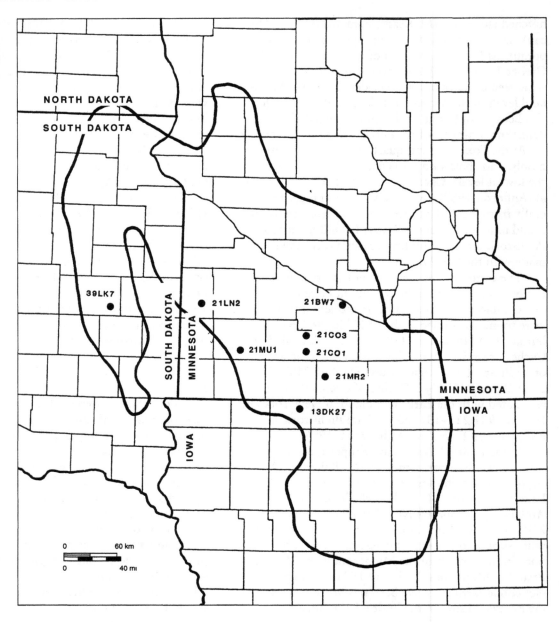

Figure 15. Locations of Mountain Lake Phase sites.

overlooking Lake Madison where a gravel pit was found in the early 1980s to contain burials (Lueck et al. 1987).

Salvage excavations in 1981 and 1985 indicated that there were 17 to 18 individuals buried in 7 to 10 graves. The burials were single primary and single and multiple secondary. Associated with the burials were numerous bifacial preforms. Some use of red ochre also was evident. Historical records and soils analysis indicate a mound had not been located at the site. Two radiocarbon dates have been obtained for the Hilde site, one on charcoal at 4040 ± 100 RCYBP (I-14,246) and one on bone at 3800 ± 110 RCYBP (I-12,298).

The Runck site (21BW7) in Minnesota's Prairie Lake Region also may be a burial of the Mountain Lake Phase. This site has been classified as Archaic based on the lack of ceramics and the presence of Parkdale Eared points (Valentine 1969). The Runck site is located on a terrace of the Minnesota River near New Ulm.

The single primary burial at the Runck site was exposed by a gravel operation in 1958 and removed along with two projectile points "from a pit" by the landowner (Valentine 1969). In 1963 a University of Minnesota team visited the site, made a surface collection, excavated a few test units, and examined the landowner's notes and photos.

The Runck burial pit apparently was covered with a layer of large cobbles and lined with smaller cobbles. No mound had ever been noticed above the burial, but the terrace had been cultivated for many years. A small mound group was still visible on a nearby, higher terrace which was also in a cultivated area.

The lower-terrace surface collection and tests yielded 48 chipped stone tools, a large quantity of chert debitage, 3 ground stone mauls, a hammer-stone, and several cores (Valentine 1969:72). The 14 projectile points were triangular unnotched, corner-notched, side-notched, and stemmed types. The Parkdale Eared points associated with the burial resemble the side-notched, concave base points from the Mountain Lake site. Parkdale Eared points were defined by MacNeish in 1958 in southeastern Manitoba and attributed to Archaic contexts. Similar points now are referred to as Oxbow points in the northern Plains (Buchner 1980:46) and date from 2500–2000 B.C. (Reeves 1973:1245).

The other points from the Runck site also resemble Fox Lake Phase examples. All of the Runck points were made of locally available cherts. The large number of flakes and the presence of a few cores indicates the site served as a lithic workshop as well as a burial site.

Dating

Only four radiocarbon dates are associated with the Mountain Lake Phase. The Pederson site produced a date of 3495 ±85 RCYBP (dendro-corrected to 1800 B.C.) from charcoal in the preceramic horizon (Lass 1980b:35). (Dendro-correction is a technique used to evaluate the accuracy of radiocarbon dating; it utilizes the patterns and spacing of tree rings preserved in wood samples from sites that represent yearly growth patterns and thus can be related to actual calendar years.) At the Fox Lake site, a bison bone date from the lowest 1982 excavation level was 2500 ±130 RCYBP (dendro-corrected to 660 B.C.) This level was the approximate interface of the pre-Woodland and Woodland horizons (Anfinson 1987b:328). The two Hilde site dates listed above indicate dendro-corrected dates of 2580 B.C. and 2240 B.C.

Fox Lake Phase
(200 B.C.–A.D. 700)

Based on the materials recovered from the 1935 testing of the Fox Lake site, Lloyd Wilford first recognized a distinct Woodland complex in southern Min-

nesota. He then proposed a single Woodland complex, the Southern Minnesota Aspect, for all of southern Minnesota, including such environmentally diverse sites as Fox Lake in the southwest and LaMoille Rockshelter (21WN1) in the southeast (Wilford 1941, 1955).

As more detailed ceramic analyses became available, distinct Woodland complexes were recognized for southeastern and southwestern Minnesota (Bonney 1962:84). Because of extensive soil disturbance at southwestern Minnesota sites, the use of wide excavation levels by Wilford, and long-term stability in many cultural elements (such as subsistence and settlement), most post-Wilford researchers did not challenge the single Woodland Phase view.

The cultural history of the Prairie Lake Region is complicated by the fact that the region's Woodland Tradition is not conveniently divided into Early, Middle, and Late periods. This results from the lack of certain ceramic and lithic attributes, the absence of well-defined Hopewell influences, the lack of horticulture, and perhaps the relatively late appearance of burial mounds. Based primarily on changes in ceramics, the Woodland Period in this region is more usefully divided into two phases, the Fox Lake Phase and the Lake Benton Phase.

The definition of two Woodland phases in the Prairie Lake Region is principally based on analyses of the Fox Lake, Pedersen, and Arthur sites. The Fox Lake site location and excavations are described in some detail because Fox Lake represents a typical Prairie Lake Region Middle Prehistoric site and a typical example of excavation techniques used in the region over the last 50 years.

Fox Lake Site

The Fox Lake site (21MR2) is the type site for the initial Woodland phase of the Prairie Lake Region. Located on an island in Fox Lake just north of Sherburn, Minnesota (Figure 16), the site was tested by Alfred Jenks in 1935, by Lloyd Wilford in 1941, and by the author of this report in 1981–82. Wilford's unpublished site report (Wilford [ca. 1946]b) summarized the 1935 and 1941 excavations. Anfinson (1987b) presented a comprehensive summary of all of the excavations.

Fox Lake is long and narrow, 5.5 km in length (east-west), and averages about .7 km in width. It is relatively shallow, averaging only about 3.5 m in depth, although two small areas near the lake's center are just over 6 m deep. During the 1930s drought, the lake level fell about 3 m, causing shallow bays to dry

Figure 16. Location of the Fox Lake site (21MR2) on the Sherburn USGS 7.5' map.

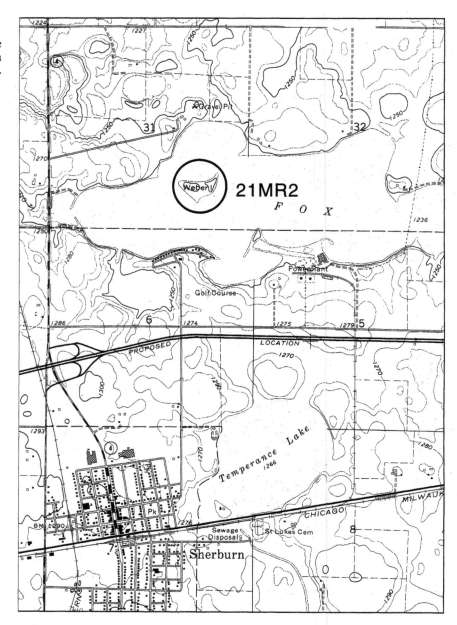

up completely. The Minnesota Department of Natural Resources classifies Fox Lake as a bullhead-panfish lake.

The island containing the Fox Lake site is about 4 ha (10 acres) in area and roughly triangular in shape, with points on the west, south, and northeast. The island's surface is relatively flat with two slight rises on the northwest and northeast. The surface drops down a steep bank to the lake, a drop of 3 m on the southwest and southeast sides and a drop of about 6 m on the north.

A narrow causeway connects the west end of the island with the mainland. The natural causeway was artificially built up in 1940 to allow vehicle and machinery access to the island. Prior to this, the causeway was exposed during periods of low water, and at even the highest lake levels it was never covered by more than a meter of water. Aerial photographs from 1938 show a second causeway extending from the northeastern end of the island to the mainland; this causeway is now inundated by at least a meter of water.

About .8 ha in the center of the island were farmed from the early 1930s through the 1950s. A small house, now gone, was located at the western edge of the field. The cultivation exposed artifacts that brought the site to the attention of local collectors and ultimately to archaeologists.

The island's vegetation is characterized by an open, weed-covered center surrounded by trees and brush. The former field is dominated by various grasses and ragweed (*Ambrosia psilostachya*). Major tree species include green ash, American elm, and black walnut (*Juglans nigra*); most of the elms died because of Dutch Elm disease. The understory vegetation is densest on the island's east side, and at places it is almost impassable. A major component of this barricade is prickly ash (*Zanthoxylum americanum*). Several deer live on the island year-round. Geese nest there in great numbers in the warm season. Walnuts attract numerous squirrels. When Joseph Nicollet's Expedition of 1838 passed by Fox Lake in late September, botanist Karl Geyer said the Dakota referred to the lake as *Omanhu Wita* or "Lake with the Walnut Island" (Geyer 1838:127; Nicollet 1976:128).

Two burial mound groups were mapped in the vicinity of the Fox Lake site by Theodore Lewis in 1889 (Winchell 1911:102). The first group (21MR8), near the shore just west of the site, contained five circular mounds. The largest was 24.5 m in diameter and 1.4 m high with a flat top. The second group (21MR9) was near the shore just northwest of the site and consisted of three circular mounds. The largest was 15 m in diameter and .75 m high. Neither group is visible today, having been plowed down. A scatter of lithic chipping debris is evident in the field between the two mound sites.

Other sites in the vicinity include a Woodland habitation site on a small island across the lake to the southeast of the Fox Lake site. A single 1 x 1 m test unit was excavated on this island in 1981, but it yielded little cultural material. Another Woodland habitation site has been documented by surface collections on a former island in Temperance Lake, 2.4 km to the south.

The Fox Lake site was first examined by archaeologists on July 24, 1935. Jenks and Wilford of the University of Minnesota made a surface collection in the small field, which was planted in corn. They also excavated one test unit. Wilford's unpublished report (Wilford [ca. 1946]b), his field notes, and his students' field notes do not describe the exact location and size of the test unit, reporting only that it was a "shallow trench" at the west end of the field.

The ceramics recovered by the 1935 excavations were all grit tempered, except for a single, small, shell-tempered sherd. On the basis of this brief work at the Fox Lake site, Wilford proposed a Fox Lake Focus in his doctoral dissertation two years later (Wilford 1937:247). The Fox Lake site is the only southwestern Minnesota archaeological site mentioned in the text of Wilford's dissertation, although the Cambria site (21BE2) was alluded to when he mentioned the presence of a Mill Creek-like manifestation (Wilford 1937:274).

On July 28, 1941, Wilford returned to the Fox Lake site and spent five days excavating with one student assistant and three WPA laborers. Four 10 x 10-foot (3.7 x 3.7 m) squares were opened in a north-south line at the west end of the field north of the 1935 trench (Wilford [ca. 1946]b:1). The field was not in crop at the time. The two northernmost squares (3 and 4) were described in field notes as being in a recently plowed area; the two southernmost squares (1 and 2) were in a previously cultivated area. The approximate location of these squares and the 1935 trench is shown in Figure 17.

The 1941 units were excavated in 8-inch (20 cm) levels, the levels numbered 1 through 4 from the surface down. Levels 1 and 2 were excavated in all four units, but the third and fourth levels were excavated only in Squares 1 and 4. Stratigraphy pits were excavated in the northeast and northwest corners of Square 2 "in order to record the elevations to subsoil for the contour map" (Wilford [ca. 1946]b:2). As with most of Wilford's site reports, no mention was made of the excavated soil being screened. Generally, Wilford appears to have screened most of the soil at habitation sites using 1/2-inch (1.3 cm) or 3/8-inch (1 cm) screen.

The second 8-inch level (20–40 cm) of the 1941 excavations was the richest in cultural material, according to Wilford; the first (0–20 cm) and third (40–60 cm) levels contained moderate amounts, and very little was recovered from the fourth level (60–80 cm). The only feature noted for all four squares was "an arrangement of stones as a firehearth" in Level 2 of the northeast corner of Square 4. A picture of this feature is the only site photograph on file at the University of Minnesota for the 1941 excavations. The subsoil depth (C horizon) varied from 70 cm to 95 cm. The average was about 79 cm.

A total of 1,414 sherds were recovered by the 1941 excavations. All are grit tempered, except for 8 shell-tempered sherds from Level 1. About 94 percent of the sherds have cordmarked surfaces. The chipped stone artifacts include 7 projectile points, 2 point tips, 6 end scrapers, 6 side scrapers, and 8 knives. Two greenstone celts (or axlike tools) and a mano (or hand-held grinding stone) also were recovered. As for faunal

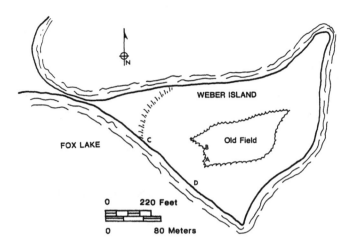

Figure 17. Locations of excavation units at the Fox Lake site. A=1935 trench, B=1941 squares, C=1981 Unit 1, D=1981–82 Units 2 and 3.

remains, Wilford was typically brief: "Some animal bones were present. All of modern species, including some fish bones, but no artifacts of bone" (Wilford [ca. 1946]b:2).

Wilford concluded that the Fox Lake site was essentially a Middle Woodland site:

> No significant differences were found in the distribution of artifact and pottery types throughout the four levels. It is therefore concluded that little or no modification of the culture occurred during this period of occupancy by the group responsible for this manifestation. An occurrence of shell-tempered pottery in the upper levels indicated that this culture antedated that of the culture responsible for such pottery (Wilford [ca. 1946]b:3).

Based on Wilford's observation that there was little evidence for cultural change through perhaps 50 cm of occupation, the Fox Lake site appeared to be ideal for reexamining cultural stability in the Prairie Lake Region. Furthermore, most of the site was undisturbed except for the cultivated area in the island's center. An excavation employing modern methods could better assess the intercomponent relationships through time by providing detailed information on subsistence patterns and, perhaps, charcoal for reliable radiocarbon dates.

In August 1981 the author of this report returned to the Fox Lake site for some additional testing to better assess the site's potentials. A 1 x 2 m unit, designated Unit 1, was laid out near the southwest corner of the island. The sod was skimmed off, resulting in a level surface about 5 cm below the modern surface.

The sod was not broken up and screened because the landowner requested that the island be left as close as possible to how it was found.

Excavation proceeded in 5-cm levels with the first level between 5 and 10 cm. The excavated soil was screened through one-quarter inch (.63 cm) hardware cloth and the recovered materials bagged according to the 5-cm level and 1 x 1 m unit of origin. Excavation was accomplished, for the most part, by careful skimming with flat-nosed shovels. Trowels were used when artifacts or features were noticed *in situ*. Soil samples were taken of features and charcoal concentrations.

As excavation proceeded on Unit 1, a second 1 x 2 m unit was laid out about 100 m southeast of the first unit. Unit 2 was about 5 m northeast of a steep bank which descended about 3 m to the surface of the lake. The Wilford locale was about 45 m northeast of Unit 2. Excavation methods employed on Unit 2 were similar to those described for Unit 1, except 10-liter soil samples were removed from alternating 5-cm levels in the center of Unit 2N.

The soil samples removed from Unit 2N were processed on the site in an active water flotation-screening device similar to that described by Watson (1976). The suspended material was passed through nested 10-, 30-, and 60-micron mesh. The heavy fraction was put through 1/16-inch (.1 cm) window screen. As the percent of clay increased with the depth, the 10-micron mesh rapidly became plugged and had to be agitated constantly. This slowed down the process considerably. It took a full day of hard work to process five 10-liter samples.

Heavy rains halted excavation in Unit 1 at 45 cm and in Unit 2 at 50 cm. Little material was recovered from the deepest level in either unit. A 50 x 50 cm stratigraphy pit was then excavated in Unit 2N to a depth of 1 m. The soil from this pit was screened, but no cultural materials were recovered.

In general, cultural materials were more abundant in Unit 2 than Unit 1. Concentrations of fire-cracked rock and cobbles were apparent between 20 and 40 cm below the surface. Unit 1 contained several oval charcoal-laden features interpreted to be burned roots. Small, isolated fragments of older looking charcoal also were found in both units.

The soils of both units consisted of dark brown to black sandy loam in A horizon, gray-brown clayey loam in B horizon, and yellow, clayey, coarse sand in C horizon. The A horizon in Unit 2 extended to about 65 cm below the surface, but it ended at about 40 cm in Unit 1. A slight textural change at about 22 cm in Unit 2 may indicate some mixing of soils between the horizons of each unit. The B horizon extended from

65 to 95 cm in Unit 2. Although the depth of the C horizon was not defined in Unit 1, the soils in general appeared to be shallower; it is likely that it may be significantly above 95 cm.

Site-processed soil samples from Unit 2N were examined later in the laboratory for possible cultural remains. The flotation samples were disappointing. They yielded only a small amount of wood charcoal, a few uncharred seeds, and some charred and uncharred walnut shells. The heavy fraction yielded fish bone, a few small flakes, pottery crumbs, and small bone fragments from a variety of small and large mammals.

In August 1982, the Fox Lake site was revisited to gain a larger sample of cultural materials, to attempt to identify discrete cultural horizons, to obtain material for radiometric dating, and to search for features. A 3 x 3 m unit, designated Unit 3, was staked out just southeast of Unit 2. The northwest corner of Unit 3 was the southeast corner of Unit 2. The southwest corner of Unit 3 was about 2 m from the bank edge. Excavation proceeded as in Unit 2 except 10-liter soil samples were taken from each 5-cm level in the center of 3C. These soil samples were processed later in the lab by flotation and water screening through 1/16-inch mesh.

Nine 5-cm levels were excavated until heavy rain once again foiled attempts to take the entire 3 x 3 m unit down deeper than 50 cm. Level diagrams in Figure 18 illustrate rock concentrations found between levels 4 and 9 (20–50 cm). Square 3NE was excavated in two more 5-cm levels to a depth of 60 cm. Few artifacts were recovered. These lowest levels appeared to contain only small quantities of bone, lithic debris, fire-cracked rock, and a few small sherds. Overall, the soil profile of Unit 3 was identical to that of Unit 2. Although it was a disappointment not to finish excavating the unit into till, it was clear that artifact densities were very low below 50 cm.

Pedersen Site

The Pedersen site (21LN2) is on an island near the northeast side of Lake Benton, 145 km northwest of the Fox Lake site (Figure 19). The site is about 4 ha in size. At low lake levels, it is connected to the shore by a narrow causeway.

The Pedersen site was first excavated by Lloyd Wilford in 1956 (Wilford 1961). Wilford opened four 10-foot squares on the northern part of the island, using six-inch excavation levels. Five levels were excavated completely in all squares, and deeper sample levels were excavated in sections of the units. In one unit, subsoil was 1.7 m below the surface. No features were

noted except for rock layers in two of the squares in the third and fourth levels (12–24 inches). In his unpublished report, Wilford concluded that the site was principally a Woodland Period habitation, although Cambria and Oneota components also were present.

Extensive excavations at the Pedersen site were carried out by G. Joseph Hudak of the Science Museum of Minnesota in 1973 and 1974. In 1973 the excavations involved eleven 1 x 2 m units, as well as 2 large block excavations each approximately 5 x 8 m. The excavations were all on the north half of the island, most in the immediate vicinity of Wilford's excavations. Sampling methods of the 1974 excavations have not been discussed in any published reports, although analyses of the faunal remains and the ceramics are available (O. Shane 1978; Hudak 1976).

Photographs of the 1973 excavations show rock features similar to the ones noted by Wilford. Five radiocarbon dates have been obtained for the Pedersen site (Lass 1980a; Hudak 1976). The landowner has an extensive collection of artifacts from the site which reportedly contains several Paleoindian points.

Arthur Site

The Arthur site (13DK27) is located 40 km southwest of the Fox Lake site on the east side of Lake Okoboji East. The site is on a relic beach above the lake and is bisected by a gully. The site is not on a peninsula or island like most other major Middle Prehistoric sites, but extensive woodlands were present in the gullies.

Excavations in 1980 consisted of about 50 square meters, most in 1 x 1 m and 2 x 2 m units (Tiffany 1982b). Features encountered included rock clusters and a few pits. Four cultural horizons were described: Late Paleoindian, Archaic, Woodland, and Late Prehistoric. The cultural horizons were all in the A soil horizon, and there was considerable horizon mixing. No radiocarbon dates are available.

Other Fox Lake Phase Sites

There are at least 35 documented habitation sites in the Prairie Lake Region with Fox Lake Phase components (Figure 20). Sixteen of these sites have been excavated, with minimal testing at another six. Most excavated sites are in southwestern Minnesota. Besides Fox Lake and Pedersen, Lloyd Wilford excavated Fox Lake Phase habitation sites at Tuttle Lake (21MR1), Big Slough (21MU1), Synsteby (21BW1), and Johnson (21JK1). Important Fox Lake sites in South Dakota

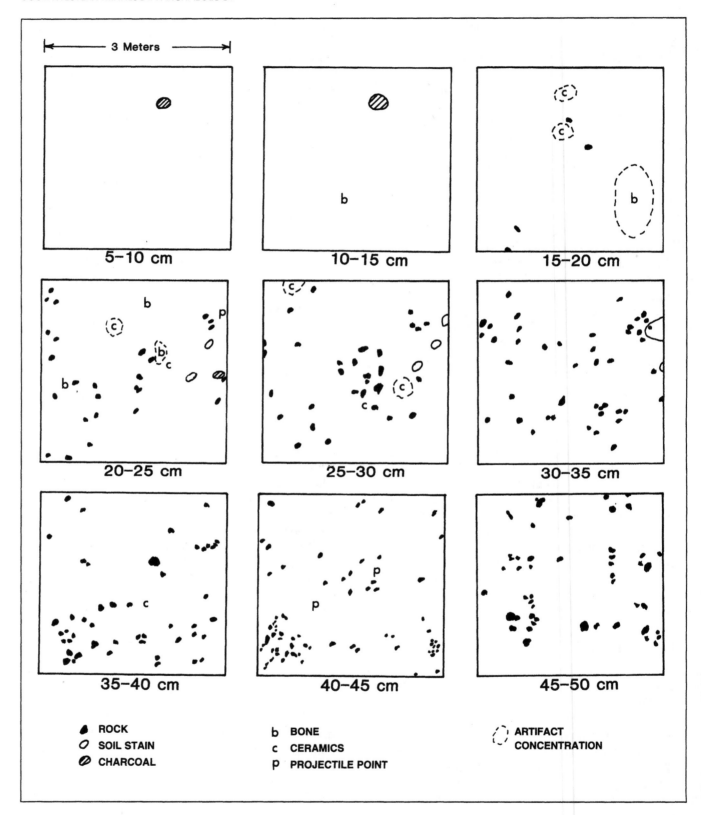

Figure 18. Top-view diagrams of levels from the 1982 excavation of Unit 3 at the Fox Lake site showing the locations of features, cobbles, and selected artifacts.

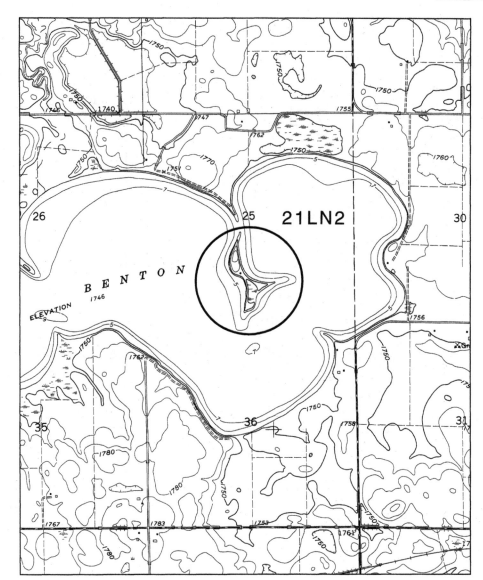

Figure 19. Location of the Pedersen site (21LN2) on the Tyler USGS 7.5' map.

are Oakwood Lakes (39BK7), Winter (39DE5), Waubay Lakes (39DA7), and Christiansen's Point (39LK18). In Iowa, the only other excavated Fox Lake site in addition to the Arthur site is the Crim site (13ET403).

As illustrated in Figure 20, there is a notable scarcity of Fox Lake sites in west-central Minnesota and north-central Iowa. This may reflect the limited survey and excavation done in these areas rather than an actual paucity of sites.

Technology
Ceramics The earliest ceramics found in the Prairie Lake Region resemble *LaMoille Thick* ceramics

defined in southeastern Minnesota (cf. Wilford 1954c; Hudak and Johnson 1975). The southwestern Minnesota examples are not common and usually feature well-defined vertical cordmarking on the exterior of thick (ca. 10 mm) sherds. Decoration usually is limited to a single horizontal row of fingernail impressions on the rim. Unlike *LaMoille*, the earliest southwestern Minnesota ceramics have interiors that are smooth, not cordmarked.

Thick, fingernail-impressed sherds have been found at the Fox Lake (Anfinson 1987b:322), Mountain Lake (Wilford 1962:13), and Kunz sites (21WW8) (Anfinson 1979:118). The use of fingernail impressions is associated with Early and Middle

53

Figure 20. Locations of Fox Lake Phase habitation sites.

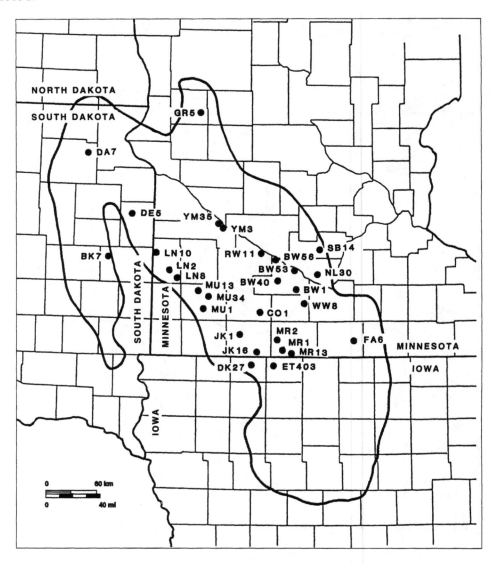

Woodland ceramics in northeastern Iowa (Logan 1976:89), west-central Illinois (Griffin 1952:100; Fortier et al. 1984:68), and southern Wisconsin (C. Mason 1964:159; Hurley 1966:228–23; Hurley 1975:223; Geier 1978:240). The Fox Lake ceramic tradition is in part an outgrowth of such ceramics.

For archaeologists, wares are the uppermost category in the ceramic classification hierarchy. They are compared on the basis of similarities in basic manufacturing attributes such as vessel form, paste composition, and surface treatment (Lehmer 1954a:41). Wares may be subdivided into types where several attributes, usually decorative, consistently co-occur. Types may

then be subdivided into varieties, often based on the presence of one particular attribute.

The most important reason for this typological analysis is to develop a simple method of comparing ceramics between sites. This helps to determine cultural relationships. As James Deetz (1967:51) pointed out, types need not be perfect representations of the mental templates of the potters, as long as they are useful to the "main aim of typology, that of classification which permits comparison."

In the Prairie Lake Region, type definition of Woodland ceramics has been relatively recent. While cordmarked-trailed rims have long been recognized as an informal type in southwestern Minnesota, it was not until Hudak's (1974, 1976) study of Pedersen site (21LN2) ceramics that enough data was assembled to formally define a Woodland type in the region. Even Hudak, however, avoided defining formal types, preferring to call his categories of co-occurring attributes ceramic "series."

Prior to Hudak's analysis, Rachel Bonney (1965) looked at materials gathered by Lloyd Wilford from six southern Minnesota sites (Fox Lake, Mountain Lake, Pedersen, Tuttle Lake, Johnson, Tudahl). She divided the rims into five categories based on surface treatment and the presence or absence of decoration (Undecorated Cordmarked, Decorated Cordmarked, Fabric Impressed, Undecorated Smooth, Decorated Smooth). These categories were then subdivided into 18 classes based on rim form, decoration, and temper. While Bonney's study was the first to illustrate the diversity in the Woodland ceramics of southern Minnesota, it is not especially useful because of the unwieldy classification scheme and its inability to recognize time differences within the Woodland sequence. It also includes ceramics from two distinct regions.

Most current studies of ceramics from Woodland sites in the Prairie Lake Region are based on Hudak's (1976) Pedersen site analysis. His five series were formalized into types and slightly expanded in *A Handbook of Minnesota Prehistoric Ceramics* (Anfinson 1979). There are three initial Woodland types: *Fox Lake Trailed* (Hudak Series B)—thick-walled, conoidal vessels with cordmarked bodies decorated with trailed lines on the rim, often accompanied by bosses (knoblike protrusions) and interior cordwrapped stick impressions; *Fox Lake Vertical Cordmarked* (Hudak Series C)—thick-walled, conoidal vessels with vertically cordmarked bodies occasionally decorated below the lip with exterior bosses and/or interior cordwrapped stick impressions; and *Fox Lake Horizontal Cordmarked* (Hudak Series D)—thick-walled, conoidal vessels with horizontal cordmarked bodies occasionally partially smoothed and lacking exterior or interior decoration.

There are two terminal Woodland types: *Lake Benton Cordwrapped Stick Impressed* (Hudak Series A)—subconoidal vessels with walls of moderate thickness, cordmarked lower bodies, smoothed upper bodies, and rims with exterior cordwrapped stick impressions in vertical, horizontal, and/or oblique bands; and *Lake Benton Vertical Cordmarked* (Hudak Series E)—subconoidal vessels with moderately thick walls and vertically cordmarked bodies lacking interior or exterior decoration.

When the Fox Lake site rims and near-rims were examined initially by the author (Anfinson 1987b), it was immediately apparent that a much greater range of Woodland ceramics was present than was represented by the Pedersen site types; even the ceramics that generally fit the Pedersen types had variations not present at the Pedersen site. For example, Hudak reported no single-twisted cord-impressed sherds at Pedersen. Benn (1982) had a similar problem using the Pedersen series with the Arthur site ceramics from northern Iowa. He dealt with the problem by defining a number of new Fox Lake and Lake Benton types and revising several existing types. He also formalized Fox Lake and Lake Benton into wares.

Benn's (1982) analysis of the Arthur ceramics is detailed and provocative, although the published data is sorted by types only. This makes attribute stratigraphy and comparisons to the Fox Lake and Pedersen site ceramics more difficult. Benn divided the Woodland ceramics at Arthur into ten types belonging to four wares. Half of Benn's types were defined elsewhere, but five new types were defined. Fox Lake Ware is represented by: *Fox Lake Trailed* (62 sherds) with varieties *Early* (11 sherds), *Middle* (10 sherds), and *Late* (14 sherds); *Fox Lake Cordwrapped Stick Stamped* (1 sherd); and *Fox Lake Cordmarked* (13 sherds).

A new type (of an undefined but inferred Arthur Ware), *Arthur Cord Roughened* (40 sherds), Benn believed to be transitional·between the initial and terminal Woodland phases. Terminal Woodland Lake Benton Ware types include *Lake Benton Dentate Stamped* (7 sherds), *Lake Benton Cordwrapped Stick* (139 sherds), *Lake Benton Plain* (10 sherds), and *Lake Benton Cordmarked* (3 sherds). Terminal Woodland Loseke Ware types at Arthur are *Late Woodland Cord Roughened* (2 sherds) and *Missouri Bluffs Cord Impressed* (13 sherds). Overall, initial Woodland types accounted for 26 percent of the ceramics, transitional types 14 percent, and terminal Woodland types 60 percent.

While Benn's Arthur site study pointed out a number of inadequacies in the regional use of the Pedersen types, his new types and revisions of existing types usually were based on small sample sizes. This is a problem throughout the northeastern Plains, where few Woodland sites have been excavated intensely and recovered sherds are usually small fragments of the original vessels. Vessel forms and decorational patterns are often a best guess. Rims and near-rims, with quite different decorative treatments and classed as two discrete types, may be in fact from the same vessel. Ceramic types often are little more than rim types.

Hudak (1976) used thickness as *the* attribute differentiating initial and terminal Woodland ceramics at the Pedersen site. He subdivided the thin (<8 mm) and thick (≥ 8 mm) ceramics into five series, based on surface treatment and exterior decorative attributes. The three thick series were Series B (cordmarked/trailed), Series C (vertical cordmarked/undecorated), and Series D (horizontal cordmarked-smoothed/undecorated). The thin-series ceramics were Series A (cordmarked-smoothed/cordwrapped stick-impressed or smooth/cordwrapped stick-impressed) and Series E (vertical cordmarked/undecorated). These series were defined using only the 1973 data, while the published totals for each category included the sherds from 1974. The series totals accounted for only 57 percent of the Pedersen ceramics. The ceramics that did not fit the five Series definitions were not discussed in Hudak's published analysis.

While Hudak's Series B and D exhibit clear stratigraphic associations with the lower Woodland levels at the Pedersen site, Series A, C, and E reflect bimodal distributions. An overview of the Pedersen site ceramics is presented in Table 3, which includes previously unpublished data provided by Hudak (personal communication 1986). The overall totals suggest a bimodal ceramic distribution, with peaks in levels 3 and 8. Surface treatment/exterior decoration attributes indicate vertical cordmarked/undecorated ceramics are the most common (26 percent), followed by vertical cordmarked-smoothed/cordwrapped stick-impressed or smooth/cordwrapped stick-impressed (23 percent), smooth/bossed, punctated or undecorated (15 percent), vertical cordmarked/trailed (10 percent), and vertical cordmarked/bossed (4 percent). With regard to exterior decoration alone, cordwrapped stick impressions are the most common (26 percent), followed by bossing (18 percent), trailing (11 percent), and punctating (2 percent). There are only a few single-twisted cord impressed and dentate-impressed sherds at Pedersen. Interior cordwrapped stick impressions occur on 15 percent of the rim sherds.

Stratigraphically, most ceramic attributes are found in most excavated levels at Pedersen, but several trends are apparent: thin walls (<7 mm), smooth surfaces, and lip notching in the upper levels with horizontal cordmarking in the middle levels. Thick walls (8 mm) and bossing are found in the lower levels. The failure of Hudak's Series A, C, and E rims to exhibit clear stratigraphic patterning appears to be a result of the arbitrary use of a definition that used an 8 mm thickness attribute. While there is a definite thinning of ceramics through time at the site, some initial Woodland ceramics are less than 8 mm thick, and some terminal Woodland ceramics may be more than 8 mm thick.

At the Fox Lake site, the lower level Woodland ceramic attributes (Table 4) include wide-trailed lines, bosses, punctates, lip decoration (tool impressions, cordwrapped stick), and thicker body walls. The upper-level attributes include narrow-trailed lines, cordwrapped stick decorations, smooth exterior surfaces, cordmarked lips, and thinner body walls (Anfinson 1987b:323–26). A bimodal stratigraphic distribution of Woodland ceramics is not apparent at the Fox Lake site; there is some mixing of attributes stratigraphically and even on individual sherds.

The one attribute at the Fox Lake site that usually differentiates initial Woodland from terminal Woodland ceramics is the use of sand versus crushed-rock temper. While Hudak did not differentiate these types of grit temper at the Pedersen site, an examination of the collection at the Science Museum of Minnesota indicated that almost all vertically cordmarked/trailed (Series B), thick (≥ 8 mm), vertically cordmarked (Series C), and horizontally cordmarked-smoothed (Series D) rims were sand tempered. Most exterior cordwrapped stick impressed sherds (Series A) and thin, vertically cordmarked sherds (Series E) at the Pedersen site have crushed-rock temper. The temper analysis apparently confirms the usefulness of Hudak's basic initial Woodland types. Benn (1982) noted a similar association of sand tempering with initial Woodland ceramics at the Arthur site.

As at Fox Lake and Pedersen, the Arthur site ceramic attributes are scattered throughout the stratigraphy of the site. Certainly, this is a result of variable soil deposition and soil disturbance. Most pits at Arthur appear to be of post-Fox Lake origin, thus mixing the initial Woodland ceramics with later ceramics. Some stratigraphy is apparent, however. *Fox Lake Trailed* and *Fox Lake Cordmarked* are found primarily at the lower levels. Meanwhile, *Arthur Cord Roughened* is most representative in the middle levels, and Lake Benton types, *Late Woodland Cord Impressed*, and Oneota make up the majority of types found in the upper levels.

The use of trailing over cordmarking is the originally recognized hallmark of Fox Lake ceramics. The use of trailed-over cordmarked ceramics in the Midwest usually is associated with Early Woodland complexes, especially Black Sand ceramics from western Illinois and adjacent areas. Although still not well defined, Black Sand vessels are small conoidal jars with rounded lips, fine grit temper, walls averaging 6 mm in thickness, and vertically cordmarked exterior surfaces. Exterior rim and upper shoulder decorations

Level	HUDAK'S SERIES					SURFACE TREATMENT, DECORATIVE ATTRIBUTES							SELECTED ATTRIBUTES								
	A (Tn,Cm/Sm-Sm,CWS)	B (Tk,VCm,Tr-Bs,InCWS)	C (Tk,VCm,Und)	D (Tk,HCm/Sm,Und)	E (Tn,VCm,Und)	VCm,Tr	VCm,Bs	VCm,PCt	VCm,Und	VCm-VCm/Sm,CWS	HCm-HCm/Sm,Bs-PCt-Und	Sm,Bs-PCt-Und	HCm	Bs	PCt	CWS	Tr	Interior CWS	Lip Notch	Thickness	Sample Total
1	5			1	3		1		5	5	2	3	2	3		5	1	3	2	6.7	17
2	5		2		2				4	5	1	8	1			5	1	3	3	6.8	19
3	7	2	2	1	5	3	2		8	7	3	6	3	5		7	3	2	5	6.9	29
4	2	1	2		3	2			5	2		4		1		4	2	4	2	7.3	15
5	2		1	1	2	2			4	2	5	3	5	5		2	3	1	1	7.4	17
6	7		2	1	5			1	7	7	1	4	1		1	7			3	6.4	20
7	7	1	2	2	4	1	2	1	8	7	5	6	5	7	1	8	2	6	4	7.5	32
8	9	3	3	4	7	4	1		12	10	6	2	6	5		11	5	6	1	7.9	37
9	3	3	5	1	1	3			6	3	4		4	4		4	3	5		7.5	16
10	3	4	1		1	6	1		1	4	3	3	3	7	1	6	6	4	1	8.0	18
11												3	3	1		1				8.0	4
12						1										1				8.0	1
13																					0
14						1								1		1	1			8.0	1
15												2				1				7.5	2
Total	49	14	20	14	33	22	8	2	60	52	33	41	33	40	4	60	26	34	22		227
%	21	6	9	6	15	10	4	1	26	23	15	18	15	18	2	26	11	15	10		100

Table 3. Pedersen site (21LN2) rim sherds by level and selected attributes from the 1973 and 1974 excavations. Data from Hudak (1976; personal communication 1986). Abbreviations: Tn=Thin, Cm=Cordmarked, Sm=Smooth, CWS=Cordwrapped stick, Tk=Thick, VCm=Vertical cordmarked, Tr=Trailed, Bs=Bossed, In=Interior, Und=Undecorated, HCm=Horizontal cordmarked, PCt=Punctate.

consist of horizontal, oblique, and vertical trailed lines. Often, these are in combination with a single row of bosses on the upper rim (Griffin 1952:98; Struever 1968:149; Munson 1982:7–8). The five possible Black Sand ceramic dates from the Peisker site in Illinois range from 625 ± 110 B.C. to 230 ± 130 B.C., with a mean between 400 to 300 B.C. (Struever 1968:142).

Trailed-over cordmarked ceramics are widespread in the western Midwest. Besides *Fox Lake Trailed* and *Black Sand Incised*, there are *Spring Hollow Incised* in northeastern Iowa (Logan 1976), *Brock Lake Incised* in southwestern Wisconsin (Keslin 1958:203–05), *Nokomis Trailed* in north central Wisconsin (Salzer 1974:47), and *Crawford Trailed* and *Valley Embossed/Trailed* in western Iowa and eastern

Nebraska (Benn 1981a, 1981b). All of these types are poorly dated but generally associated with Early Woodland or early Middle Woodland components.

Isolated finds of trailed-over cordmarked ceramics have been noted in east-central Minnesota at the Anderson site (21AN8), the Aqua Lane site (21AN20), and in the Snake River Valley (Caine 1969). They have been reported in north-central Minnesota at the White Oak Point site (21IC1) (Lugenbeal 1982:15), the Black Bear site (21CW96) (Birk 1986:76), and 21BK33.

At the Naze site (39SN246) in eastern North Dakota on the James River, trailed-over cordmarked ceramics were found associated with a possible house structure dated by a series of radiocarbon samples to 550–410 B.C. (Gregg 1987, 1990). The intriguing presence of apparently early ceramics in such a west-

	CORD-MARKED TRAILED		CORDMARKED			CORD-WRAPPED STICK		SINGLE-TWISTED CORD		SMOOTH			MISCELLANEOUS						UNID	ONEOTA	TOTAL
	Wide	Narrow	Bossed	Punctate	No Ext Dec	Only CWS	Punctate	Only STC	CWS	No Ext Dec	Punctate	Bossed	Dentate	CombStp	Combed	KnotCrd	Fingernail	Trailed			
1935																					
Surface	0	1	0	0	3	0	0	0	0	1	0	0	1	1	0	0	0	1	0	0	8
Trench	1	0	0	5	2	4	0	6	2	1	0	0	0	0	0	0	0	0	0	0	21
Total	1	1	0	5	5	4	0	6	2	2	0	0	1	1	0	0	0	1	0	0	29
%	7		34			14		28		7			10						0	0	100
1941																					
0–20 cm	4	5	1	3	2	6	1	0	1	3	0	0	0	0	1	0	0	2	0	3	35
20–40 cm	17	14	4	9	12	34	7	0	0	8	11	1	3	1	1	1	0	1	4	1	129
40–60 cm*	17	1	2	2	6	4	3	1	0	2	1	0	0	0	0	0	0	0	4	0	43
60–80 cm*	0	1	0	0	0	0	0	0	0	0	0	0	0	0	0	0	1	0	2	0	4
Total	38	21	7	14	20	44	11	1	1	13	12	1	3	1	2	1	1	3	13	4	211
%	28		19			26		1		12			5						6	2	100
1981–1982																					
5–10 cm	1	2	0	0	0	0	0	0	1	0	1	0	0	0	0	0	0	0	2	0	7
10–15 cm	0	1	0	0	2	1	0	0	0	0	0	0	0	0	0	0	0	0	0	0	4
15–20 cm	2	0	0	0	1	2	0	0	0	0	0	0	0	0	0	0	0	1	0	0	6
20–25 cm	1	6	0	0	1	0	0	0	0	0	0	0	0	0	0	0	0	1	2	0	11
25–30 cm	2	10	0	1	0	2	0	0	0	0	0	0	0	0	0	0	0	0	1	0	17
30–35 cm	0	12	2	0	0	3	0	0	0	1	0	0	0	0	0	0	0	0	0	0	18
35–40 cm	1	11	1	0	3	0	0	0	0	0	0	0	0	0	0	0	0	0	1	0	17
40–45 cm	1	2	0	0	2	0	0	0	0	0	0	0	0	0	0	0	0	0	0	0	5
45–50 cm	0	1	0	0	0	0	0	0	0	0	0	0	0	0	0	0	0	0	0	0	1
50–55 cm	0	0	0	0	0	0	0	0	0	0	0	0	0	0	0	0	0	0	0	0	0
55–60 cm	0	0	0	0	0	0	0	0	0	0	0	0	0	0	0	0	0	0	0	0	0
Total	8	45	3	1	9	8	0	0	2	1	1	0	0	0	0	0	0	2	6	0	88
%	60		15			9		2		2			2						7	0	100
No provenience	0	1	0	0	0	1	0	0	0	0	0	0	0	0	0	0	0	0	0	0	2
Total	47	68	10	20	34	57	11	7	5	16	13	1	4	2	2	1	1	6	19	4	330
%	35		19			21		4		9			5						6	1	100

Table 4. Vertical and horizontal distribution of rim and near-rim sherds from the Fox Lake site by surface treatment/decoration categories. Abbreviations: CWS=Cordwrapped stick, STC=Single-twisted cord, UNID=Unidentified, No Ext Dec=No exterior decoration, CombStp=Comb-stamped, KnotCrd=Knotted cord. *Levels sampled differently than other levels in the same unit.

ern location has led to suggestions of an Early Plains Woodland horizon in the northeastern Plains (Gregg and Picha 1989). However, there is no evidence for such a horizon in the Prairie Lake Region.

While the earliest Fox Lake ceramics appear to be dominated by Early Woodland attributes (thick walls, cordmarked exteriors, trailing, and bossing), some Havana influences soon appear in Fox Lake. (Havana ceramics, originally defined in west central Illinois, are Middle Woodland ceramics decorated with dentate, crescent, or ovoid stamping on the rim in combination with panels on the shoulders often filled with stamping or trailed lines.) Havana influences are suggested by the use of cordwrapped stick and dentate impressions, but remain limited, with little evidence of zoning, a lack of ovoid or crescent stamps, and the rarity of beveled lips.

The Heymans Creek site, located on a lower terrace in the Minnesota River Valley north of New Ulm in Nicollet County, has yielded a partial vessel that shows strong Havana influences (Figure 21). The 7 cm thick, grit-tempered, subconoidal vessel has a smooth exterior surface and a flat lip. There is a single row of bosses 15 cm below the lip. The neck has triangular zoned panels outlined with trailed lines and filled with horizontal rows of fine dentate stamps (Skaar 1991).

Hopewell influences are even more limited than Havana in the Prairie Lake Region. There is a lack of Hopewell vessel forms, curvilinear lines, and limited smoothing and brushing. The only Hopewell-like sherd in the University of Minnesota collections from southwestern Minnesota is a large rim from the Johnson site (21JK1). It features cordwrapped stick impressions on the upper rim and curvilinear trailed lines on the lower rim. The decorated area has been smoothed, but the lower vessel is cordmarked.

Based on the ceramics from the Fox Lake, Pedersen, and Arthur sites, Fox Lake Phase ceramics may be characterized this way: moderate to small-sized conoidal to subconoidal vessels with bold exterior cordmarking that is usually vertically oriented, but occasionally oblique or horizontally oriented; the horizontally cordmarked vessels are often partially smoothed; and a few Fox Lake rims feature complete smoothing. Vessel walls are relatively thick (6–12 mm), and the paste is sand tempered. Lips can be round or flat, rims everted or inverted slightly. About two-thirds of the vessels have some exterior rim decoration, notably trailing, bossing, punctating, and dentate or cordwrapped stick stamping in order of importance. These decorative attributes can appear alone or in combination. Occasional interior decoration features short, vertically oriented tool or cordwrapped stick impressions in a single band immediately below the lip. Occasional lip decoration with tool or cordwrapped stick impressions can give the lip a notched appearance. Five Fox Lake types are recognized here: *Fox Lake Trailed, Fox Lake Vertical Cordmarked, Fox Lake Horizontal Cordmarked, Fox Lake Smooth,* and *Fox Lake Cordwrapped Stick.*

Fox Lake Trailed pottery is divided into two varieties, *Wide Line* and *Narrow Line.* The *Wide Line* (Figures 22 and 23) is characterized by trailed lines ≥ 2 mm wide, usually in horizontal bands with tool-impressed lips. Bosses are common; punctates are occasional; and interior decoration is rare. The *Narrow Line* variety (Figures 24 and 25) has lines <2 mm wide, usually in complex motifs involving horizontal, vertical, and oblique orientations. There are few punctates and bosses, only occasional interior decoration (usually cordwrapped stick impressions), and no lip

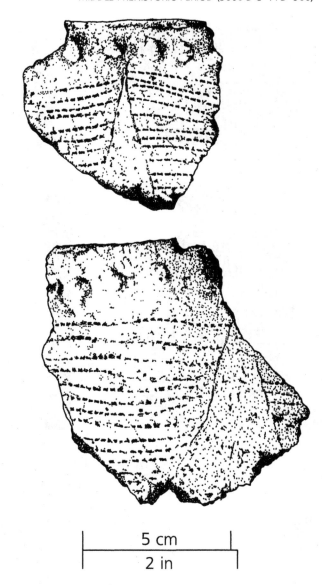

5 cm
2 in

Figure 21. Rim sherd from the Heymans Creek site in Nicollet County (drawing by Mary Beth Skaar).

decoration, except occasional cordmarking. *Wide Line* lips can be round or flat, but *Narrow Line* lips are almost always flat.

Benn (1982) defined three *Fox Lake Trailed* varieties at the Arthur site—*Early, Middle,* and *Late.* The *Early* variety is characterized by wide-trailed lines (2.9 mm average) or bold gashes on rims or shoulders, with some bosses and lip notching. The *Middle* variety has somewhat narrower lines (1.7 mm average) in parallel horizontal and oblique patterns (e.g., crisscross, filled-in triangles), with some use of bosses, punctates,

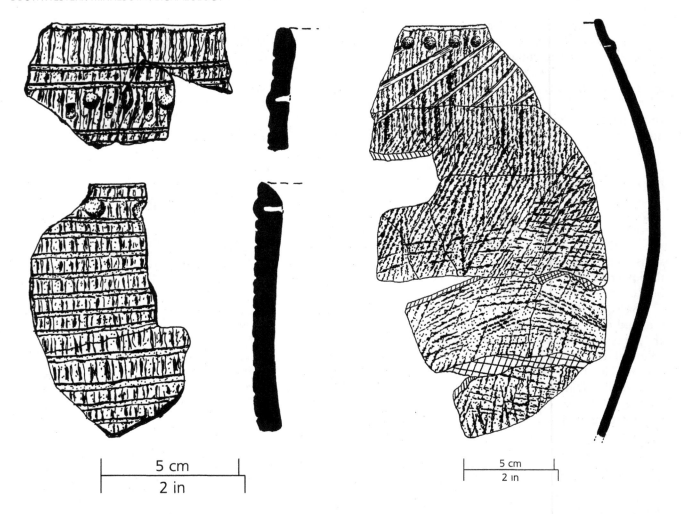

Figure 22. *Fox Lake Trailed, Wide Line* sherds from the Fox Lake site.

Figure 23. *Fox Lake Trailed, Wide Line* partial vessel from the Arthur site (from Benn 1982).

lip notching, and interior cordwrapped stick impressions. The *Late* variety is characterized by even narrower lines (1.5 mm average) in complex patterns (e.g., filled-in triangles), with some use of punctates. There is a trend from the *Early* to the *Late* variety toward thinner walls, less bold cordmarking, partially smoothed exteriors, finer paste, and a more curved rim profile.

The other two originally defined (Anfinson 1979:80) Fox Lake types, *Fox Lake Vertical Cordmarked* and *Fox Lake Horizontal Cordmarked*, were based on Hudak's (1976) Series C and D ceramics from the Pedersen site. *Fox Lake Vertical Cordmarked* rims (Figure 26) can be undecorated or feature occasional bosses, punctates, and/or interior cordwrapped stick impressions. *Fox Lake Horizontal Cordmarked* rims (Figures 27 and 28) usually are partially

smoothed and often undecorated, especially on the exterior; they occasionally have exterior punctates and/or cordwrapped stick impressions, but rarely are trailed.

Benn (1982) lumped these two Fox Lake types into a single type, *Fox Lake Cordmarked*, contending that there are no clear attribute associations to justify two types. Benn went on to define *Arthur Cord Roughened*, however, which has horizontal cordmarking as its principal distinction. Benn (1982:72) admitted the similarity of Arthur Ware to Fox Lake Ware, noting that Arthur lacks trailing. While Hudak's (1976) Series D ceramics featured horizontal cordmarked/smoothed exteriors and Benn's *Arthur Cord Roughened* has bold horizontal cordmarking, *Fox Lake Horizontal Cordmarked* was defined as having both kinds of surface treatments (Anfinson 1979:80).

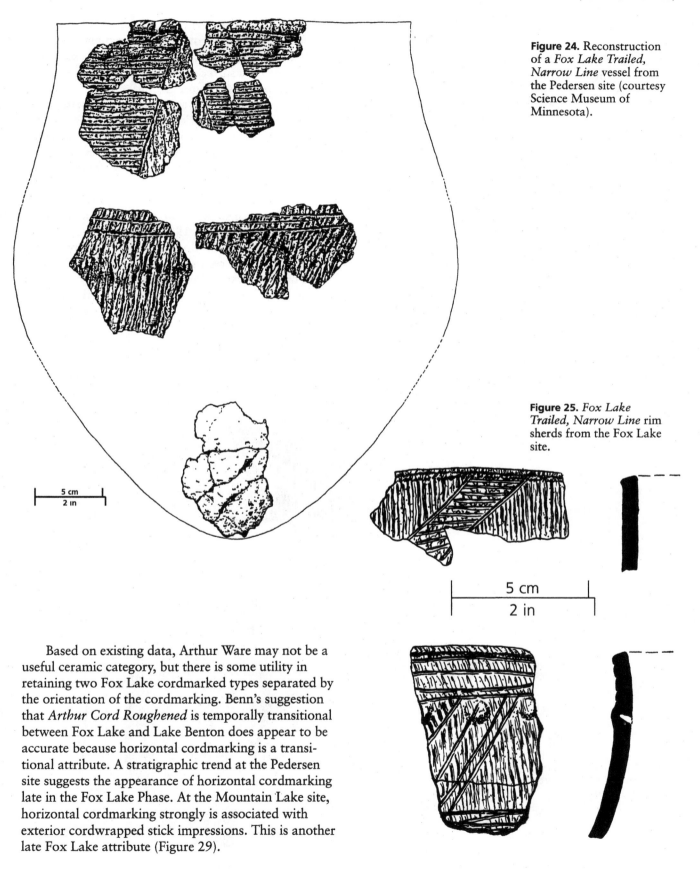

Figure 24. Reconstruction of a *Fox Lake Trailed, Narrow Line* vessel from the Pedersen site (courtesy Science Museum of Minnesota).

5 cm
2 in

Figure 25. *Fox Lake Trailed, Narrow Line* rim sherds from the Fox Lake site.

5 cm
2 in

Based on existing data, Arthur Ware may not be a useful ceramic category, but there is some utility in retaining two Fox Lake cordmarked types separated by the orientation of the cordmarking. Benn's suggestion that *Arthur Cord Roughened* is temporally transitional between Fox Lake and Lake Benton does appear to be accurate because horizontal cordmarking is a transitional attribute. A stratigraphic trend at the Pedersen site suggests the appearance of horizontal cordmarking late in the Fox Lake Phase. At the Mountain Lake site, horizontal cordmarking strongly is associated with exterior cordwrapped stick impressions. This is another late Fox Lake attribute (Figure 29).

Based on examinations of the Woodland ceramics from the Fox Lake, Pedersen, and Mountain Lake sites, a previously undefined Fox Lake type, *Fox Lake Smooth*, is suggested. The rim and upper shoulder of these vessels is completely smoothed. Rim decoration is present on most sherds. There are bosses, punctates, and occasional cordwrapped stick or dentate stamping (Figure 30).

Benn (1982) also proposed a *Fox Lake Cordwrapped Stick* type, which features horizontal cordmarking, exterior horizontal rows of cordwrapped stick impressions, and angular punctates. While his sample size is somewhat small (one sherd from the Arthur site and three from the Mountain Lake site) and other studies (e.g., Anfinson 1982b:75; Hudak 1976) have suggested exterior cordwrapped stick impressions are a hallmark of the terminal Woodland phase of the Prairie Lake Region, a close examination

of the Fox Lake, Pedersen, and Mountain Lake ceramics appears to justify Benn's type. An expanded definition is in order, however, and should include some vertical cordmarked surfaces, smoothing, and more decorative variation (Figure 29 and 30).

The presence of sand-tempered, thick sherds with exterior cordwrapped stick impressions at the above listed sites indicates Fox Lake affiliations. At the Pedersen site, one large rim (Figure 31) features exterior trailing, bosses, and cordwrapped stick impressions over a smooth surface. The radiocarbon date directly associated with this sherd was 1135 ± 90 RCYBP: (dendro-corrected to A.D. 920) (Lass 1980b; Hudak, personal communication 1986).

A number of chronological trends are apparent in Fox Lake ceramics regardless of the varying usefulness of the proposed types. Vessel walls gradually got thinner, although they still remained relatively thick. Smoothing of the cordmarked exterior appeared late

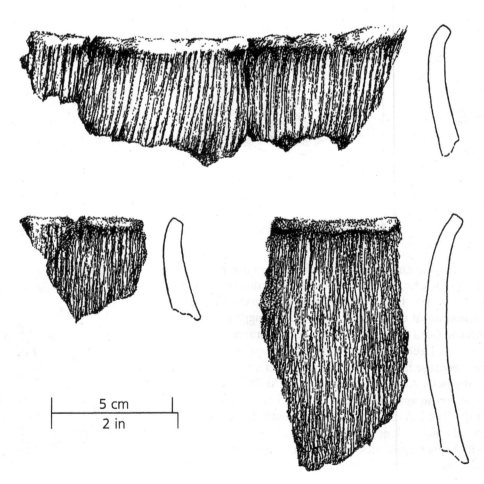

Figure 26. *Fox Lake Vertical Cordmarked* rim sherds from the Pedersen site (from Hudak 1976).

5 cm

2 in

in the phase, but unsmoothed, bold cordmarking remained popular. Wide-trailed lines in simple patterns were common early, while narrow-trailed lines in complex patterns were used late in the phase. Horizontal cordmarking appeared, but it did not displace vertical cordmarking. Bosses were more common than punctates in early Fox Lake, but the reverse became true later. Cordwrapped stick impressions were restricted to lips and interiors early in the phase, but they appeared on exteriors late in the phase.

Geographic trends also are apparent in Fox Lake ceramics. *Fox Lake Cordmarked Trailed* sherds account for at least half of the Fox Lake ceramics at the Fox Lake and Arthur sites, but account for only about 20 percent of the Fox Lake ceramics at the Big

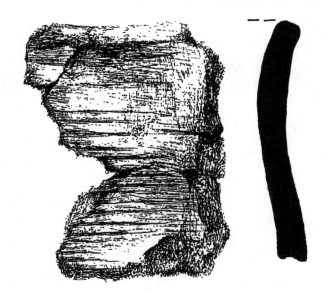

5 cm
2 in

Figure 27. *Fox Lake Horizontal Cordmarked* rim sherd from the Pedersen site (from Hudak 1976).

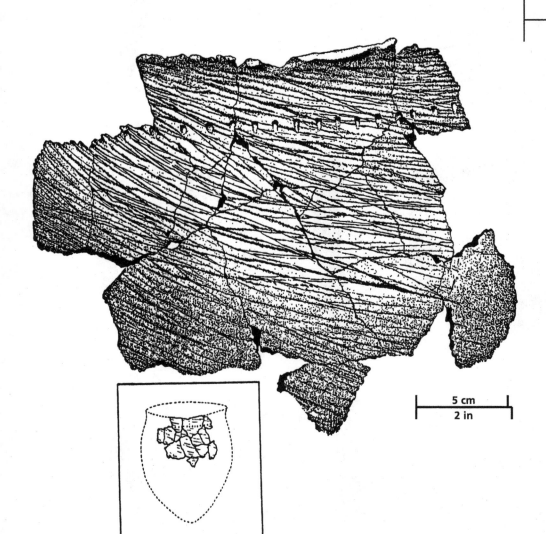

5 cm
2 in

Figure 28. Partially reconstructed *Fox Lake Horizontal Cordmarked* vessel from 21BW38 (from Anfinson 1987b).

Figure 29. *Fox Lake Cordwrapped Stick Impressed* sherds from the Mountain Lake site.

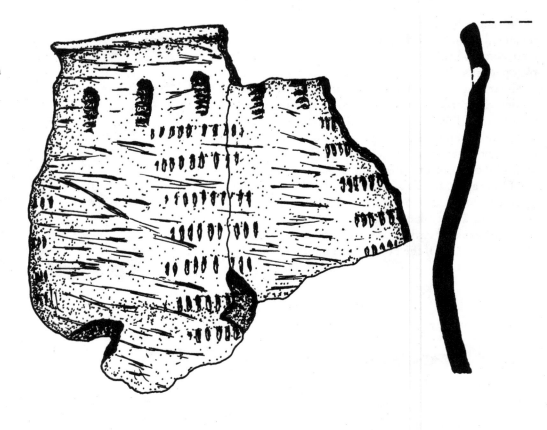

Figure 30. *Fox Lake Smooth* rim sherds (top row) from the Pedersen site (left) and Fox Lake site (right) and *Fox Lake Cordwrapped Stick Impressed* rim sherds (bottom row) from the Fox Lake site (Pedersen rim from Hudak 1976).

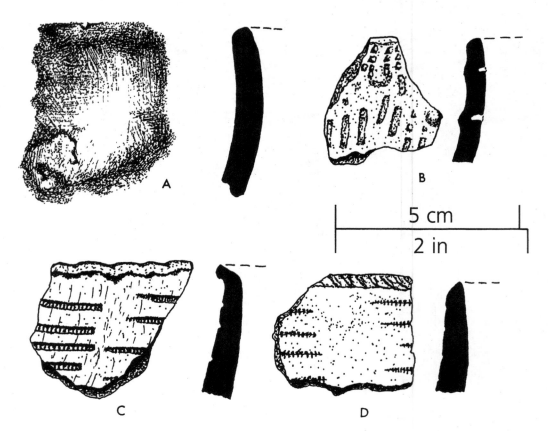

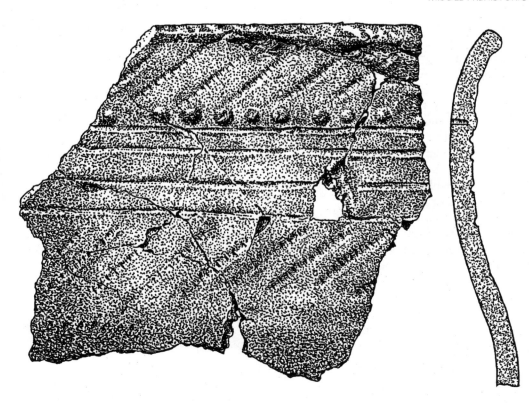

Figure 31. Sherds from the Pedersen site showing combination of trailing, cordwrapped stick impressions, and bosses (courtesy of the Science Museum of Minnesota).

5 cm

2 in

Slough and Pedersen sites and less than 10 percent of the Fox Lake ceramics at eastern South Dakota sites. The Mountain Lake and Synsteby sites have high percentages (25–40 percent) of *Fox Lake Cordmarked Trailed* sherds, but not as high as Fox Lake and Arthur. Thus, the type became less popular moving east to west and south to north in the Prairie Lake Region.

Fox Lake Vertical Cordmarked was more predominant in the western Prairie Lake Region. *Fox Lake Horizontal Cordmarked* was most popular in the central part of the region. *Fox Lake Cordwrapped Stick Impressed* never accounted for more than 10 percent of Fox Lake ceramics at any site, but seems to decrease in abundance moving east to west. *Fox Lake Smooth* was also a minor type at all sites, but it was more common in the western Prairie Lake Region.

As noted earlier, recorded Fox Lake sites are rela-tively uncommon in west-central Minnesota. Excavated habitation sites in general are rare in this part of the Prairie Lake Region. This is unfortunate because it is a major ceramic transition zone. An extensive surface collection from the Levin site (21KH93) in southern Kandiyohi County has yielded no *Fox Lake Trailed* sherds. However, it does appear to contain other Fox Lake types, including *Fox Lake Vertical Cordmarked*. The Levin site also contains single-twisted cord, cordwrapped stick, dentate, and undecorated ceramics. Some do not resemble any of the currently defined types in Minnesota.

In general, Fox Lake ceramics appear to document a relatively stable ceramic manufacturing tradition lasting perhaps a thousand years. Thick vessel walls, sand temper, oriented cordmarking, and conoidal vessels are dominant throughout the Fox Lake Phase.

Decorative techniques indicate a gradual change in preference and elaboration, but punctates (tiny depressions), bosses, trailed lines, and cordwrapped stick stamping were in use throughout the phase.

Lithics Of the excavated Prairie Lake Region sites with major Fox Lake Phase components, the Pedersen site currently may be the most reliable indicator of projectile point associations; it has both the largest sample and perhaps the best stratigraphic integrity. Data from other sites is also necessary, however, because the Pedersen site sample probably does not represent either the full range of types or the most statistically common types for the phase as a whole. In general, four styles of projectile points appear to be associated with the Fox Lake Phase: stemmed, side-notched, corner-notched, and triangular unnotched. Within each of these styles there is a good deal of variation in size and outline.

The projectile points from the Fox Lake site (Figure 32) generally represent a good cross-section of Fox Lake Phase styles. Unfortunately, only ten points have been recovered by excavations. In outline, four are stemmed, four are side-notched, one is corner-notched, and one is triangular unnotched. It is interesting that the largest stemmed point (Figure 32G) and the triangular point (Figure 32B) are from the lowest excavation levels of the most recent excavation (Anfinson 1987b:298). All of the Fox Lake site points are made of chert, except for one of Tongue River Silica.

Based on Hudak's (1974) data from 1973 excavations at the Pedersen site (Table 5), stemmed points were common early in the Fox Lake Phase. Of the ten stemmed points from the Fox Lake levels (7–10), eight have expanding stems and two straight stems. These points vary in length from 25 mm to 74 mm (42 mm average) and vary in basal width from 8 mm to 18 mm (14 mm average). The stemmed points, especially the expanding stemmed variety, appear to be a direct carryover from the preceding Mountain Lake Phase.

The other early Fox Lake projectile-point style at Pedersen is corner-notched; six points of this type are from Fox Lake levels. These points are of a more uniform size than the stemmed points; lengths range from 20 to 25 mm (29 mm average) and widths range from 12 to 14 mm (13 mm average).

Triangular unnotched points dominate the upper Fox Lake levels at the Pedersen site, with seven of the nine points from the upper two levels. These points range in length from 17 to 28 mm (22 mm average) and range in width from 12 to 17 mm (15 mm average). All are isosceles in outline, with an average length 1.5 times the width.

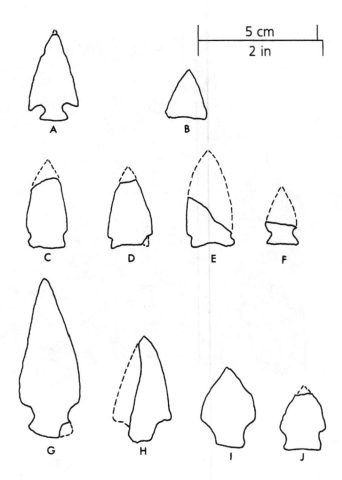

Figure 32. Outlines of projectile points from the Fox Lake site.

There are five side-notched points from the Fox Lake levels at the Pedersen site. They show a good deal of variety in form. One features an "eared" appearance with a deeply concave base. Of the other four, two have straight bases, one is slightly concave, and one is slightly convex. They are all isosceles in outline with lengths ranging from 20 to 36 mm (25 mm average) and widths from 14 to 16 mm (15 mm average).

Wilford's 1956 excavations at the Pedersen site produced 82 projectile points, of which 67 were considered classifiable (Wilford 1961:25). Of these, 22 are stemmed (20 expanding, 2 straight), 3 are corner-notched, 22 are side-notched, and 20 are triangular unnotched. Wilford noticed differences in the horizontal distribution of the points but could determine no significant differences in stratigraphy. Part of the apparent lack of stratigraphic differences in Wilford's sample is probably a result of his use of six-inch (15 cm) levels; it also may be partially a result of his

	PROJECTILE POINTS											OTHER TOOLS					RAW MATERIALS — DEBITAGE				RAW MATERIALS — CHIPPED TOOLS			
Level	Corner Notched	Straight Stem	Expanding Stem	SN/Deep Concave Base	SN/Shallow Concave Base	SN/Straight Base	SN/Convex Base	Eq Triangle Unnotched	Is Triangle Unnotched	Total	Fragments	Scrapers	Knives	Other	Total Non-ProjPt	Total Chipped	Chalcedony	Chert	Quartzite	Total	Chalcedony	Chert	Quartzite	Total
1									1	1	1		4		4	10	4	38		42	1	5		6
2	1		1	1			2			5	2	9	2	1	12	19	35	395	6	436	4	14		18
3	3		1			1	2	1	1	9			1		1	10	28	210	4	242	3	7		10
4	2		1	1		4	1		4	13		8	3		11	24	36	335	2	373	4	18	2	24
5			1	1					1	3	2	2	1	1	4	9	50	345	5	400		8		8
6							1		1	2	1		3		3	6	4	370		374		6		6
7	1		2				1		4	8	2	3	1		4	14	17	50	4	71	3	10		13
8		1	1		1				3	6	3	4	2	1	7	16	34	320	1	355	2	13	1	16
9	1	1	1	1		1			2	7	1	9	5		14	22	50	224		274	3	19		22
10	4		4			1				9	3	14	4	2	20	32	27	168		195	8	22	1	31
11			2							2			3		3	5	24	95		119	1	3	1	5
12			1							1						1	17	75	4	96	1			1
13														1	1	1	3	6		9	1			1
14													2		2	2							2	2
15										0					0	0				0				0
Total	12	2	13	5	2	7	5	7	13	66	15	49	33	6	88	169	329	2631	26	2986	31	127	5	163
%	18	3	20	8	3	11	8	11	20	100		29	20	4	52	100	11	88	1	100	19	78	3	100

Table 5. Projectile points and other chipped stone tools from the 1973 Pedersen site (21LN2) excavations by level and selected attributes. Data from Hudak (1974). Abbreviations: SN=Side-notched, Eq=Equilateral, Is=Isoceles, ProjPt=Projectile point.

assumption that certain forms (e.g., triangular unnotched) were associated with only one component (the youngest).

A detailed study of the points from the 1956, 1973, and 1974 excavations of the Pedersen site would be very useful in determining Prairie Lake Region point styles through time. The sample size is almost 200 points from excavated contexts in a site containing Archaic, initial Woodland, terminal Woodland, Plains Village, and Oneota components. Many more points in the landowner's collection suggest an Early Prehistoric horizon (Hudak, personal communication 1986).

The Mountain Lake site has produced at least 66 projectile points; 15 are from the 1957 excavation (Wilford 1962) and 51 from the 1976 excavation (Timothy Ready, personal communication 1986). There is limited evidence for stratigraphic seriation, however. The 1957 excavation used six-inch (15 cm) levels, and the 1976 excavations centered on what appeared to be a Late Prehistoric house, thus confusing the stratigraphy. Based on overall artifact densities and ceramics, the major component at the Mountain Lake site is the Fox Lake Phase occupation, with less intensive preceramic (Mountain Lake Phase), terminal Woodland, and Oneota occupations. Of the relatively complete points, there are 9 lanceolate, 17 side-notched with deeply concave bases, 16 triangular unnotched, and 5 stemmed. The lanceolate points and some of the stemmed points appear to have preceramic associations. Some of the small triangular points have Oneota associations. Other points are probably Woodland, mainly Fox Lake Phase. Of particular note are the numerous side-notched points with deeply concave bases (see Figure 14, second row from top).

At the Arthur site, where 36 relatively complete points were recovered, Duane C. Anderson and Spriestersbach (1982) associated stemmed, corner-notched, and side-notched points with the initial Woodland component. This association was based more on similarities to other midwestern types of assumed contemporaneity than site stratigraphy. The triangular unnotched points at Arthur are all assigned to the Late Prehistoric, but they show a great deal of variety in form. The larger isosceles points came mainly from middle and lower excavation levels.

At the Big Slough site, the 1971 excavations recovered 52 projectile points (Anfinson 1977:90). The points show approximately equal numbers of corner-notched/stemmed, triangular, and side-notched varieties. Large unnotched triangular and large side-notched points were found in the lower levels associated with Fox Lake pottery. At the Oakwood Lakes site, the Fox Lake levels featured stemmed, corner-notched, and side-notched points (Nowak 1981).

In general, the projectile points of the Fox Lake Phase display more eastern affinities early in the phase and more western affinities late in the phase. There is, however, a good deal of geographic variation within the Prairie Lake Region. Contracting stem points are not common in Fox Lake, especially in the western part of the region. Stemmed points in general are rare in the west. The stemmed points of the early Fox Lake Phase usually have expanding stems resembling western Midwest types such as *Monona Stemmed* (Wittry 1959), *Stueben Stemmed* (Montet-White 1968:76), *Durst Stemmed* (Wittry 1959), and *Apple Blossom Stemmed* (Cook 1976:170).

Unnotched triangular projectile points almost invariably are ascribed to the Late Prehistoric in the Midwest and Plains. A rare exception is Neuman (1975:91), who associated them with the Plains Woodland Sonota complex. While some points listed as unnotched triangular are no doubt preforms, there is a clear association of moderate-sized, usually isosceles triangular unnotched points with the Fox Lake Phase.

Side-notched points exhibit perhaps the greatest variety in the Fox Lake Phase. Forms resembling such Plains varieties as Avonlea, Besant, Hanna, and Oxbow are present (cf. Frison 1978). An Oxbow-like form seems to be associated strongly with Fox Lake. Points resembling contemporary side-notched types from the Midwest such as *Raddatz Side-Notched* (Wittry 1959) and the various Middle Woodland points (e.g., *Manker Notched*, *Gibson*), illustrated in Montet-White (1968:179), are rare.

Corner-notched points clearly are associated with the Fox Lake Phase, but here, too, the affinities are more with the west than the east. The closest affinities may be with Pelican Lake points (cf. Kehoe 1974), but there is a good deal of variety. Well-defined corner-notched examples do not appear to be a dominant Fox Lake type. Notably lacking are Snyders and Norton points associated with the Midwestern Middle Woodland (cf. Montet-White 1968).

In part, the great variety in size and form of Fox Lake projectile points may reflect the introduction of the bow and arrow during the phase. More than 10,000 years old in the Old World, they do not appear to have entered the New World until about 3000 B.C. (Blitz 1988). The bow and arrow were first used in the North American Arctic and slowly spread southward reaching the northeastern Plains perhaps around A.D. 500–600. Benn (1983) dated their appearance in western Iowa to about A.D. 300; Frison (1978:223) dated their introduction in the High Plains to about A.D. 500.

The other chipped stone tools associated with the Fox Lake Phase appear to be common midwestern and Plains forms of scrapers, knives, drills, flake tools, and choppers. No definitive type of these tools appears exclusively attributable to the Fox Lake Phase.

The relative percentages by site of various lithic tools based on inferred function may give some indication of a site's predominant function and even seasonality. The Fox Lake and Oakwood Lakes sites have low percentages (<15 percent) of projectile points, while Pedersen, Arthur, Big Slough, Synsteby, and Mountain Lake have relatively high percentages, with Pedersen featuring 50 percent. Scrapers of both end and side forms are the most numerous stone tools at every Prairie Lake Region Woodland habitation site except Pedersen. They usually account for half the chipped tools. Non-projectile point bifaces, most of which were probably used as knives, usually account for about 20 percent of the chipped stone samples. Specialized tools for drilling, punching, and engraving have very low percentages at most Fox Lake Phase sites. Nevertheless, utilized flakes not dealt with in most analyses may have served these functions.

In general, the chipped stone tool assemblages from Prairie Lake Region sites reflect an emphasis on animal dispatching and processing (cutting meat and scraping hides). It also should be noted that all of the sites discussed are multicomponent, so overall tool percentages may not reflect accurate individual component percentages. Most of the sites have major initial Woodland components, however, and seem to have relatively consistent tool percentages stratigraphically.

Ground stone tools associated with the Fox Lake Phase include full-grooved mauls, grooved and ungrooved celts/axes, hammer-stones, grinding stones, nutting stones, and abrading/sharpening stones. Use of ground stone tools was not extensive, with each site producing only a few examples. Excavations at the Fox Lake site have yielded only 2 grinding stones, 2 celts, 3 hammer-stones, and 2 sharpening stones. The Pedersen site excavations produced only a single ground stone maul. The Arthur site excavations recovered 5 milling stones (2 manos used for grinding seeds and nuts, 3 metates), 2 sharpening stones, 1 celt, and 1 nutting stone. The Oakwood Lakes site yielded 7 hammer-stones, 3 grooved mauls, and 2 celts. The Synsteby site produced 1 grooved axe and 1 celt. The 1957 excavation at the Mountain Lake site uncovered a single milling stone.

Raw material types for Fox Lake Phase chipped stone tools are reflected in both the debitage and the tools. Lithic debris from the initial Woodland levels at the Fox Lake site (Anfinson 1987b:290) is dominated by chert (67 percent), with lesser amounts of quartzite (19 percent), chalcedony (11 percent), and silicified sediment (3 percent). The chert, quartzite, silicified sediment, and much of the chalcedony appear to be from local till sources. At least half of the chalcedony is Knife River Flint, but this material too can be found in the till. Tools from the Fox Lake levels at the type site reflect a raw material preference similar to the debitage with respect to chert, but reversed percentages of chalcedony (22 percent) and quartzite (11 percent).

At the Pedersen site, chert accounts for 85 percent of the Fox Lake Phase debitage, with 14 percent chalcedony and only 1 percent quartzite and silicified sediment. Stone tools at Pedersen are 78 percent chert, 20 percent chalcedony, and 1 percent quartzite/silicified sediment. Twelve of the 16 chalcedony tools (primarily scrapers) are listed as being Knife River Flint (Hudak 1974).

Local materials also predominated the Arthur site, although some chert associated with the Woodland occupations may have been imported from central and southwestern Iowa (D. C. Anderson and Spriestersbach 1982:116). The presence of a small amount of obsidian at the Big Slough, Arthur, and Synsteby sites indicates some distant trade or travel. These examples, however, may not be associated with Fox Lake components. An obsidian point from the Big Slough site is a small side-notched form, while the Synsteby site yielded a straight-stemmed obsidian point. The Arthur site produced only an obsidian flake.

High-quality raw materials (e.g., chalcedony) usually were reserved for unifacial tools (i.e. scrapers) or projectile points. Little of this material was wasted, as

indicated by low relative debitage percentages and high percentages of utilized flakes. Knife River Flint commonly makes up less than 10 percent of the tools and less than 5 percent of the debitage at most sites, except the Oakwood Lakes site where 18 percent of the chipped stone tools are Knife River Flint (Nowak 1981).

Overall, the Fox Lake Phase features a wide variety of lithic artifact forms. Raw materials are predominantly from local sources, but non-local percentages increase moving south and west in the region where sites are closer to quarries in adjacent regions. Stemmed points were the most popular form early in the phase, with triangular, side-notched, and corner-notched forms gradually replacing the stemmed varieties. The chipped stone tools reflect a hunting economy, but the presence of a few grinding stones indicates some vegetal food processing.

Bone and Shell Artifacts Bone artifacts are not common at the multicomponent Woodland sites in the Prairie Lake Region. The few bone artifacts that have been found at these sites are difficult to assign to a specific component because of stratigraphic mixing. No shell artifacts have been recovered by excavations at any major initial Woodland habitation site in the Prairie Lake Region.

At the Fox Lake site, Wilford ([ca. 1946]b) did not notice any bone tools. However, a later analysis by Lukens (1963:169–70) found four carnivore jaw elements that had been trimmed or lightly engraved. All of the bone artifacts came from levels below 20 cm. No bone artifacts were found by the 1981 and 1982 excavations at Fox Lake.

At the Pedersen site, Wilford (1961:32) found a bone awl and a triangular bone pendant; no stratigraphic depth was noted in his report. Hudak (1974: Appendix 1) listed 11 bone artifacts from the Pedersen site, but depicted 17 artifacts in Plate 14. The list included 7 mammal-bone awls, 3 worked teeth (2 beaver incisors and 1 canine), and 1 bird-bone bead. All were found associated with fire hearths containing Fox Lake ceramics. Hudak's Plate 14 included what appear to be several bone pendants.

The Big Slough site yielded a bone awl from the earlier excavations (Wilford [ca. 1954]a). The 1971 excavations recovered 2 needles, 5 awl fragments, 1 bird-bone bead, 1 polished hawk humerus, and a bison metapodial flesher (Anfinson 1977:54). Three of the awls, the bead, and the polished humerus were from levels associated with Fox Lake ceramics.

At the Mountain Lake site, Wilford (1962:22–23) recovered a bird-bone bead and a split mammal long-bone tool that has one square end and one convex end. At Sysnsteby, Wilford (1962:49) found a bone chisel and 2 worked mammal long-bones. At the Johnson site, Wilford (1962) recovered 2 bone beads from lower levels. No bone tools were recovered at the Arthur site in Iowa (Tiffany 1982b:192).

Subsistence

Detailed subsistence studies have been undertaken at six sites with major Fox Lake Phase components: Fox Lake, Big Slough, Mountain Lake, Pedersen, Arthur, and Oakwood Lakes. Study comparisons of the results must be done with caution because of differential sampling methods and analytical techniques (cf. Anfinson 1986). Each of these sites also is multi-component and evidences extensive soil disturbance, further complicating cultural-temporal comparisons.

At the Fox Lake site, the initial Woodland levels of the 1981 and 1982 excavations contained identifiable elements belonging to bison (11), deer (6), dog/wolf (3), muskrat (29), badger (2), raccoon (4), beaver (11), fox (3), skunk (9), mink (1), gopher (2), northern pike (18), bullhead (4), Canada goose (1), duck (1), and painted turtle (14). The only significant difference between the Fox Lake Phase levels and the lower levels was the presence of deer and dog/wolf. While bison clearly dominated the potential edible meat, fish and muskrat dominated the minimum numbers of individuals (Anfinson 1987b:283). The only non-charcoal botanical remains recovered from the Fox Lake levels at the type site were a few uncharred walnut shells, probably deposited recently by rodents.

At the Pedersen site most of the soil from the 1973 and 1974 excavations was dry screened through half-inch mesh. Many small remains, particularly fish, probably were not recovered. The Fox Lake levels yielded a variety of mammals (12 species), fish (6 species), birds (4 species), and turtles (2 species). These finds were dominated by bison (108 elements—6 individuals), muskrat (54 elements—5 individuals), bullhead (290 elements—34 individuals), and perch (104 elements—18 individuals) (O. Shane 1982).

The 1976 excavations at the Mountain Lake site featured recovery methods similar to those carried out at Pedersen, and the site yielded a similar Fox Lake Phase faunal assemblage (O. Shane 1978, 1982). Mountain Lake initial Woodland levels contained 11 mammal species, 5 fish species, 5 bird species, and 1 turtle species. Bison dominated the mammals with 50 identifiable elements from three individuals, but there were fewer muskrat (4 elements—2 individuals), and fish (11 elements from 7 individuals) than the Fox Lake and Pedersen sites. No subsistence related floral

remains have been reported at either Mountain Lake or Pedersen.

At the Big Slough site, the Fox Lake levels featured bison (139 elements), muskrat (56 elements), dog/wolf (11 elements), turtle (17 elements), and bullhead (39 elements), as well as smaller amounts of deer, beaver, badger, raccoon, skunk, gopher, duck, goose, crane, owl, northern pike, and mussels (Anfinson 1982a). The lowest stratigraphic levels at Big Slough were dominated by the same species but had less variety. No subsistence related floral remains could be attributed to the Fox Lake levels.

At the Arthur site, it is difficult to separate the Fox Lake Phase faunal remains from those of other components. Overall, bison (112 elements—6 individuals) and muskrat (35 elements—12 individuals) were the dominant mammals, with nine other mammal species present (Semken 1982). Fish remains were abundant, with minimum numbers of 92 bass, 82 northern pike, 40 bullheads, 34 perch, 26 walleye, 15 sunfish, 8 crappies, and at least 1 individual of five other species (Vondracek and Gobalet 1982). No subsistence-related botanical or mussel remains were recovered.

At the Oakwood Lakes site, vertical comparisons also were difficult. There were widespread disturbances but little inter-component variation. Overall, bison dominated the faunal remains with 270 elements from 19 individuals. Seven other mammal species were recovered, but no muskrat were found (L. Alex 1981). Fish remains were numerous, with bullhead the dominant species (1,083 elements from 62 individuals). Five other fish species were present, and the recovery of at least 121 minnows indicates that netting was used to catch at least some of the fish (L. Alex 1981:292). Four duck elements from 3 individuals were present. No turtle remains were recovered, but 3 mussel shells may indicate the use of shellfish. Some carbonized plant remains were recovered at Oakwood Lakes, including 16 maize fragments, 4 *Chenopodium* seeds (representing a genus of mealy herbs and forbs), 1 wild rose seed, 1 hawthorn seed, 1 *Ambrosia* seed, and 1 marsh elder seed (Haberman 1981). The maize was associated with the late component (Plains Village).

The above sites have notable similarities. Bison were important at all sites, although their overall importance to the diet may be overemphasized by assumptions that humans always used all edible meat. Most of the bison bone from these sites was shattered, indicating marrow and/or bone grease extraction. Small numbers of cranial, vertebral, and rib elements at all of the sites except Arthur indicate kill sites some distance from habitation sites.

A diversity of other mammals also typifies these sites; muskrats dominated this group at every site except Oakwood Lakes. Deer and elk were present only in modest amounts. Fish had some importance at every site, although the numbers of species and dominant species varied considerably. The importance of fish at some of the sites (e.g., Pedersen, Mountain Lake) would increase if finer scale recovery techniques had been employed. Considering the region's potentials, it is surprising that waterfowl remains were present in only modest amounts. Turtles also were present in small amounts. Mussel remains were uncommon. The lack of subsistence-related floral remains may be the most deceptive archaeological result of these excavations. It may be explained by the poor preservation of remains from plants like tubers, although some fault probably lies in recovery techniques.

Settlement Pattern

Twenty-six of the known Fox Lake sites are on lakes, while the other 9 are on rivers or streams. The site locations usually feature water on at least two sides. To date, these sites include 11 on islands, 7 on peninsulas, and 5 on isthmuses. Of the other 3 lake sites, 2 are on prominent hills and 1 is on a bench bisected by a ravine. Of the 9 riverine sites, 4 are at river/stream junctions; others are on either high or low terraces adjacent to a ravine.

These locations suggest that protection was a key element in village location, protection from prairie fires being the most plausible explanation. Such protection served a dual purpose; not only were the village inhabitants and their belongings protected from quick moving, frequent prairie fires, but the trees that were also protected could be used for constructing shelters and tools and for firewood. Protection from hostile humans would have been an added benefit.

The seasonality of habitation sites is open to some debate. While the fish, waterfowl, and turtle remains may indicate warm-season use of these sites, there is little to suggest that they were not occupied in the winter as well. Some of the sites would have been exposed in the winter, as the leafless trees and frozen lakes would have done little to stop the fiercely cold winter winds. The major river-valleys offered humans more protection from the elements, as well as protecting game animals. The presence of some Fox Lake sites in these locations may suggest a winter settlement pattern. Few of the riverine sites have been excavated, however, and most riverine areas have not been surveyed extensively. At the Hildahl site (21YM35) on a lower terrace of the Minnesota River Valley, fish, turtle, and muskrat remains (Dobbs 1979) indicate that river-valley locations were not exclusively winter habitations.

Hudson (1979) discussed a Fox Lake Phase house structure found by the 1976 excavations at the Mountain Lake site. Subsequent analysis by Timothy Ready of the Science Museum of Minnesota suggested that the structure is of Late Prehistoric rather than Fox Lake affiliation (Ready, personal communication 1986).

Gregg (1990) described an early Woodland house found at the Naze site (32SN246) in eastern North Dakota. A reconstruction suggests that the structure was conical in shape with multiple central support posts set in footing trenches packed with daub. Perimeter support poles could then be leaned against the central supports and the exterior covered with bark and/or hides.

Mortuary Treatment

The apparent lack of widespread burial-mound use in at least the early part of the Fox Lake Phase is a major factor differentiating the Prairie Lake Region from adjacent regions. Just north of the region, charred logs from the Morrison Mound site (21OT2) have been dated to 690 B.C. (E. Johnson 1964b). In northern Minnesota, Laurel mounds date as early as 20 B.C. (D. L. Anderson 1979:121). In eastern North Dakota, the Jamestown Mound (39SN22) dates to A.D. 20 (Snortland-Coles 1983), and in northeastern Iowa the Sny-Magill mound site (13CT18) has a date of 550 B.C. (Tiffany 1981:61). Within the Prairie Lake Region, the earliest radiocarbon date from a mound is A.D. 875 from the Round Mound site (21TR1) on Lake Traverse. The nearby DeSpiegler mortuary site (39RO23) had a date of A.D. 550, but the presence of a mound or mounds at the site is undocumented (E. Johnson 1964b).

Stronger evidence for the lack of burial mounds in the Fox Lake Phase is the lack of Fox Lake ceramics. Not only are they lacking in direct association with mound burials, but they have not been found in even the mound fill. The few ceramic vessels associated with burials in the Prairie Lake Region are terminal Woodland or Late Prehistoric types. Decorated sherds in the fill of Prairie Lake mounds almost always are stamped with exterior cordwrapped stick or single-twisted cord impressions.

Mounds are not uncommon in the region but are limited to certain areas. As illustrated in Figure 33, concentrations of mounds are restricted largely to the Minnesota and middle Des Moines river valleys. However, smaller groups appear near four major lake belts in eastern South Dakota or southwestern Minnesota.

Figure 33. Distribution of mounds in and around the Prairie Lake Region plotted by township.

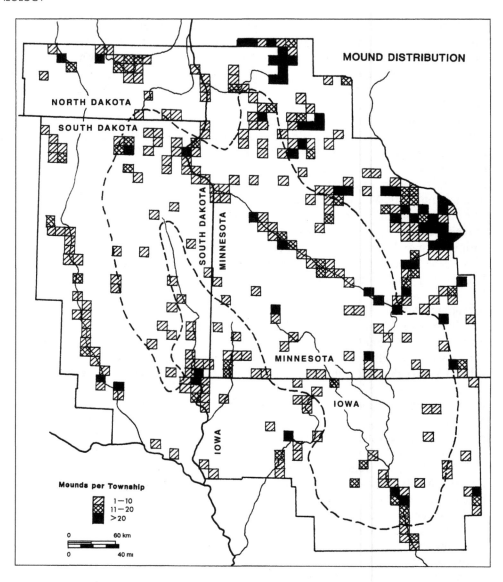

The Prairie Lake Region's interior has a notable scarcity of mounds. The exceptions are at a few major lakes like Lake Shetek or the Chain of Lakes in Martin County.

If concentrations of less than 50 mounds per township are filtered out (Figure 34), only 2 townships in the Des Moines River Valley at the extreme southern end of the region remain. However, immediately east of the region, there are numerous townships with more than 50 mounds each. The Prairie Lake Region is clearly a transition zone between the high-density mound area of central/eastern Minnesota—northeastern Iowa and the low-density mound area of the Missouri Coteau in the central Dakotas.

A study of external features of mounds in Minnesota (Anfinson 1984) indicated that Prairie Lake Region mounds are concentrated on the upper terraces of the Minnesota River Valley. Most mounds in the region tend to be circular, with relatively large basal diameters (12–18 m) and low heights (.3–1.5 m). Most appear alone or in small groups of two to five mounds. Linear mounds are present but not common. Effigy mounds are unknown.

Based on projectile-point form, the best candidate for a Fox Lake mortuary site is the Alton Anderson (21WW4) site in southwestern Minnesota (Figure 35). The Alton Anderson site was excavated by the Minnesota Historical Society in 1971 after human bone was exposed in a gravel pit north of Madelia (Lothson 1983). The site consisted of two discrete burial areas

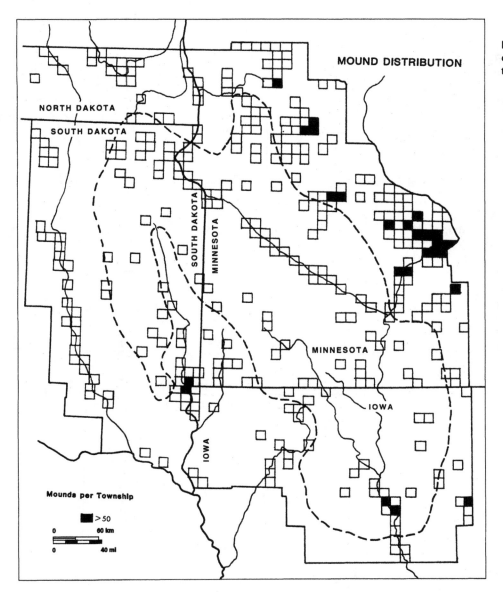

Figure 34. Townships with 50 or more mounds in and around the Prairie Lake Region.

on a ridge near a small lake. No mounds were apparent, but the area had been plowed for many years. Of the more than 30 individuals recovered, 12 were adult males, 12 adult females, 6 children, and 2 young adults. Almost all of the adults were relatively young. Most burials appeared to be in shallow pits. The dominant burial form was flexed or semi-flexed primary, although a few secondary burials also were present.

Associated with the Alton Anderson burials were numerous projectile points, a number of other chipped stone tools, shell pendants, a few bone tools, elk teeth, and a little red ochre. The presence of a few nineteenth-century trade goods and a catlinite pipe indicates a late component at the site, probably associated with the secondary burials. No early ceramics were

recovered. An attempt to radiocarbon date some of the bone was apparently unsuccessful because of intense carbonate contamination; the date of 4760 ± 100 RCYBP (dendro-corrected to 3560 B.C.) appears to be much too early.

Lothson (1983) classified the projectile points into eight groups which are either side-notched or triangular unnotched in form. A high percentage of the points are made of brown chalcedony. Lothson believed the points are related to the Besant-Avonlea complex of the northern Plains and the primary burial mortuary form related to the Arvilla complex. He dated the site between A.D. 600 and 1000.

Rather than seek a distant affinity for the Alton Anderson site, it seems much more useful to look closer to home. The projectile points clearly resemble

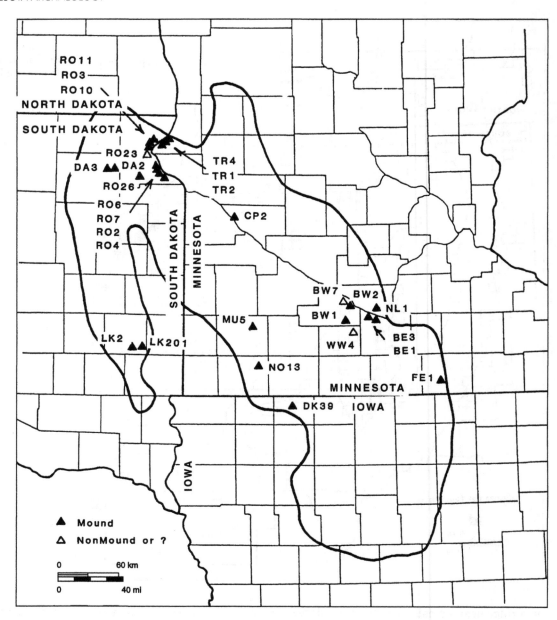

Figure 35. Locations of excavated Woodland burial sites in the Prairie Lake Region.

Fox Lake Phase points, especially the triangular unnotched varieties. The high percentage of brown chalcedony (Knife River Flint) points is greater than at any of the Fox Lake habitation sites but this may simply reflect specialized mortuary treatments. Shell artifacts are not associated with Fox Lake habitation sites but appear to be associated with mortuary sites.

The Runck site (discussed above under the Mountain Lake Phase) could represent an early Fox Lake Phase burial if projectile-point form is considered. The Alton Anderson site may be a late Fox Lake Phase burial site. Alton Anderson indicates more outside contacts than Runck, and Alton Anderson may very

well be the forerunner to mound burial in the Prairie Lake Region.

Dating

There are 18 radiocarbon dates from excavated sites in the Prairie Lake Region that appear to be associated with the Fox Lake Phase. Twelve of these dates (see Table 1, Chapter 1) are from the Oakwood Lakes site (13BK7), where the initial Woodland component appeared to be the most intensive period of site use (Hannus 1981:312). Unfortunately, soil disturbance was extensive and diagnostic initial Woodland materials sparse, so the context of the dates is far from ideal.

In addition, all of the dates are from bone, which is generally not as reliable as charcoal as a dating material. The Oakwood Lakes dates ranged from 260 B.C. to A.D. 785, strongly correlating with the temporal range of the Fox Lake Phase (200 B.C.–A.D. 700).

At the Fox Lake site, four radiocarbon dates were excavation levels containing significant amounts of initial Woodland ceramics (Anfinson 1987b:329). One of these dates, 790 ±70 RCYBP (A.D. 1260), is clearly not of Fox Lake age, but it was from a charcoal sample in the heavily turbated 30–35 cm level. Two other charcoal dates fit the predicted temporal range for the Fox Lake Phase: 1430 ±70 RCYBP (A.D. 640) and 1270 ±70 RCYBP (A.D. 780). A bison bone date was 1480 ±130 RCYBP (A.D. 580).

At the Pedersen site, two radiocarbon dates from the Fox Lake horizon were 2050 ±80 RCYBP (80 B.C.) and 1135 ±90 RCYBP (A.D. 920) (Lass 1980b:36). The latter date was associated with a large rim sherd exhibiting both Fox Lake and Lake Benton characteristics (see Figure 31). The Winter site (39DE5) had two radiocarbon dates from features directly associated with an initial Woodland occupation: 1950 ±70 RCYBP (A.D. 50) and 1180 ±70 RCYBP (A.D. 860) (Haug 1983b).

Only a single radiocarbon date from a mortuary site is of Fox Lake age, but no typical Fox Lake materials were associated. Human bone from a flexed primary burial at the De Speigler site (39RO23) associated with a small dentate stamped vessel yielded a date of 1350 ±110 RCYBP (A.D. 660) (E. Johnson 1964b:41–42).

Lake Benton Phase
(A.D. 700–1200)

A major transition for the cultures of the Midwest and northern Plains occurred between A.D. 400 and 500. In the Midwest, it is denoted by the decline of Hopewell and the rise of numerous local complexes collectively called Late Woodland (cf. Fitting 1978:52–55). This transition is evidenced by changes in subsistence-settlement patterns, lithics, ceramics, and mortuary practices. In the northern Plains, it is marked by the transition from the spear/dart to the bow and arrow, which promoted a climax in communal pedestrian bison hunting in the northwestern Plains (Frison 1978:223).

In the Prairie Lake Region, change is less evident at this time, certainly than in the eastern Midwest. While there may have been a shift to the bow and

arrow and increasing but still limited use of burial mounds, the subsistence-settlement pattern does not appear to change. Ceramic evidence indicates only gradual shifts in decorational styles and technique preferences. By A.D. 700, however, more dramatic changes are evident in ceramic technology, and the use of burial mounds appears to be widespread. These changes in ceramics and mortuary practices mark the end of the Fox Lake Phase and the beginning of the Lake Benton Phase. The Lake Benton Phase may have survived well into the Late Prehistoric Period, co-existing and probably interacting with Plains Village and Oneota complexes.

Lake Benton Phase Sites

Twenty-five sites containing Lake Benton Phase components currently are recorded in the Prairie Lake Region (Figure 36). The type site for this phase is the Pedersen site (21LN2) on Lake Benton, described previously. Other major Minnesota Lake Benton habitation sites include Synsteby (21BW1), Walnut Lake (21FA6), Tuttle Lake (21MR1), Fox Lake (21MR2), Big Slough (21MU1), Johnson (21JK1), Mountain Lake (21CO1), Boy Scout Hill (21LN10), Gautefald (21YM1), Gullickson (21YM2), and Artichoke Island (21BS23). South Dakota Lake Benton sites are Oakwood Lakes (39BK7), Waubay Lakes (39DA7), Winter (39DE5), and Hartford Beach (21RO5). In Iowa, the Arthur site (21DK27) is the only recorded Lake Benton Phase site.

As with Fox Lake Phase sites, Lake Benton Phase sites are notably scarce in the west-central Minnesota and Iowa areas of the Prairie Lake Region. While much of this results from the lack of concentrated archaeological work, Lake Benton is also more difficult to recognize than Fox Lake. Lake Benton ceramics are related closely to other wares, especially the St. Croix-Onamia series in central Minnesota. Until extensive excavations and detailed ceramic analyses are completed at Woodland sites in west-central Minnesota, the distribution of Fox Lake and Lake Benton sites north of the Minnesota River will not be completely understood.

Technology

Ceramics The widespread use of exterior cord-wrapped stick impressions and the disappearance of attributes like trailed lines and bosses are currently the best-known indicators of Lake Benton Phase beginnings. The ceramic attributes that differentiate Lake Benton and Fox Lake ceramics go beyond decoration, however. There are significant differences in

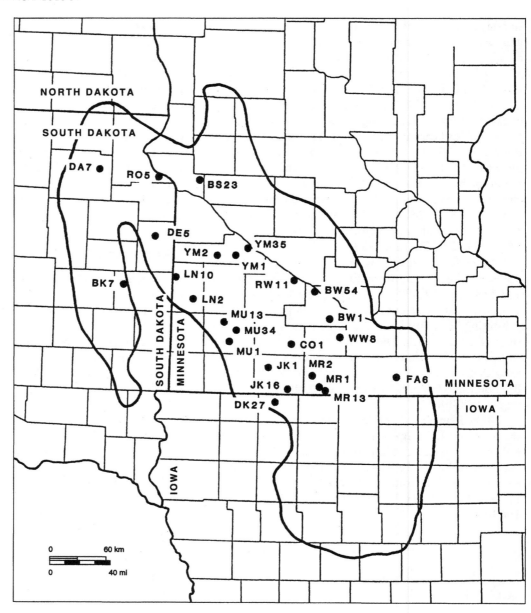

Figure 36. Locations of Lake Benton Phase habitation sites.

manufacturing techniques. While the decorational changes are important, they seem to be more gradual. Some manufacturing traits appear to have undergone a more abrupt shift. These changes include the use of crushed rock as opposed to sand temper, the greatly increased use of surface smoothing, and thinner vessel walls.

Initially, two ceramic types were proposed for the terminal Woodland phase in the Prairie Lake Region, *Lake Benton Cordwrapped Stick Impressed* and *Lake Benton Vertical Cordmarked* (Anfinson 1979:110). These types largely were based on Hudak's (1976) Series A and E ceramics from the Pedersen site. Benn

(1982) then proposed two additional types, *Lake Benton Dentate* and *Lake Benton Plain,* based on his analysis of the Arthur-site ceramics. Anfinson (1987b) confirmed the usefulness of these four types.

Based on studies by Hudak (1976), Anfinson (1979, 1987b), and Benn (1982), Lake Benton ceramics are characterized by the following attributes: moderate-sized, subconoidal vessels with moderately thick walls (6–7 mm) and crushed-rock temper. Rim orientation is slightly inflaring to slightly outflaring, and rims are usually slightly curved in profile. Lips can be round or flat. Some wall thickening can occur in the shoulder. Exterior surfaces of the mid-body usually feature well-defined vertical cordmarking, probably produced by a cord-rolling rather than cord-paddling technique. Rims and upper shoulders of decorated vessels usually are smoothed, and a small percent of body sherds also can be smooth. Interior surfaces are usually smooth but, occasionally, vertically cordmarked. Vessel exteriors can be undecorated or feature cordwrapped stick impressions, dentate impressions, and/or punctates on the rim and upper shoulder. Bosses are known but rare. There is occasional interior cordwrapped stick decoration. Up to one-half of the lips have cordmarking, with some lips having cordwrapped stick impressions.

Lake Benton Cordwrapped Stick Impressed vessels feature bands of oblique, horizontal, and/or vertical cordwrapped stick impressions on smoothed rims and upper shoulders (Figure 37). Single horizontal rows of punctates are occasional on the lower rim. This type is differentiated from *Fox Lake Cordwrapped Stick Impressed* on the basis of temper (crushed rock instead of sand), the diameter of the stick (somewhat larger in Lake Benton), the depth of the impression (shallower in Lake Benton), to some degree wall thickness (thinner in Lake Benton), and rim form (Lake Benton is more curved and less vertical).

The similarity of *Lake Benton Cordwrapped Stick Impressed* to St. Croix-Onamia ceramics found in central Minnesota previously has been pointed out (Hudak 1976:3; Anfinson 1979:110; Caine 1983:215). Onamia ceramics originally were defined by Elden Johnson, based on materials from the Lake Mille Lacs area (Bleed 1969:26). Onamia ceramics also are linked closely to St. Croix ceramics. Caine (1983:214) believed that there are two basic St. Croix types and one Onamia type within a single ceramic series which dates between A.D. 500 and 800.

Similarities between Onamia and Lake Benton ceramics include the use of oblique and horizontal bands of cordwrapped stick or dentate impressions, subconoidal vessels, and crushed-rock temper. There are also differences. Lake Benton has more variation in rim orientation, finer cordwrapped stick stamps, the widespread use of punctates made with angular or circular tools, and distinct vertically oriented cordmarking on the vessel body. There also may be differences in decorational motifs and lip treatment (E. Johnson 1986). Despite differences, Lake Benton and Onamia ceramics are related closely, though Lake Benton seems to persist later in time.

Lake Benton Vertical Cordmarked is a direct carry-over from *Fox Lake Vertical Cordmarked*. Besides ware differences between the two types (e.g., temper, thickness, vessel form), *Lake Benton Vertical Cordmarked* lacks exterior decoration, such as bosses and punctates, and interior cordwrapped stick decoration (Figure 38). The only decoration occasionally found on the Lake Benton type is cordwrapped stick impressions on the lip. Lake Benton also has cordmarking on the lip; this is rare in Fox Lake.

Dentate stamping is not a common Lake Benton decorative technique, and *Lake Benton Dentate Impressed* was defined on the basis of only seven sherds from the Arthur site (Benn 1982:59). Nevertheless, it does appear to be a useful type for the Prairie Lake Region. The Arthur sherds feature fine-toothed dentate impressions in patterns similar to *Lake Benton Cordwrapped Stick Impressed* in horizontal and oblique bands (Figure 39). One *Lake Benton Dentate Impressed* sherd from the Arthur site has cordwrapped stick impressions on the lip. Two others have a single row of punctates on the rim. Several sherds of this type were recovered from the Fox Lake site.

The other new Lake Benton type defined by Benn (1982:61) is *Lake Benton Plain* based on 10 sherds from the Arthur site. These rims lack decoration of any kind. Half have smooth surfaces, and the other half are cordmarked-smoothed (Figure 39). The rims tend to be thinner and straighter than other Lake Benton types. Hudak (personal communication 1985) believed that such a type exists at the Pedersen site. He tentatively designated it Series F, which he characterized as thin, smooth, and plain (undecorated).

The Lake Benton ceramics at the Fox Lake site account for 17 percent of the total sample of rims and near-rims. The *Cordwrapped Stick Impressed* type make up 69 percent of the Lake Benton sherds with 15 percent *Plain*, 12 percent *Vertical Cordmarked*, and 4 percent *Dentate*. At the Pedersen site, 46 percent of the rims are probably Lake Benton types, with 47 percent *Cordwrapped Stick*, 31 percent *Vertical Cordmarked*, and 22 percent *Plain*. Apparently, no *Lake Benton Dentate* is present at Pedersen.

Less detailed information about Lake Benton ceramic distributions is available for most other sites, but some general observations can be made. The Big Slough site has a major Lake Benton component dominated by the *Vertical Cordmarked* type, significant amounts of the *Cordwrapped Stick* type, a little of the *Plain* type, and no *Dentate*. At the Mountain Lake and Synsteby sites, there are small Lake Benton components with *Cordwrapped Stick* and *Vertical Cordmarked* types. The Oakwood Lakes site also has a minor Lake Benton component with *Vertical Cordmarked* and perhaps *Plain* and *Dentate* types present. The Winter (39DE5) and Waubay Lakes (39DA7) sites

Figure 37. Partial restoration of a *Lake Benton Cordwrapped-stick Impressed* vessel from the Pedersen site (from Hudak 1976).

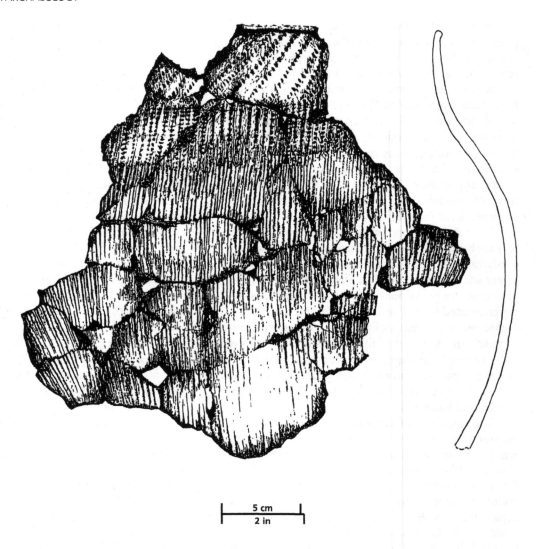

| 5 cm |
| 2 in |

may have major Lake Benton components, dominated by the *Cordwrapped Stick Impressed* type.

The geographical trends of Lake Benton ceramics are less distinct than Fox Lake ceramics, but a few are apparent. The *Cordwrapped Stick Impressed* type is found at almost every site, but it decreases in relative abundance moving east to west in the Prairie Lake Region. The Lake Benton sherds at the Arthur site are about 90 percent this type; the Pedersen site has 47 percent and the Big Slough site about 30 percent. *Dentate Impressed* sherds also decrease in abundance moving east to west, but they never account for more than 5 percent of the Lake Benton sample at even the eastern sites. More of the *Dentate* type also appears to be present in west-central Minnesota north of the Minnesota River and in Iowa than in southwestern Minnesota and South Dakota. *Vertical Cordmarked* and *Plain* types appear to increase in relative abundance moving east to west.

The temporal trends of Lake Benton Phase ceramics are difficult to document even with the relatively large sample and good vertical control at the Pedersen site. As illustrated in Table 3, exterior cordwrapped stick decoration represents a bimodal distribution stratigraphically at Pedersen, as do vertical cordmarked and smooth-surfaced sherds. This probably reflects the use of these attributes by Lake Benton and Fox Lake people. The use of trailing, bosses, punctates, and interior cordwrapped stick impressions decreases, but lip decoration appears to increase reaching its peak in Lake Benton times. In general, through time Lake Benton vessels became thinner walled, more globular, and had less decorative variety on the exterior and more decoration on the lip. The *Vertical Cordmarked*, *Dentate*, and *Cordwrapped Stick* types may be early types, while the *Plain* type may be late.

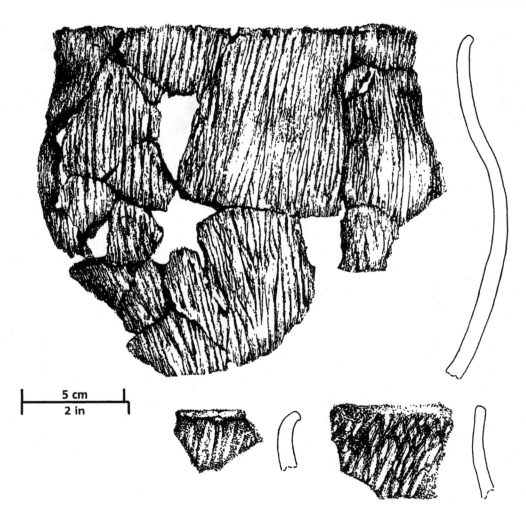

Figure 38. *Lake Benton Vertical Cordmarked* rims and partial vessel from the Pedersen site (from Hudak 1976).

5 cm
2 in

Small amounts of single-twisted cord impressed ceramics found in the upper levels at Prairie Lake Region sites are apparently contemporary with Lake Benton ceramics, but they do not appear to be a Lake Benton type. The fact that such ceramics were never very important in the region is a major factor in differentiating the region from others to the west, south, and east. Benn (1983:83) believed the appearance of single-twisted cord impressed ceramics is the distinguishing trait of the late Late Woodland Period in the western Prairie Peninsula. This decorative attribute is widespread in Late Woodland contexts in the Midwest, as evidenced by such ceramics as Maple Mills/Canton Ware from Illinois (Fowler 1955:219), *Madison Cord Impressed* from Wisconsin (Hurley 1975:225), *Lane Farm Cord Impressed* from northeastern Iowa (Logan 1976:134), and Loseke Ware from the east-central Plains (Benn 1981a, 1981b).

Single-twisted cord impressions also are associated with early Plains Village ceramics, including the Initial and Extended Middle Missouri variants in the central Dakotas (Lehmer 1971:73), Mill Creek in northwestern Iowa (Ives 1962), and Cambria in southwestern Minnesota (Knudson 1967).

Single-twisted cord impressed ceramics are found at most Prairie Lake Region habitation sites, but they rarely account for more than 5 percent of the rims/near-rims. At the Arthur site, the 13 single-twisted cord impressed sherds were classified by Benn (1982:69) as *Missouri Bluffs Cord Impressed*, a type of Loseke Ware. Tiffany (1982b:193) disagreed with this assessment. He contended that the sherds are not large enough to determine vessel form and if the sherds are from sub-globular rather than globular vessels, they may date as early as A.D. 450.

Although the single-twisted cord impressed sherds

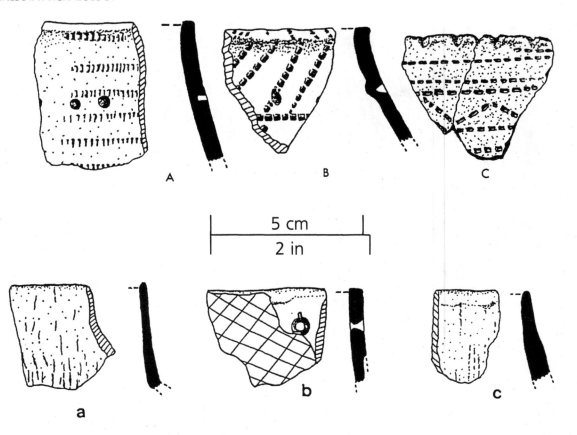

Figure 39. Top Row: *Lake Benton Dentate* rim sherds from the Arthur (A and B, from Benn 1982) and Fox Lake sites (C). Bottom Row: *Lake Benton Plain* rim sherds from the Arthur site (from Benn 1982).

from the Fox Lake site are also too small to determine vessel form, they appear to have closer affinities to western rather than eastern ceramics. Two of the Fox Lake site sherds have a horizontal row of broad, short, cordwrapped stick stamps immediately below the lip. These are followed by a band of horizontal single-twisted cord impressions (Figure 40). Benn (1981a, 1981b) listed this as a characteristic of Loseke Ware. Some single-twisted cord impressed sherds from the Fox Lake site and other sites in the Prairie Lake Region may be related to Plains Village rather than Woodland types.

Lithics The Pedersen excavations of 1973 yielded 27 projectile points from levels 2–4 (Table 5). These levels had the strongest Lake Benton ceramic affiliations. Hudak (1974) classified 12 of these points as side-notched, 8 as unnotched triangular, 6 as corner-notched, and 1 as stemmed. One of the most significant lithic differences between the Lake Benton levels and the levels below is the paucity of stemmed and isosceles triangular points. The presence of 3 out of 5 side-notched points with deep concave bases in the Lake Benton levels may indicate a continuation of this form from the Fox Lake Phase.

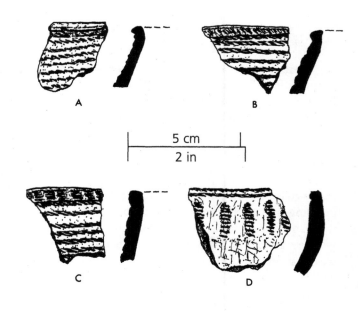

Figure 40. Selected single-twisted cord impressed rims (A-C) and near-rim (D) from the Fox Lake site.

Side-notched points dominate the Lake Benton levels, but there is great variety in these points in outline and size. Lengths vary from 15 to 43 mm (28 mm average) and basal widths from 8 to 19 mm (14 mm average). Basal profiles feature 5 straight, 3 deeply concave ("eared"), 1 slightly concave, and 3 convex. One of the side-notched points is made of Knife River Flint, and 1 is agate. The rest are chert.

Some of the corner-notched points could be described as side-notched on the basis of the photographs in Hudak (1974). The range in length of the corner-notched points is 21–41 mm (36 mm average), and the range in basal width is 12–17 mm (15 mm average). Three of the 6 points are made of Knife River Flint. The other 3 are chert. Of any point type at the Pedersen site, points classified as corner-notched have the highest percentage (42 percent) made of Knife River Flint.

The triangular unnotched points from the Lake Benton levels at Pedersen feature 7 equilateral and 1 isosceles. Although 4 of the 7 equilateral points have broken tips (so original dimensions were estimated), the only points of this type from the site are from the Lake Benton levels. Lengths of the equilateral points vary from 14 to 16 mm (15 mm average) and widths vary from 12 to 17 mm (17 mm average). Five of the points are of chert, 1 is agate, and 1 is quartz. The single isosceles point from these levels is 32 mm by 20 mm and is of chert.

Wilford noticed no projectile point stratigraphy at the Pedersen site where he recovered 67 points in 1956. The lack of stratigraphy in his analysis may be mainly a result of the use of only two major categories of points, notched/stemmed and triangular. Distribution of triangular points at the site particularly puzzled Wilford:

> Simple triangular points were found in every level. . . . From the evidence of the arrow points it would appear that the Pedersen site was contemporary with the Mississippian culture at all stages (Wilford 1961:26).

Wilford was unaware that triangular points also are associated with the initial Woodland phase in the Prairie Lake Region.

At the Mountain Lake site, the stratigraphy of the area excavated in 1976 seems to have been severely mixed by a Late Prehistoric dwelling. Therefore, the presence of lanceolate, side-notched deep-concave base, other side-notched, corner-notched, and triangular points in the upper levels is not surprising. Wilford's upper levels at the site featured triangular points and side-notched points with deep concave bases. The

Arthur site, like Pedersen, had side-notched, corner-notched, and equilateral unnotched triangular points in the upper excavation levels. The 1981 and 1982 excavations at the Fox Lake site yielded a single corner-notched point from the Lake Benton levels.

It is difficult to determine precisely Lake Benton point associations at most sites because Fox Lake and Lake Benton levels have been mixed. Too, most sites have a Plains Village and/or Oneota component that may be contemporary with the Lake Benton component. Many of the equilateral triangular points and some of the side-notched points from these sites are no doubt associated with Plains Village and/or Oneota cultures. The strongest Lake Benton projectile point associations appear to be with small side-notched points with straight to slightly concave bases. These commonly are referred to as Plains Side-Notched (Kehoe 1966) and typified by the Avonlea type (see Figure 14, second row, second from right; Figure 32F). Some corner-notched points and perhaps side-notched points with deep concave bases also may have continued to be used.

As with the Fox Lake Phase, the Lake Benton Phase appears to have no non-projectile point chipped stone tools exclusively associated with it. Lake Benton has the general hunting-oriented tool kit with end scrapers, side scrapers, regular and irregular shaped knives, a few specialized drilling and engraving tools, and a wide variety of flake tools. One difference between the Fox Lake Phase and Lake Benton may be the relative abundance of projectile points. At the Pedersen site, there are apparently equal percentages (36 percent) of projectile points and scrapers in the Fox Lake levels. In the Lake Benton levels, there are 55 percent projectile points and only 17 percent scrapers. This could reflect the change-over to the bow and arrow (where more losses of points occurred during hunting so more were needed). On the other hand, it might indicate some intensification of projectile hunting rather than trapping, netting, or gathering.

With regard to raw materials, the Lake Benton Phase indicates a continued reliance on local till sources. The debitage from the Pedersen site (Table 6) shows almost identical percentages of chert (89 percent), chalcedony (10 percent), and quartzite (1 percent) in the Lake Benton and Fox Lake levels. The raw material percentages for the tools show a slight increase in the use of chalcedony (14 percent Fox Lake, 21 percent Lake Benton), but the percentage of chalcedony that is Knife River Flint actually declines (25 percent Fox Lake, 17 percent Lake Benton). The Fox Lake site also fails to indicate any significant dif-

SITE	Mound Excavated	Mounds in Group	Mound Shape	Mound Diameter(m)	Mound Height(m)	Hydrologic Location	INITIAL BURIALS					Cultural Association	Intrusive Burials
							MODE	TYPE	#	GRAVE GOODS	FEATURES		
Schoen #2(21BS1)	1	1	C	12.2	.8	L	PrimFlex	Surf,ShPit	2	None	Cbl	PV	x
Schoen #1(21BS2)	1	1	C	12.2	1.2	L	PrimFlex	ShPit	3	None		PV	
Lindholm(21BS3)	1	2	C	15.0	.6	L	PrimFlex	ShPit	11	Cer,Shl	O	PV	x
	2		C	15.0	.6	L	PrimFlex	ShPit	2	None		PV	
Miller(21BS4)	1	1	C	9.2	.3	L	PrimFlex	Surf	4	Cer,Lth		PV	
Holtz(21BS5)	1	1	C	?	?	L	Primary	ShPit	4	None		?	
Hanel(21BEI)	4	8	C	11.0	.6	R	?	ShPit	?	None		?	
	5		C	9.8	.6	R	?	ShPit	?	None		?	
	6		C	9.8	.6	R	PrimFlex	ShPit	?	None		?	x
	7		C	8.6	.6	R	?	ShPit	?	None		?	
	8		C	7.4	.6	R	?	ShPit	?	None		?	
Judson I(21BE148)	1	1	C	20.5	2.3	R	Secondary	Pit		1+ Shl	Cbl,Wd,O	WL	
Judson II(21BE3)	2	3	L	-	.3	R	PrimFlex	Pit	7		O	PV	
Lewis(21BE6)	1	5	C	21.5	.9	R	PrimEx	ShPit	4	Cer		On	x
	2		C	18.4	.6	R	?	?	1			PV	x
Harbo Hill(21BE10)	1	7	C	12.1	.8	R	?	?	?		O	?	
Synsteby(21BW1)	1	2	C	14.0	.3	L	Secondary	ShPit		7+ Shl,Lth		WL	
	2		C	18.4	.5	L	Secondary	ShPit	11	None		WL	
Sievert(21BW2)	4	5	C	14.0	1.7	R	Secondary	Pit	11+	None	O	WL	
	5		C	13.0	.8	R	Primary	Surf	1	None		WL	
Saienga(21CP2)	1	1	E	-	1.2	R	?	ShPit	1+		Cbl	WL	
Albert Lea(21FE1)	1	13	C	9.2	.8	L	PrimFlex	Surf?	?			WL	
	4		C	9.2	.3	L	Secondary	Pit	?			WL	
Camden(21LY2)	1	1	C	12.2	2.5	R	Primary	?	1	Cer		On	
Lake Shetek(21MU5)	14	15	C	18.4	.8	L	Secondary	Pit	11	None		WL	x
	15		C	18.4	.8	L	Secondary	Pit	3	None		WL	x
Poehler(21NL1)	6	26	C	18.4	1.8	L	Sec,Prim	Fill	3	Shl	O	WL	?
Wolff(21NO13)	1	1	E	-	1.2	L	Secondary	Surf,Pit	11	Shl,Bn	Hth	WL	x
Round Mound(21TR1)	1	1	E	-	2.0	L	Sec,Prim	Surf	52	Bn,Lth	Hth,Cbl,O	WL	x
Wilson(21TR2)	3	3	E	-	1.0	L	PrimFlex	?	1+	Shl,Bn	O	Ar	
K Group(21TR3)	1	3	C	?	?	L	PrimEx	ShPit	?	None		?	
Fire(21TR4)	1	1	C	2.0	1.7	L	Secondary	Surf	3	Lth	Hth,Wd	WL	
Palmer(39DA2)	L	10	C	3.0	2.1	L	Secondary	Pit	1+	None	Hth	WL	?
Enemy Swim(39DA3)	L	7	C	?	?	L	Secondary	Pit	3	None		WL	x
Madison Pass(39LK2)	L	2	C	18.4	1.0	L	Secondary	Pit	10	Shl		WL	x
Spawn(39LK201)	1	1	C	24.5	.7	L	Primary	Pit	6	None	Hth,O	WL	x
Griner/Madsen(39R02)	1	2+	C	12.2	1.3	L	Secondary	Pit	1+	None	Hth	WL	x
	2		C	10.6	1.0	L	Secondary	Pit	3	None	Cbl	WL	
Buchanan(39R03)	1	5	C	14.7	1.8	L	Secondary	Pit	9	None		WL	x
Hartford Beach(39R04)	1	3+	C	16.6	1.8	L	PrimFlex	Pit,Surf	14+	Shl,Bn,Pp	Cbl,Brk,O	PV	x

Table 6. Mound excavations in the Prairie Lake Region. Abbreviations: *Mound Excavated* L=Largest; *Mound Shape* C=Circular, E=Elongated; *Hydrological Location* L=Lake, R=River; *Mode* PrimFlex=Primary flexed, PrimEx=Primary extended; *Type* ShPit=Shallow pit; *Grave Goods* Cer=Ceramics, Shl=Shell, Lth=Lithics, Bn=Bone, Pp=Projectile point, Cpr=Copper, Brk=Bark; *Features* Cbl=Cobbles, O=Ochre, Wd=Wood, Hth=Hearth; *Cultural Association* PV=Plains Village; WL=Woodland, On=Oneota, Ar=Arvilla.

SITE	Mound Excavated	Mounds in Group	Mound Shape	Mound Diameter(m)	Mound Height(m)	Hydrologic Location	INITIAL BURIALS					Cultural Association	Intrusive Burials
							MODE	TYPE	#	GRAVE GOODS	FEATURES		
Hiawatha Beach(39R06)	1	1	c	6.1	1.0	L	PrimFlex	Pit	1	Cer,Lth		PV	x
Hunters(39R07)	1	1	C	10.7	1.0	L	Secondary	Pit	3		Hth,Wd	WL	
Dougherty(39R010)	2	8	C	13.5	.6	L	Secondary	Pit	9	Shl,Bn,Lth	O	WL	x
	3	2	C	15.3	?	L	Prim,Sec	Surf,Pit	2	Cpr		WL	
	4	1	C	9.2	.3	L	?	?	2	None		?	
	5	1	C	15.3	1.3	L	?	Surf,Pit	2	None		?	
	6	1	C	?	?	L	?	?	1			?	
Medberry(39R011)	L	4	C	?	?	R	Primary	?	1	Shl		?	
Sisseton(39R026)	1	1	E	-	.8	R	Secondary	Fill	6	Lth	Cbl,Hth,Wd	WL	
Kallstrom(39R0301)	1	1	C	15.3	?	L	Primary	Surf	8	Shl,Bn,Brk	Cbl	?	
Okoboji(13DK39)	1	1	C	16.5	1.8	L	Secondary	Pit	1+	?	Hth	WL	x
Gypsum Quarry(13WB1)	1	3	C	14.0	1.0	R	?	?	?	?	O	PV	x

Table 6 (continued). Mound excavations in the Prairie Lake Region. Abbreviations: *Mound Excavated* L=Largest; *Mound Shape* C=Circular, E=Elongated; *Hydrological Location* L=Lake, R=River; *Mode* PrimFlex=Primary flexed, PrimEx=Primary extended; *Type* ShPit=Shallow pit; *Grave Goods* Cer=Ceramics, Shl=Shell, Lth=Lithics, Bn=Bone, Pp=Projectile point, Cpr=Copper, Brk=Bark; *Features* Cbl=Cobbles, O=Ochre, Wd=Wood, Hth=Hearth; *Cultural Association* PV=Plains Village; WL=Woodland, On=Oneota, Ar=Arvilla.

ferences in raw-material usage between the Fox Lake and Lake Benton phases (Anfinson 1987b:294).

Subsistence

Subsistence patterns of the Lake Benton Phase appear to show no significant differences from that of the Fox Lake, although the quality of the data is somewhat poorer. Orrin Shane's (1982) faunal analysis of the Pedersen site included only the material from the Fox Lake component. The Arthur and Big Slough sites both have major Lake Benton components but also have somewhat confused stratigraphies. If most of the faunal remains from Arthur are associated with the terminal Woodland component (as are most of the ceramics), the basic Lake Benton subsistence pattern featured a variety of mammals (dominated by bison and muskrat) and fish. The same assumption can be made at the Big Slough site where a similar faunal inventory exists, although the stratigraphy suggests a slight increase in bison and a decrease in fish and birds through time (Anfinson 1982a).

In general, Lake Benton people had the same faunal exploitation patterns as those in the preceding Fox Lake Phase. Namely, they relied on no particular species, but utilized large mammals, small mammals, and fish. Bison always dominated the potential edible meat totals, but all of the meat may not have been used, especially when kill sites were distant from campsites. Bison were probably the most important species in a varied inventory.

There is no evidence for Lake Benton use of horticulture, although there was widespread use of horticulture in contemporary Plains Village, Oneota, and Midwestern Late Woodland cultures. At the Nelson site (21BE24), southwest of Mankato on the Blue Earth River, corn was found in association with Late Woodland ceramics that closely resemble Effigy Mound types from Wisconsin (Scullin 1981). While this site is within the Prairie Lake Region, it is definitely not a Lake Benton site. Lake Benton peoples probably did make extensive use of native plants, but like Fox Lake, the most important plant foods (e.g., tubers, legumes) would have left remains that have since completely decayed.

Settlement Pattern

Lake Benton settlement patterns are almost indistinguishable from Fox Lake. If the distribution of Lake Benton sites (Figure 36) is compared to that of Fox Lake sites (Figure 20), it is clear that most Lake Benton sites are also Fox Lake sites. There are, however, notable exceptions at the Gautefald (21YM2) and

Hartford Beach (39RO5) sites. These have major Plains Village components and Lake Benton components but apparently lack Fox Lake aspects.

As with the Fox Lake Phase sites, most Lake Benton sites are on lakes. Usually, these are on peninsulas, islands, or isthmuses. Once again, site locations appear to have been chosen for defensive advantages, but this defense may have been against prairie fires rather than other humans. Too, locations may simply reflect where significant patches of woodland existed. The presence of a Lake Benton component at the Hartford Beach site is particularly interesting since it features an artificial fortification ditch that probably was built by the Plains Village inhabitants (Haug 1982).

Mortuary Practices

Most burial mounds in the Prairie Lake Region appear to be temporally if not culturally associated with the Lake Benton Phase. This observation is based on a lack of initial Woodland ceramics either in the mound fill or associated with original mound burials and a lack of mound radiocarbon dates of Fox Lake age. Of the 54 mounds from 37 excavated mound sites in the region (Table 6), 32 mounds from 23 sites probably are associated with the Woodland Tradition. Most of the other mounds have Plains Village associations.

The excavated Woodland mound sites share a number of characteristics. Almost all of the mounds are circular in outline. A few are elongated slightly. They typically have moderate to large basal diameters (9–25 m range, 15 m average) and relatively low heights (.3–3 m range, 1.2 m average). The mounds are found alone or in small groups. The average group size is 4 mounds, and the largest is 26. The 26-mound group (21NL1) is at the eastern margin of the Prairie Lake Region, with the next largest group containing only 15 mounds. All but 4 of the mound groups are located on lakes, and there is rarely a habitation site associated.

The dominant burial mode is clearly multiple secondary burials in shallow pits. One to 12 individuals can be associated with the initial burial phase: the average is 6 individuals. Both sexes and all age groups can be represented. Evidence of cremation or charring is rare. Grave goods are not common, but when present they are usually shell ornaments (e.g., beads, pendants). Red ochre, hearths, and cobble concentrations are occasionally present. Many of the mounds contain additional burials that date to the Late Prehistoric and Historic (contact) age.

The few Woodland ceramics found in Prairie Lake Region mounds are usually not complete vessels. Usually, they are not associated directly with burial pits. However, many of the sherds do appear to be associated with initial mound construction. Large rim sherds have been found at the Poehler, Saienga, and Fire mounds. At the Poehler site (21NL1) on the south side of Swan Lake east of New Ulm, ceramics from the fill of Mound 6 featured horizontal rows of dentate stamps on a smooth rim and upper shoulder, with interior cordwrapped stick impressions (Wilford et al. 1969:30, 65). The vessel form is subconoidal with a high, outflaring rim and an outwardly beveled, flat lip. Vessel wall thickness varies from 6 to 9 mm and is tempered with crushed rock. Vertically oriented cordmarking is present on the body below the decorated zone. About a third of the vessel was found in a very fragmented form.

At the Saienga site (21CP2) near Lac qui Parle on the Minnesota River, burials made during the contact period severely disturbed original burials in the mound. Fragments of a partially restored vessel were present in the mound fill. This vessel featured dentate stamps in horizontal and oblique bands on a smooth rim and upper shoulder, with tool impressions on the lip (Wilford et al. 1969:48, 72). The vessel form is similar to the Poehler vessel, and the Saienga vessel also has a vertically cordmarked body. The rim sherds are about 5 mm thick. Other decorated sherds in the mound fill at Saienga included small cordwrapped stick and single-twisted cord impressed sherds.

The Fire Mound (21TR4) on a high bluff above the east side of Lake Traverse yielded a single rim sherd recovered from the mound fill. It had vertical, oblique, and horizontal cordwrapped stick impressions on the rim exterior, as well as interior impressions. The vessel form is different from the Saienga and Poehler vessels, having a short rim that is probably from a more globular vessel (Wilford et al. 1969:46, 71).

Other Prairie Lake Region mounds containing Woodland ceramics include the Lake Shetek mounds (21MU5) and the Spawn Mound (39LK201). Lake Shetek mounds 14 and 15 had a few small near-rims with single-twisted cord impressions (Wilford et al. 1969:39). The Spawn Mound contained a single near-rim with single-twisted cord impressions (Howard 1968:136). The Sisseton Mound (39RO26) yielded five cordmarked body sherds 4–8 mm thick, with an associated radiocarbon date of 830 RCYBP ± 85 (dendro-corrected A.D. 1220) (Sigstad and Sigstad 1973b).

Mention also should be made of the DeSpiegler site (39RO23) located on a ridge between the Little Minnesota River and the Big Stone-Traverse lake basin. A salvage excavation by the University of Minnesota in 1953 encountered 24 burial pits containing over 40 individuals (E. Johnson 1973:44–57). No mounds were apparent at the site, but the area had been cultivated prior to the opening of the gravel pit which disturbed the burials. The burial forms at DeSpiegler featured secondary and partially disarticulated primary burials. The site has been classified as an Arvilla site. The DeSpiegler burials were re-interred by South Dakota in 1987, although some additional analysis was performed at the University of North Dakota prior to the reburial. This analysis has not been published.

Associated with the burials at DeSpiegler were stone tools, bone tools, a copper awl, faunal remains, and shell ornaments. Two mortuary vessels also were found directly associated with primary burials. Both have been classified as *St. Croix Stamped* (E. Johnson 1973:57, 85; Caine 1983:215). The vessels are sub-conoidal in form with oblique dentate impressions on a cordmarked-smoothed rim and upper shoulder. One has vertical cordmarking on the body; the other has horizontal cordmarking.

While neither vessel was available for examination, the descriptions and photographs indicate that the vessels are indeed more closely related to St. Croix/Onamia ceramics than Lake Benton ceramics. The vertical cordmarking is less distinct than on most Lake Benton vessels, and the use of horizontal cordmarking is rare in Lake Benton. The dentate impressions were made with a larger tool than is usual for *Lake Benton Dentate*. Two radiocarbon dates were obtained for materials directly associated with the horizontally cordmarked vessel. One on bone was 1350 RCYBP ± 110 (A.D. 660). The other, on bark, was 670 RCYBP ± 100 (A.D. 1290) (E. Johnson 1964b:41–42). Root contamination made the bark date somewhat suspect.

Besides the radiocarbon dates from the DeSpiegler and Sisseton Mound sites, the Round Mound site (21TR1) on the east side of Lake Traverse yielded a radiocarbon date of 1025 RCYBP ± 110 (A.D. 1010) from decayed wood near a central burial pit (E. Johnson 1964b:43–44). The Round Mound featured 52 secondary human burials with associated bison burials (Wilford 1970:1–6).

In general, Lake Benton burial practices are not much better known than Fox Lake. There is a lack of diagnostic materials, reliable radiocarbon dates, and excavated mounds from the Prairie Lake interior. Most of the ceramics from mounds of Lake Benton age in the region yield dentate-stamped ceramics, while this type is rare at the habitation sites. This may be a result of mortuary specialization or mound con-

struction by non-Lake Benton people. The overwhelming burial form from mounds in the Prairie Lake Region is secondary burial, and it is assumed that at least some of these are Lake Benton. It does not appear that Lake Benton people practiced the bison ceremonialism apparent in Sonota complex burials (Neuman 1975:94) and at sites along the northern edge of the Prairie Lake Region, such as the Fingerson Mound (21PO2) and the Round Mound (21TR1) (Wilford et al. 1969:41; Wilford 1970:1–6).

Dating

Only six radiocarbon dates are available associated with Lake Benton levels at habitation sites in the Prairie Lake Region. The four possible Lake Benton dates from mortuary sites are discussed above. The phase is thought to begin about A.D. 700 and last until perhaps A.D. 1200.

Features containing terminal Woodland ceramics at the Winter site (39DE5) yielded charcoal dated to 1180 ±70 RCYBP (A.D. 860) and 1110 ±70 RCYBP (A.D. 940) (Haug 1983b). At the Pedersen site, animal bone samples associated with Lake Benton ceramics produced dates of 1135 ±90 RCYBP (A.D. 920) and 705 ±80 RCYBP (A.D. 1280) (Lass 1980b:36). At the Fox Lake site, where the stratigraphy seemed more disturbed than at the Pedersen site, dates of 1210 ±70 RCYBP (A.D. 780) and 790 ±70 RCYBP (A.D. 1260) were obtained from charcoal samples from middle excavation levels associated with both initial and terminal Woodland ceramics (Anfinson 1987b:329).

Perspective on the Middle Prehistoric Period

The Middle Prehistoric Period began with the Mountain Lake Phase about 3000 B.C. The Mountain Lake Phase featured the beginnings of a subsistence-settlement pattern where village sites were located on islands and peninsulas in the lakes. There was a balanced use of upland and lowland resources.

Contemporaneous with the Mountain Lake Phase was the Late Archaic Period in the Midwest. The Late Archaic featured multiseasonal base camps, permanent habitations, specialized plant gathering and horticulture, multiregional exchange networks, the initial use of burial mounds, and some use of pottery (Phillips and Brown 1983). Overall, the period was one of a fairly sedentary lifestyle. The Mountain Lake Phase has certain features of the Late Archaic, including a more sedentary lifestyle and lanceolate projectile points. There is no evidence in Mountain Lake, however, for intensive plant gathering, horticulture, ceramics, mound burial, or interregional exchange.

The Mountain Lake Phase in the Prairie Lake Region is clearly not Late Archaic as defined in the Midwest. There is no evidence for increased dependence on vegetal foods, the beginnings of agriculture, mound burial or multiple internments, and increased river-bottom utilization. The increased use of lake-related resources in the Mountain Lake Phase may be a result of shallow lake stabilization following the thermal maximum. This may have encouraged increased sedentism, which is the one Archaic trait that holds true in the Prairie Lake Region. The phase can be distinguished from the initial Woodland phase only by the use of ceramics in the latter and the use of small lanceolate projectile points in the former.

The High Plains at this time was dominated by the McKean complex (Greiser 1985; Frison 1978). This is defined by the presence of projectile points of the Mallory, McKean, Duncan, and Hanna types, which feature concave bases on lanceolate, stemmed, or side-notched forms. A wide variety of animal remains are found at many McKean sites, along with vegetal food remains and large numbers of grinding tools. Stone-lined roasting pits are also common. Overall, McKean people had a more diverse diet than previous Plains groups and utilized a wide variety of settlement locations.

Areas around the Prairie Lake Region show varying similarities to eastern and western influences, although the period is poorly known in all of the regions. Some occupation of the valleys of the upper Mississippi and central Des Moines rivers is evidenced by stemmed and medium-sized lanceolate points. The upper and lower sections of the James River Valley yield points closely resembling McKean complex types. Copper artifacts, which probably indicate some participation in interregional trade networks, are found in all of the adjacent regions except the lower James River, the Big Sioux River, and the central Des Moines River areas. There is no evidence for the pre-Woodland use of ceramics, horticulture, or burial mounds in any of the regions immediately adjacent to the Prairie Lake Region.

In general, it appears as if the regions to the north, south, and east of the Prairie Lake Region participated to some degree in Midwestern Late Archaic interaction, while the regions to the west were influenced by the McKean complex. The Prairie Lake Region culture experienced significant subsistence and settlement changes at this time, but the root cause appears to

have been a changing environment rather than widespread cultural interaction. The Prairie Lake Region had neither strong western or eastern ties at this time.

The appearance of the Woodland Tradition in the Midwest is identified by the intensification and elaboration of patterns begun in the Archaic. This included more elaborate mortuary ritual, improved technology (e.g., better-made ceramics), more intensive horticulture, more cooperative production, and more regional interaction. These factors are reflected in increased sedentism and social stratification. The Woodland Period in the Midwest began as early as 1000 B.C. and climaxed in Middle Woodland times which are associated with the Hopewell Interaction Sphere. The sphere had a limited presence on the Plains and was waning ca. 300 B.C.–A.D. 400; its influence largely was gone by A.D. 1000.

The beginning of the Woodland Tradition in the Prairie Lake Region is marked by the introduction of ceramics. The appearance of pottery about 200 B.C. denotes the beginning of the Fox Lake Phase and the end of the Mountain Lake Phase. The source of ceramic technology is obviously to the southeast of the Prairie Lake Region. This cultural diffusion appears to involve just ceramics. The subsistence and settlement patterns, lithic technology, and mortuary practices of the Fox Lake Phase did not change appreciably from the Mountain Lake Phase. The only other trait besides the addition of ceramics that differentiates the two phases is the replacement of lanceolate and stemmed points with side-notched, corner-notched, and triangular unnotched points.

In surrounding areas adjacent to the Prairie Lake Region, Early Woodland also was not well developed. In southeastern Minnesota there is a ceramic type, *La Moille Thick*, resembling the earliest thickwares of the Midwestern Early Woodland, but only a few sites have yielded the pottery (Gibbon 1986). Trailed-over cordmarked ceramics are present in most of the adjacent regions but, like Fox Lake, these ceramics appear to be temporally of early Middle Woodland age.

A notable exception is the Naze site (32SN246) in southeastern North Dakota where cordmarked/trailed ceramics and small corner-notched points were dated to 550–410 B.C. (Gregg and Picha 1989; Gregg 1990). While the Naze site has been used to define an Early Plains Woodland horizon in the northeastern Plains, this horizon is defined only by the presence of early ceramics. There is no connection to intensified mortuary ritual, large stemmed projectile points, and the incipient horticulture which defines Early Woodland in the eastern Midwest. Burial mounds do not seem to be used anywhere on the eastern Plains border in Early

Woodland times, but they were in use in most regions except the Prairie Lake Region by early Middle Woodland. Horticulture was of very limited importance in the northeastern Plains during the Middle Prehistoric Period.

Munson (1982) proposed that sand-tempered, cordmarked, trailed/embossed ceramics in the western Midwest were all representative of the Black Sand Tradition. This began somewhere in the northwestern Midwest during the Early Woodland Period (ca. 500 B.C.). By 400–300 B.C., Black Sand had extended into the Illinois River Valley where there was limited Havana interaction. Munson believed that within several hundred years, Black Sand retreated to the northwest and only weakly participated in the Hopewell Interaction Sphere. He characterized Black Sand sites in west-central Illinois as seasonal camps whose residents spent the rest of the year in northeastern Iowa, southwestern Wisconsin, and southern Minnesota. This would include the makers of Fox Lake, Brock Lake, and Spring Hollow ceramics in the Black Sand Tradition.

While there is certainly some relationship between most of the trailed-over cordmarked ceramics of the Midwest, there are a number of problems with Munson's Black Sand theory:

1) He assumes that all users of sand-tempered/cordmarked/trailed ceramics represent a homogeneous cultural group.

2) While dating for all of these complexes is generally poor, Fox Lake seems significantly younger than Black Sand; *Fox Lake Trailed* sherds at the Pedersen site dated to 80 B.C. and perhaps even A.D. 920. At the Fox Lake site, the initial Woodland levels have dates as late as A.D. 400–700. Available Black Sand dates are all several hundred years B.C.

3) There are significant differences between the various cordmarked/trailed types. *Fox Lake Trailed* differs from *Black Sand Incised* in its widespread use of interior cordwrapped stick stamping, motif preference, thicker walls, and perhaps slightly larger vessel sizes. Fox Lake ceramics appear to be partially an outgrowth of *LaMoille Thick* ceramics, while Munson believes Black Sand ceramics are not related to *Marion Thick*.

4) Black Sand lithic associations (e.g., contracting stem and large side-notched points, pebble manos) and mortuary associations (e.g., use of mounds) do not appear to be Fox Lake traits.

5) The geographical area involved in Munson's Black Sand region is enormous. It is difficult to believe that the initial Woodland inhabitants of southwestern Minnesota spent part of the year in west-central Illinois and abandoned the Prairie Lake Region. Not only are year-round subsistence resources available in the Prairie Lake Region, but population densities would have to be incredibly low for southern Minnesota, southwestern Wisconsin, northern Iowa, and western Illinois to be almost the exclusive domain of Black Sand people utilizing a seasonal round incorporating the entire region.

There is a lack of extensive evidence for the Hopewell Interaction Sphere on the eastern Plains north of present-day Kansas City (Benn 1983). A few Hopewell elements have been noted in southeastern Minnesota, northeastern Iowa, and south-central Iowa. However, even in these Plains border regions close to major Hopewell expressions in southwestern Wisconsin and western Illinois, the Hopewell Interaction Sphere operated only peripherally. The Woodland phases of the Prairie Lake Region appear to have been excluded particularly from Hopewell interaction. This may explain why few exotic materials (e.g., obsidian, copper, marine shells) have been found in excavated sites in the Prairie Lake Region. It also may explain the very limited mortuary ceremonialism found, as well as the lack of Hopewell ceramic and lithic influences.

The demise of the Hopewell Interaction Sphere between A.D. 300–400 is the usually accepted signal for the beginning of the Late Woodland in the Midwest. Numerous regional complexes developed that were less elaborate than Hopewell in their material culture and mortuary ceremonialism. Most Late Woodland cultures are identified by their ceramics; these are typified today by globular forms, thin walls, and exterior surface treatments featuring complex woven-cord impressions. Localized subsistence-settlement patterns also are important. Horticulture often played an important role. Smaller projectile points indicate the universal acceptance of the bow and arrow. Such points are also evident on the High Plains, where they signal the beginning of Late Prehistoric times. The use of ceramics also appears for the first time on the northwestern Plains, although in a limited way.

In the areas surrounding the Prairie Lake Region, the widespread changes apparent at this time are reflected variously. The complex cord technology associated with Late Woodland ceramics is present in the Effigy Mound complex to the east of the Prairie Lake Region and to the north in Brainerd and Blackduck ceramics. During the Late Woodland Period to the south and southwest, single-twisted cord decoration is a hallmark of the period. In the Prairie Lake Region neither fabric-impressed nor single-twisted cord-impressed ceramics are common, although some changes in the ceramics denote the beginning of the terminal Woodland Lake Benton Phase.

Ceramic changes include a switch from sand to crushed-granite temper, a thinning of vessel walls, a slight change in vessel form to a more subconoidal shape, the abandonment of trailing and embossing, and the dominance of cordwrapped stick impressions as exterior decoration. St. Croix-Onamia ceramics similar to Lake Benton Phase ceramics are found in the area immediately northeast of the Prairie Lake Region. These probably were made early in the Lake Benton Phase. St. Croix-Onamia ceramics developed into Kathio-Clam River ceramics in central Minnesota, a type not found in the Prairie Lake Region.

The lithic changes associated with the acceptance of the bow and arrow are evident in the Prairie Lake Region and the adjacent areas. Some Lake Benton Phase projectile points closely resemble Avonlea forms on the Plains, with side-notching and slightly concave bases. There also is, however, some continuation of corner-notched points and side-notched points with deep concave bases. No changes in raw material types or basic tool kits are evident between the Lake Benton and Fox Lake phases.

Subsistence-settlement patterns do not appreciably change in the terminal Woodland Period in the Prairie Lake Region, but major changes were apparent in adjacent regions. There was widespread use of horticulture and an attendant development of storage technology in the Late Woodland complexes to the east

and south. To the north, wild rice was harvested intensively and stored for the first time. There is no evidence for horticulture in the Lake Benton Phase. Even though some large wild rice beds may have been present in the Minnesota River Valley and a few eastern lakes, there is no evidence for the use of wild rice in the Prairie Lake Region.

While mortuary ritual became less important in the Midwest in Late Woodland times, it seems to have become more important on the northeastern Plains in the late Middle Prehistoric. The Arvilla complex (ca. A.D. 600–900), the Sonota complex (ca. A.D. 100–600), and the Devils Lake–Sourisford complex (ca. A.D. 900–1400) all suggest this. In the Prairie Lake Region, the widespread use of mound burial may have begun in the Lake Benton Phase, but burial treatments were relatively simple and featured multiple secondary burials in shallow pits with few grave goods. The mounds themselves were also relatively simple, usually being moderate-sized, low, conical earthworks found alone or in small groups. No effigy mounds have been found in the Prairie Lake Region. An egalitarian society may be reflected by the inclusion with little differentiation of all age groups and both sexes in the mound burials.

As the Woodland Period waned, new subsistence options and technologies fostered population growth and cultural diversity. Tensions between the various groups also increased, however, and life in the Prairie Lake Region became more complex.

Chapter 6

Late Prehistoric Period (A.D. 900–1650)

Significant cultural changes are apparent in the Prairie Lake Region beginning about A.D. 900. These changes can be seen in ceramics that differ greatly from Woodland ceramics in form and decoration. A new subsistence-settlement pattern focused on gardening and rivers, and new cultural orientations appeared. During the Late Prehistoric era, Plains Village and Oneota complexes replaced earlier cultures.

The "new" cultures of the Prairie Lake Region did not immediately displace the Woodland culture. They adapted or adopted practices already developed by earlier inhabitants, particularly a lacustrine-oriented Middle Prehistoric subsistence-settlement pattern. Ceramic attributes, lithic types, and mortuary practices also show some continuity. In sharp contrast to the preceding period, the Late Prehistoric in the Prairie Lake Region seems to represent an example of E. Leigh Syms's (1977) Co-Influence Sphere model, with many different groups utilizing the region, some year-round and others only seasonally.

Radiocarbon dates associated with Woodland ceramics from the Pedersen, DeSpiegler, and Sisseton Mound sites indicate that Woodland peoples inhabited the Prairie Lake Region until at least A.D. 1200. Woodland use of the region was not limited to Lake Benton people. This is indicated by the presence of single-twisted cord ceramics around the region's periphery and ceramics closely resembling early Late Woodland central Minnesota types in the area north of the Minnesota River.

The Plains Village pattern originally was described by Donald Lehmer in the early 1950s (Lehmer 1954a, 1954b). It is usually considered to encompass two early traditions, Central Plains and Middle Missouri, and one later tradition, Coalescent, which blends the earlier two (cf. Caldwell and Henning 1978:125; A. Johnson and Wood 1980:38–39).

These complexes occupied the eastern half of the northern and central Plains. The southern Plains also featured village cultures in the Late Prehistoric (cf. W. Wedel 1964:206; Baugh 1986), but they rarely are included in discussions of the Plains Village pattern because they have neither been studied as extensively nor consolidated into larger traditions.

The characteristic Plains Village lifeway featured semi-permanent villages on river valley terraces with adjacent river bottom gardens. Many of the village sites were fortified. Villages contained sturdy, rectangular, semisubterranean houses, as well as numerous large storage/trash pits. Globular ceramic jars were used, exhibiting blends of Woodland and Mississippian traits. Arrowheads were small and triangular, with or without notching (W. Wedel 1964:205–6; A. Johnson and Wood 1980:38).

The best-studied early Plains Village tradition of the northern Plains, the Middle Missouri Tradition, has been divided into three "variants": Initial, Extended, and Terminal (Lehmer 1971). Only the Initial Variant is widespread in the northeastern Plains, while the later two variants largely are limited to the Missouri River trench. The Initial Variant appeared in the northeastern Plains about A.D. 900. It was almost completely abandoned by Plains Village peoples by A.D. 1300 (R. Alex 1981; D. C. Anderson 1986). However, protohistoric Plains Village sites are known in eastern North Dakota (Wood 1971; Michlovic and Schneider 1988; Gregg 1987).

Four complexes make up the Initial Variant: Over, Mill Creek, Great Oasis, and Cambria, with at least two Over phases and two Mill Creek phases (Henning 1973, 1983a; Caldwell and Henning 1978:130). Two of these complexes, Great Oasis and Cambria, currently are recognized in the Prairie Lake Region. Both were defined initially by Lloyd Wilford following excavations at the respective type sites in southwestern Minnesota, and both are considered here to be Late Prehistoric phases.

A third Plains Village phase, the Big Stone Phase, originally proposed by James Haug (1983a) on the basis of excavations at the Hartford Beach site (39RO5) and reconnaissance surveys in northeastern South Dakota, is further developed here. The need for the Big Stone Phase and perhaps additional Plains Village phases results from the unsatisfactory practice of classifying all non-Great Oasis Plains Village sites in Minnesota as Cambria.

Besides terminal Woodland and Plains Village complexes, the other major Late Prehistoric complex evident in the Prairie Lake Region is Oneota. The Oneota Tradition is a widespread manifestation originally defined in northwestern Iowa (Orr 1914). Oneota distribution generally concurs with the Prairie Peninsula of the Midwest. Oneota is evident as early as A.D. 900, although most dates are after A.D. 1000 and some are from the time of early European contact (Dobbs 1982).

Oneota components usually are defined by the presence of shell-tempered ceramics from globular jars with straight rims and wide-trailed line decoration. Other Oneota traits are large horticultural villages with numerous storage/trash pits, small unnotched projectile points, catlinite pipes, and catlinite plaques (Henning 1983b). Oneota sites are found from the James River Valley of the Dakotas in the west to northern Indiana in the east and from central Minnesota in the north to central Missouri in the south. Henning (1983b) defined four Oneota "group continuities" or micro-traditions: South-central Wisconsin, Northwest Iowa, Upper Mississippi River Valley, and Central Missouri. Oneota peoples are linked to ethnographically known Siouan speakers such as the Ioway, Oto, Missouri, Winnebago, Osage, and Kansa (Springer and Witkowski 1982).

Great Oasis Phase
(A.D. 900–1200)

Great Oasis is one of the earliest and most widespread Plains Village phases. Great Oasis ceramics are found in eastern and central South Dakota, northern Iowa, southwestern Minnesota, northeastern Nebraska, and even western Illinois (Henning 1971). Great Oasis ceramics have been reported from southern Manitoba (Nicholson 1989). The densest concentration of Great Oasis sites is in northwestern Iowa.

There is some disagreement as to whether or not Great Oasis should be considered part of the Middle Missouri Tradition. It does have stronger Woodland influences than other Initial Variant phases and lacks certain Middle Missouri traits such as fortified villages (Tiffany 1983). There seems to be general agreement, however, that Great Oasis is ancestral to Initial Middle Missouri.

Great Oasis Site

Great Oasis was first defined in 1945 by Lloyd Wilford following excavations at 21MU2 in northwestern Murray County, Minnesota (Wilford 1945b). The name Great Oasis was Joseph N. Nicollet's name for the large wooded area in the southwestern Minnesota prairie that was protected from prairie fires by several large adjoining lakes (cf. Nicollet 1976:66). The lake complex was drained in 1911, and the lake bed and parts of the wooded island/isthmus are now farmed.

The Great Oasis type site (21MU2) originally was referred to by Wilford as the Great Oasis site, but subsequent references (Wilford [ca. 1954]b, 1955) called it the Low Village, in honor of the local landowner. Confusion regarding the site name was compounded in 1971 when excavators of a western locale of the site (Figure 41) referred to that location as the Thompson site (21MU17) and to the eastern location as the Nelson site (21MU2) (Hudak 1972b). Sites 21MU2 and 21MU17 are both considered here to be part of one site, the Great Oasis site.

Wilford excavated at the Great Oasis site in 1941, 1950, and 1955. The 1941 and 1950 excavations were described in a detailed unpublished report (Wilford [ca. 1954]b), but the 1955 excavations were described only in field notes on file at the University of Minnesota. The 1941 excavations consisted of eight 10 x 10-foot units near the southeast edge of the island (Figure 41). The 1950 excavations were a 20 x 20-foot area divided into four 10-foot squares 92 m north of the 1941 excavations. The 1955 excavations consisted of three 10 x 10-foot units at the top edge of the old lake bank just east of the southernmost 1941 excavations. In addition, Wilford excavated seven 2 x 6-foot trenches along the base of the bank in 1955 in an apparent search for burials. No cultural materials or burials were encountered by these trenches.

In 1971 a joint University of Minnesota-University of Nebraska expedition led by Dale Henning excavated three 10 x 10-foot units at the Great Oasis site. Two of the units were in the western locale (Thompson). The other unit was in the eastern locale (Nelson)

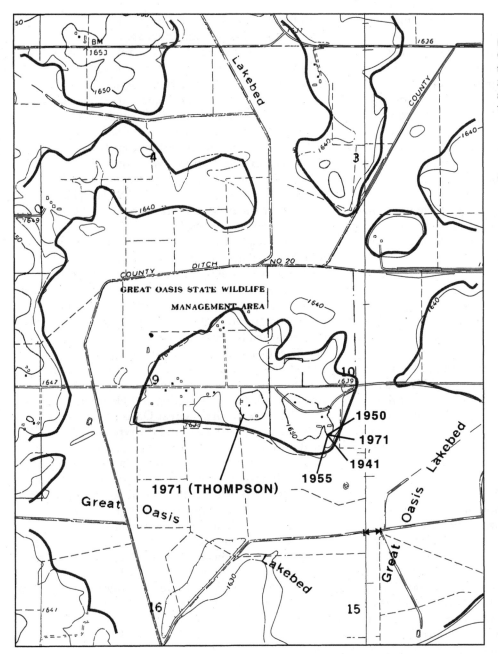

Figure 41. Location of the Great Oasis site (21MU2) on the Balaton SW and Hadley USGS 7.5' maps showing the original lake shoreline (heavy line) and excavation areas.

between Wilford's 1941 and 1950 excavations. The 1971 excavations have not been reported, although there are field notes about the Thompson area units on file at the University of Nebraska (Hudak 1972b).

Wilford's excavations at the Great Oasis site yielded large amounts of Great Oasis ceramics and a few Woodland, Cambria, and Oneota sherds. The Woodland sherds are almost all Lake Benton types (*Cord-wrapped Stick Impressed*, *Vertical Cordmarked*) with

perhaps a few Fox Lake sherds. Wilford interpreted the Woodland and Cambria sherds to be contemporary with the Great Oasis component, but he believed the Oneota sherds to be later (Wilford [ca. 1954]b:30). Wilford noted numerous storage/trash pits during his 1941 and 1950 excavations.

The 1971 excavations at the Thompson locale west of Wilford's units yielded fewer ceramics, lithics, and pits. There appeared to be more bone, principally

91

bison bone. The ceramics from this area are mostly shell tempered, although a few Great Oasis sherds also were recovered. The 1971 10-foot square near Wilford's units encountered numerous storage/trash pits. One contained a secondary bundle burial associated with Oneota sherds.

It is unfortunate that only the ceramics from the Great Oasis site have been subjected to intensive analysis. Based on the density of artifacts and features, the site is obviously a major Great Oasis Phase village, the only one in Minnesota. The recovery of Great Oasis, terminal Woodland, Cambria, and Oneota sherds in close proximity is especially intriguing. The lack of bison scapula hoes and the site location suggest that horticulture was not practiced at the site. Portions of the site are still undisturbed.

Other Great Oasis Sites

Fewer than 10 Great Oasis sites are known in the Prairie Lake Region (Figure 42). In Minnesota the type site (21MU2) appears to be the only major site. There are smaller campsites at the Big Slough (21MU1) site and perhaps a site near the Pedersen (21LN2) site. A few Great Oasis sherds have been recovered at the Cambria site (21BE2), and a few are evident in a local collection from the Albert Lea Lake area in south-central Minnesota. The only other known Great Oasis site in Minnesota is the Pipestone Quarry site (21PP2) in the southwest corner of Minnesota just west of the Prairie Lake Region (Sigstad 1970).

In the South Dakota portion of the region, at least four Great Oasis sites are known. They are the Volunteer site (39BK8), the Winter site (39DE5), the Roy Lake site (39ML9), and 39RO42 (Buechler 1982; Haug 1977, 1982; Beissel et al. 1984:4). The Roy Lake site may be the Great Oasis site excavated near Fort Wadsworth by army surgeon Aaron Comfort in 1867 (Comfort 1978). In Iowa no Great Oasis habitation sites have been excavated in the Prairie Lake Region, but a mortuary site, the Gypsum Quarry site (13WB1), has been described (Flanders and Hansman 1961).

Technology

Ceramics Great Oasis ceramics have been divided into two wares, Great Oasis High Rim and Great Oasis Wedge Lip (Henning and Henning 1978). Both wares feature grit-tempered (usually crushed granite), well-made globular vessels with smooth to slightly polished rims and smooth or cordmarked-smoothed exterior bodies. Great Oasis High Rim vessels have straight, outflaring rims from 2 cm to 5 cm in height

with flat lips and sharp rim-shoulder junctions (Figure 43). Most rim exteriors are decorated with fine trailed lines, but some rims are plain. The trailing is usually in bands of horizontal and oblique parallel lines in the following motifs: triangle, diamond, pendant triangle, trapezoid, oblique, turkey track, maize, tree, flag and dot, and pendant chevron (Henning and Henning 1978:18, 22). The Great Oasis type site yielded High Rim sherds with primarily triangle (zigzag) or diamond (crisscross) motifs (E. Johnson 1969). These motifs also dominate the Great Oasis sherds from the Big Slough site (21MU1). (This latter is the other site in Minnesota with a Great Oasis component excavated by Wilford).

Great Oasis Wedge Lip has low outcurving rims with broad, flat, outwardly beveled lips; the rims thicken toward the lip to resemble a wedge (Figure 43), hence the ware name. The rim-neck junction also is thickened, giving this area of the vessel more strength than the High Rim ware. Wedge Lip vessels are occasionally decorated on the lip, rim, and shoulder. The lip and rim decorations are generally fine, trailed line crosshatching and/or tool impressions. Shoulder decorations are closely spaced horizontal parallel trailed lines (Henning and Henning 1978:24).

The more northern Great Oasis sites such as Chamberlain (39BR202) and the type site (21MU2) yield only very small amounts of Great Oasis Wedge Lip, while some of the northwestern Iowa sites (e.g., 13PM25) have up to 50 percent. Henning and Henning (1978:15) believed that the differential percentage in Wedge Lip as opposed to High Rim was a regional rather than a temporal variation.

The motifs and use of cordmarking on the High Rim ware may indicate Woodland antecedents. The High Rim ware closely resembles Chamberlain Ware found at Mill Creek sites and the Anderson High Rim type from Over Phase sites. Henning and Henning (1978:16) believed that Great Oasis High Rim may be ancestral to other Initial Middle Missouri high rim types.

Great Oasis Wedge Lip closely resembles Mill Creek Sanford Ware and some Over Phase Anderson Ware types. Great Oasis may be ancestral to some of these types as well. The Wedge Lip ware also resembles some Central Plains types. Great Oasis ceramics lack an S-rim ware, which is an important rim form in other Initial Middle Missouri variants. The lack of an S-rim in Great Oasis is one of the principal reasons that Tiffany (1983) did not classify Great Oasis as an Initial Middle Missouri phase.

Lithics Great Oasis Phase projectile points are usually small side-notched and unnotched triangular

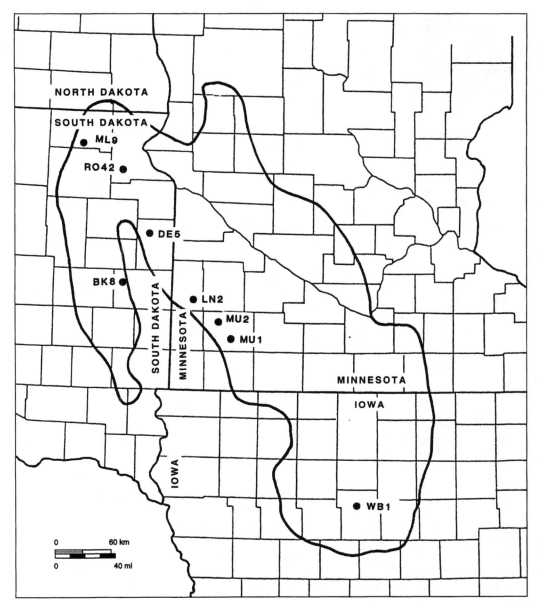

Figure 42. Locations of Great Oasis sites in the Prairie Lake Region.

varieties, although some corner-notched and even stemmed points also have been reported (Zimmerman 1985:78; Ludwickson et al. 1981:139). At the type site, the 1941 excavations recovered 13 classifiable projectile points; Wilford ([ca. 1954]b:17) described these as 10 small stemmed or barbed (side-notched or corner-notched), 2 triangular unnotched, and 1 shouldered-stemmed. The 1950 excavations yielded 12 classifiable points. These were described as 8 triangular unnotched, 2 side-notched, and 2 stemmed. Wilford attributed the triangular unnotched, side-notched, and small corner-notched points to the Great Oasis component. He also noted that the differential horizontal

distribution of points at the type site suggested "different areas of the site may have been intensively occupied at different times, though the pottery series from the two areas is much the same" (Wilford [ca. 1954]b:32).

Other Great Oasis Phase chipped stone tools include end and side scrapers, knives of various forms, choppers, gravers, drills, and flake tools. The 1941 excavations at the type site recovered 26 end scrapers, 17 side scrapers, 5 knives, 1 drill, and 3 large, crude tools which Wilford called hoes. The 1950 excavations yielded 26 end scrapers, 26 side scrapers, 5 knives, and a chopper.

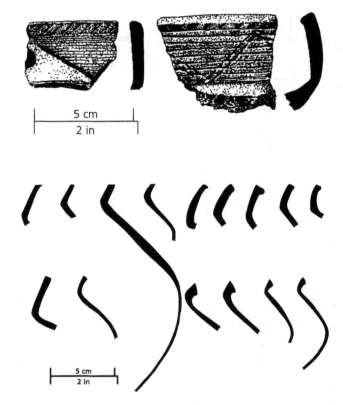

Figure 43. Great Oasis rim sherds from the type site (top) and rim profiles from *High Rim* (middle and lower left) and *Wedge Lip* (lower right) vessels (from Anfinson 1979; Henning and Henning 1978).

Raw material preferences for the small chipped stone tools at the Great Oasis type site for the 1941 and 1950 excavations indicated 76 percent (106) chert, 21 percent (29) chalcedony, and 3 percent (4) quartzite. The 1941 debitage featured 76 percent chert (half of it oolitic), 15 percent chalcedony (almost all of it Knife River Flint), and 9 percent quartzite. Ten of the 26 side scrapers from the 1950 excavations are made of Knife River Flint. The other tool categories clearly are dominated by chert. A slightly higher percentage of quartzite was found in the 1941 units, as opposed to the 1950 units. Wilford ([ca. 1954]b:31) noted the relatively low percentage of quartzite tools in general at the type site, as opposed to the 23 percent he found at the Big Slough site. This is probably a result of the predominance of Woodland components at the Big Slough site.

Ground stone tools associated with Great Oasis sites are celts, arrowshaft abraders, and hammerstones. A few manos and metates have been recovered.

The type site yielded 2 celts, 1 arrowshaft abrader, and 1 mano.

Bone and Shell Artifacts Bone tools from Great Oasis sites include awls, chisels, quill flatteners, shaft wrenches, and antler-tine flaking tools. Bison scapula hoes are rare at Great Oasis sites, even outside of the Prairie Lake Region. The type site yielded 4 bone spatulas, a bone flesher, a bone awl, and 2 crook-shaped objects made of bison scapulas. The last Wilford (1960b) later classified as sickles.

Shell objects from Great Oasis sites include dippers, beads, and pendants. Eight clam shell crosses and *Ancolusa sp.* beads were found with a Great Oasis burial near Des Moines (Knauth 1963). The type site has produced one clam shell pendant.

Subsistence

Wilford generally paid little attention to subsistence remains, and his report on the 1941 excavations at the Great Oasis site noted only that "animal bones include the bones of mammals, birds, fish and turtle carapace. Many of the bones are charred by fire. The amount of bones in the debris is relatively small. . . . The clam shells were not very numerous" (Wilford [1954]b:15).

Lukens (1963) analyzed the mammal remains from the 1941 and 1950 excavations at the Great Oasis site. He identified 234 elements from 13 species. These were bison (158), dog/wolf (20), beaver (15), lynx (11), striped skunk (9), muskrat (7), raccoon (4), pocket gopher (3), red fox (2), mink (2), badger (2), and white-tailed deer (1).

The subsistence remains from the 1971 excavations at the type site have not been identified in detail, but Hudak (1972b:10) noted that 95 percent of the faunal remains from the Thompson locale are probably bison, with a little fish, beaver, and *Canis sp.* Some charred maize kernels were recovered from the 1971 unit near Wilford's excavation area, but no cobs were found at the site.

At the Big Slough site, 20 km southeast of the Great Oasis site, the upper levels from the 1971 excavations contained mammalian remnants similar to those at the Great Oasis site. Bison, dog/wolf, muskrat, and gopher are dominant (Anfinson 1982a). Very little bird was present in the upper levels at Big Slough, but some fish, turtle, and mussel remains were recovered. Limited testing at the Volunteer site (39BK8) in eastern South Dakota in 1979 and 1980 yielded Great Oasis ceramics associated with muskrat, gopher, badger, bullhead, and walleye bones. There also were charred maize kernels (R. Alex 1980; Buechler 1982).

Great Oasis subsistence patterns outside of the Prairie Lake Region suggest a good deal of variation. At the Broken Kettle West site (13PM25) in northwestern Iowa, principal faunal remains were migratory birds, fish, deer, and small mammals. However, there was a notable paucity of bison bone (Baerreis 1970). At the Heath site (39LN15) in southeastern South Dakota, bison were clearly the most important animal (Zimmerman 1985:77). Maize kernels have been found at most Great Oasis sites, as well as some sunflowers and squash. Native seeds, nuts, and berries also have been recovered at some sites (Dallman 1970).

Settlement

Typical Great Oasis site locations outside the Prairie Lake Region are on first terraces above stream or river floodplains (Henning 1971). Patricia Williams (1975:29) suggested that most Great Oasis sites in northwestern Iowa were small, temporary campsites associated with small garden plots. Only a few large sites such as Broken Kettle West appear to have house structures. Four houses were evident at Broken Kettle West. They were rectangular in shape, 6.5–12 m long by 5–7.5 m wide, and semisubterranean; there were entryways in the southwest (C. Johnson 1973). Numerous post molds and trash pits were found inside the Broken Kettle West houses, as well as central fire hearths. A similar house was uncovered at the Heath site (Zimmerman 1985:75).

Prairie Lake Region Great Oasis sites exhibit a settlement pattern different from other regions. Prairie Lake sites occupy traditional Woodland locations on the islands, peninsulas, and isthmuses of the larger shallow lakes. While no house structures have been found at any Prairie Lake Region Great Oasis sites, the density of artifacts and storage/trash pits at the type site suggest that houses probably existed there. The lack of fortifications associated with Great Oasis sites is another reason Tiffany (1983) did not classify the phase under Initial Middle Missouri.

Mortuary Treatment

At least three Great Oasis burial sites are known, one of them within the Prairie Lake Region. The Gypsum Quarry site (13WB1) featured two mounds and a possible associated habitation area on a low terrace above the Des Moines River near the south end of the Prairie Lake Region (Flanders and Hansman 1961). One of the mounds was excavated in 1960. The mound was dome-shaped, 14 m in diameter, and 1 m high. Two Great Oasis High Rim vessels were recovered from the mound, but only fragmentary human remains were noted. The presence of single-twisted cord impressed sherds with Great Oasis trailed-line ceramics in the mound fill suggests a strong Woodland relationship.

The West Des Moines Burial (13PK1) was located on a high hill near the confluence of Walnut Creek and the Raccoon River in central Iowa (Knauth 1963). This is just south of the Prairie Lake Region. At least 18 individuals were unearthed at the site in single flexed and multiple burials. With the burials were two Great Oasis vessels, eight crosses of clam shell, *Anculosa sp.*, beads, various other artifacts, and faunal remains. At the Ryan site (25DK211) in northeastern Nebraska, Great Oasis and Woodland burials were found together (Ludwickson et al. 1981:138). The Great Oasis burials appeared to be secondary bundles; ceramics are the only apparent grave goods.

Scattered human remains have been found at several Great Oasis habitation sites (13PM50, 24CD10, 21MU2). A flexed, secondary burial was found in a trash pit at the type site in 1971, but associated shell-tempered sherds indicate that it was related to an Oneota rather than Great Oasis component.

Dating

Two radiocarbon dates were obtained by the 1971 excavations at the Great Oasis type site; 1050 RCYBP ± 60 (dendro-corrected to A.D. 990) for the eastern square and 975 RCYBP ± 65 (A.D. 1020) for the western or Thompson locale (Henning and Henning 1978:13). An earlier attempt to date charcoal from the Wilford excavations had resulted in a date of 2980 BP ± 180 (1240 B.C.) which indicates the charcoal was either contaminated or from a pre-Great Oasis component (E. Johnson 1964b:39). The Caseys Mound site (13WB6) at the southern edge of the Prairie Lake Region has a single radiocarbon date of 785 ± 100 RCYBP (A.D. 1250) (Tiffany 1981).

A few radiocarbon dates from outside the Prairie Lake Region indicate Great Oasis may be as early as A.D. 800 and persisted as late as A.D. 1250; however, the usually accepted chronological range of Great Oasis is A.D. 900 to 1200. The Broken Kettle West site (13PM25) in northwestern Iowa has yielded eight dates with the earliest at 1150 ± 55 RCYBP (A.D. 880) and the youngest at 850 ± 55 RCYBP (A.D. 1200) (Henning and Henning 1978:13). The Beals site (13CK62) yielded two radiocarbon dates associated with a Great Oasis component; 990 ± 90 RCYBP (A.D. 1020) and 690 ± 80 RCYBP (A.D. 1270) (Henning and Henning 1978:13).

Cambria Phase
(A.D. 1000–1200)

The Cambria Phase is the least-known Initial Middle Missouri Phase. Almost all of the published information has dealt with a single site, the type site (21BE2). The type site contains a complex blending of Woodland, Middle Mississippian, and Plains Village traits, especially in the ceramics. Elden Johnson (1986) presented an overview of the Cambria Phase, linking it to a Cahokia-based trade network. The Cambria type site was a dominant center in the northern extension of this network, operating through another center at Red Wing, Minnesota. In Johnson's view, these sites were involved in a network that exchanged bison meat, hides, and perhaps finished clothing for horticultural products and exotic materials (e.g., marine shells).

Cambria Site

The Cambria site (21BE2) is on an intermediate terrace 20 m above the Minnesota River about 25 km northwest of Mankato (Figure 44). The terrace is triangular with the apex pointing toward the east. The Minnesota River is to the north, and a steep ravine cut by Spring Creek runs along the south side joining the river just beyond the apex. The river bluff and the ravine provide good natural defenses on two sides. The habitation debris is concentrated near the apex of the terrace.

The Cambria site initially was reported and mapped by Newton Winchell in the early twentieth century (Winchell 1911:742). The first professional excavations were undertaken by W. B. Nickerson for the Minnesota Historical Society in 1913 and 1916 (Nickerson 1988).

Nickerson opened units in nine localities at what he called the Jones Village site. Locality 1 was the largest excavation unit, a 50 x 30-foot unit near the southeastern edge of the site. Locality 2, located nearer the site center, was a 50 x 10-foot trench. In all, Nickerson excavated more than 2,500-square feet at the Cambria site, recovering thousands of ceramic, lithic, and bone artifacts. No mention was made of screening the excavated soil. The collections are housed at the Minnesota Historical Society.

The University of Minnesota excavated at the Cambria site in 1938 and 1941 (Wilford 1945a, 1945b). In 1938 Albert Jenks and Lloyd Wilford opened several trenches. The sizes and locations of the trenches were not recorded. In 1941 Wilford excavated a 30 x 20-foot square unit with a 10 x 20-foot extension on the west end. Wilford's 1941 unit was near the site's southwest edge. Guy Gibbon of the University of Minnesota and Orrin Shane of the Science Museum of Minnesota did limited testing at the site in 1974 to obtain material for radiocarbon dating (Shane 1981).

Most of the Cambria site has been disturbed by cultivation, professional excavations, or pothunters' pits. Almost the entire site was cultivated in the late nineteenth century, although when Nickerson excavated at the site in 1913, he reported that the eastern portion had not been cultivated since 1885. This portion is currently in pasture and may have remained in pasture over the last 100 years.

Most discussions of the Cambria site are based on two master's theses from the University of Minnesota. Knudson (1966, 1967) analyzed the site's ceramics, while Watrall looked at the bone, stone, and shell (Watrall 1967, 1968, 1974). Nickerson's excellent site report on his 1913 and 1916 excavations was published in 1988. Wilford's site reports remain unpublished, although he did present a brief site summary that focused on the ceramics (Wilford 1945b).

Other Cambria Sites

It is difficult to provide a list of Cambria sites since exactly what Cambria is has never been defined clearly. Most other ceramic complexes in the Prairie Lake Region have diagnostic pottery types that allow us to define components based on the presence of such sherds. However, the great variety in Cambria ceramics, the intersite differences in the relative percentages of the types present, the small sherd sizes and small samples of possible Cambria ceramics from most sites, and the similarities of the Cambria types to other ceramic complexes in adjacent regions all combine to make most definitions of Cambria components somewhat tenuous. The exception is the presence of grit-tempered, rolled rim ceramics, but such ceramics are present only at the type site and the nearby Price and Lewis Mound sites.

Western Minnesota sites yielding non-Great Oasis Plains village ceramics often are listed as Cambria sites. Several dozen of these sites have been reported (Figure 45). Sites yielding such ceramics are concentrated in southwestern Minnesota, but Cambria ceramics also have been reported from the Silvernale (21GD3) and Bryan (21GD4) sites in southeastern Minnesota (Ready 1979) and from a few sites in Otter Tail County in northern west-central Minnesota (Lucking [1977]; Michlovic 1979).

The ephemeral "Cambria" sites in southwestern

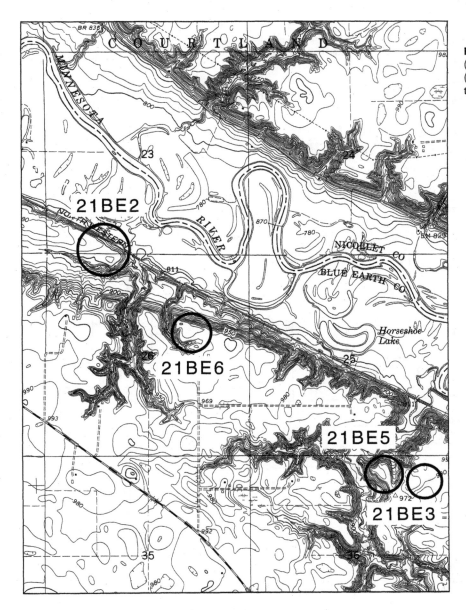

Figure 44. Locations of the Cambria (21BE2), Judson (21BE3), Owen Jones (21BE5), and Lewis (21BE6) sites on the Cambria USGS 7.5' map.

Minnesota are usually small campsites with Woodland components. The "Cambria" ceramics from these sites are often nothing more than a few thin, smooth surfaced, grit-tempered sherds. Even when rim sherds are found, there is usually little attempt to classify them according to Wilford's (1945b) or Knudson's (1967) typologies.

Except for the type site, original data on major Cambria habitation sites exists only in brief, unpublished site reports. These sites include Price (21BE36), excavated by Michael Scullin of Mankato State University in 1974 and 1975 (Scullin 1979), Owen D. Jones (21BE5), excavated by Lloyd Wilford in 1941 (Wilford 1946a), and Gillingham (21YM3), excavated

by Wilford in 1946 and 1948 (Wilford 1951). The Price and Jones sites are on the Minnesota River near the type site; Gillingham is on the Minnesota River 112 km northwest (upstream) of the type site.

Technology

Ceramics Cambria ceramics are almost all grit-tempered, globular jars with constricted necks, pronounced shoulders, and smooth surfaces. Wilford originally divided Cambria ceramics into three types based on rim form following his 1938 and 1941 excavations at the type site (Wilford 1945b). *Type A* features everted rims with trailed-line decoration primarily on the shoulder. *Type B* has S-shaped rims with

97

Figure 45. Locations of Cambria and non-Great Oasis Plains Village sites in the Prairie Lake Region.

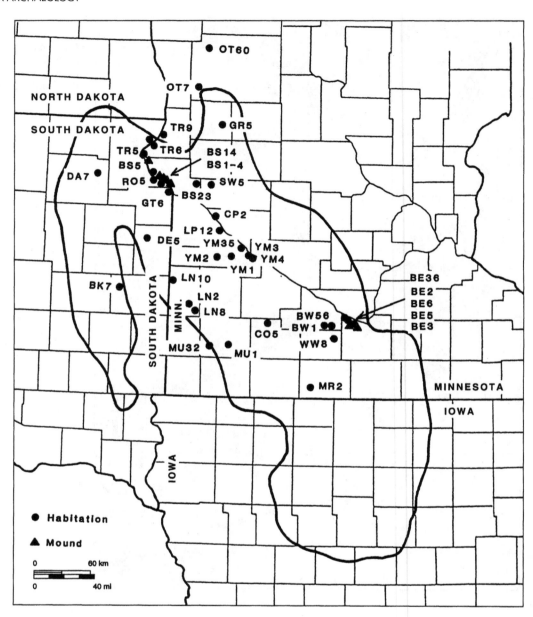

trailed-line or single-twisted cord decoration on the rim. *Type C* features rolled rims with broad trailing on the shoulder. Wilford also found small amounts of shell-tempered pottery in all his excavation levels at the Cambria site. He considered them to be aberrant Cambria sherds rather than part of an Oneota component (Wilford 1945a).

Knudson's (1966, 1967) analysis of Cambria ceramics included the sherds recovered by Nickerson and Wilford. Knudson divided the ceramics into five types, based on rim form and decoration. The types were then divided into varieties based on decoration. Knudson's scheme contained two rolled rim types that

had been defined previously at Cahokia and were included in Wilford's *Type C*; *Ramey Broad Trailed* (Figure 46) features broad trailing on the shoulder, while *Powell Plain* is undecorated. *Ramey Broad Trailed* was given a new variety name, *New Ulm*, while the Cambria variety of *Powell Plain*, the other rolled rim type, was unspecified by Knudson. The rolled rim types account for about 15 percent of the ceramics from the Cambria site.

Knudson named two everted rim types at the Cambria site that together represent Wilford's *Type A*. *Linden Everted Rim* features low to medium height rims that are outflared (Figure 47). Most of the rims

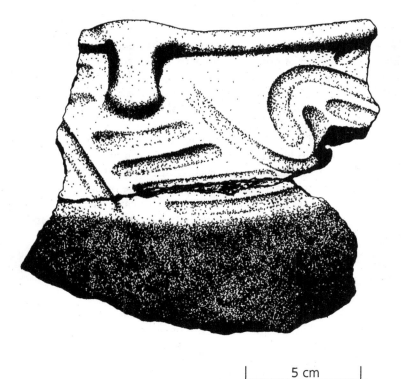

Figure 46. *Ramey Incised* vessel from the Cambria site (from Anfinson 1979, drawing by Lee Radzak).

5 cm
2 in

and shoulders are undecorated, and some vessels have loop handles. The decorated examples have trailed, single-twisted cord impressed, or finger-impressed rims; a few shoulders have trailed lines in linear or curvilinear patterns. The *Linden* type is divided into four varieties: *Linden, Nicollet, Cottonwood,* and *Searles.* The *Linden* type accounts for 64 percent of the ceramics from the Cambria site, with most in the *Linden* and *Nicollet* varieties.

The other everted rim type, *Mankato Incised,* features medium to high outflaring rims with decorations on rim interiors, rim exteriors, and shoulders (Figure 48). The decoration usually consists of trailed lines and tool impressions. There are two varieties, *Mankato* and *Butternut.* The *Mankato* type accounts for 12.3 percent of the ceramics from the Cambria site.

Knudson's single S-rim type, *Judson Composite,* has small lug or loop handles with trailed line and/or single-twisted cord decoration on some rims and shoulders (Figure 49). This type is synonymous with Wilford's *Type B.* They account for 8.7 percent of the sherds from the Cambria site, although analysis by Craig Johnson suggests that less than 1 percent of these are true S-rims.

The shell-tempered sherds from the Cambria site are associated with the *Ramey Incised* and *Linden Everted Rim* types; 13 percent of the former are shell

tempered and 1 percent of the latter. Only 1.3 percent of the Cambria site ceramics are shell tempered. Grit-tempered sherds at Cambria usually are tempered with crushed granite with some inclusions of sand. Besides the Cambria types, the site also yielded a few Woodland, Great Oasis, and Mill Creek *(Chamberlain Incised)* sherds (Knudson 1967:271).

Cambria vessel exteriors are usually completely smoothed, but 15 percent of the body sherds and 4 percent of the rims have evidence of cordmarking. Of the identified rims, 6 percent of the *Mankato Incised,* 5 percent of the *Ramey Broad Trailed,* 4 percent of the *Linden Everted,* and 4 percent of the *Judson Composite* sherds show evidence of cordmarked surface treatments. Overall, about two-thirds of the cordmarked vessels are of the *Linden Everted* type. A few polished sherds and black painted sherds also were recovered at the Cambria site.

At the Price site (21BE36), Scullin (1979) reported the following numbers of rims by Knudson's types: 1 *Powell Plain* (2 percent); 10 *Ramey Broad Trailed* (18 percent); 1 *Judson-Judson* (2 percent); 7 *Linden-Linden* (12 percent); 26 *Linden-Nicollet* (46 percent); 2 *Mankato-Mankato* (4 percent); and 10 *Mankato-Butternut* (18 percent). Comparing the relative percentages of the ceramics from the Cambria and Price sites, there is a slightly higher percentage of rolled rim

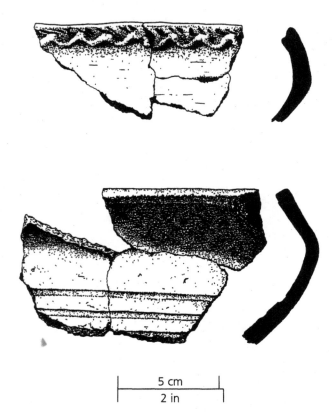

5 cm

2 in

Figure 47. *Linden Everted, Linden* (bottom) and *Linden Everted, Nicollet* (top) rim sherds from the Cambria site (from Anfinson 1979, drawing by Lee Radzak).

types and a slightly lower percentage of S-rim types at Price.

The Price and Cambria sites differ ceramically from other locations with Cambria habitation sites by the presence of rolled rim sherds. Even the nearby Owen Jones site (21BE5) excavated by Wilford contained only *Linden Everted (Type A)* varieties (Wilford 1946a). The Gillingham site (21YM3) contained 63 percent (26) rims of the everted rim *(Type A)* and 37 percent (15) of the S-rim *(Type B)* Cambria ceramics (Wilford 1951). About 80 percent of the ceramics at the Gillingham site appear to be Woodland types. Four ceramic pipes also were recovered at Gillingham.

In general, Cambria ceramics exhibit a blend of Woodland, Plains Village, Middle Mississippian, and Oneota influences. Knudson's complex classification scheme illustrates the great variety in Cambria ceramics, but this complexity somewhat obscures comparisons with ceramics from other regions. Wilford's original three types based on rim form alone make comparisons somewhat easier. It is perhaps useful to think of Wilford's types as Cambria wares subdivided by Knudson's types and varieties.

Lithics The Nickerson and Wilford excavations at the Cambria site recovered 158 relatively complete projectile points, along with 19 fragments, making up 25 percent of the chipped stone total. Watrall (1967) divided the points into four categories: isosceles triangular (unnotched), equilateral triangular (unnotched), side-notched, and miscellaneous.

The 66 (42 percent) isosceles triangular points vary in length from 19 mm to 51 mm with a 30 mm average and vary in basal width from 11 mm to 24 mm with a 15 mm average. Fifty-one of these points have straight bases and 3 have concave bases. Watrall listed 12 points as unifacially flaked. The 25 (16 percent) equilateral triangular points range in length from 15 to 38 mm (22 mm average) and range in basal width from 11 to 26 mm (17 mm average). Nineteen have straight bases, and 6 are listed as unifacial.

Of the 61 (39 percent) side-notched points, 45 have single side-notches, 3 have basal notches, 1 has double side-notches, and 1 has a serrated edge. Eleven are listed as unifacial. Most of the side-notched points are isosceles in outline. The points range in length from 14 to 34 mm (22 mm average) and vary in basal width from 11 to 21 mm (13 mm average).

Of the 6 miscellaneous points, there are 2 with distinct outlines. One is corner-notched, 35 mm in length, 21 mm in shoulder width, and 14 mm in basal width. The other point is described as a Turkey Tail, 70 mm in length and 24 mm in width. Turkey Tail points are found in Late Archaic and Early Woodland contexts in the Midwest and northeastern United States (Ritzenthaler 1967:23).

The non-projectile point chipped stone tools from the Cambria site were categorized by Watrall (1967) as: 99 blades (14 percent), 163 end scrapers (23 percent), 13 ovoid scrapers (2 percent), 225 side scrapers (32 percent), and 34 perforators/drills/gravers (5 percent). The scrapers make up 56 percent of the chipped stone assemblage.

Chert accounts for 95 percent of the raw material for the chipped stone tools at the Cambria site and 89 percent of the lithic debitage. More than three-quarters of the chert is oolitic, which Watrall (1968) believed to be from quarries in southeastern Minnesota. Some possible quarry sites are known now in the nearby Mankato area (Scullin 1979). Only 1 percent of the tools and less than 1 percent of the debitage is brown chalcedony. Other raw materials of minor importance were quartz and quartzite. A single obsidian flake was recovered.

The non-chipped stone tools from the Cambria site include 9 grooved stone mauls, 7 celts, 33 ham-

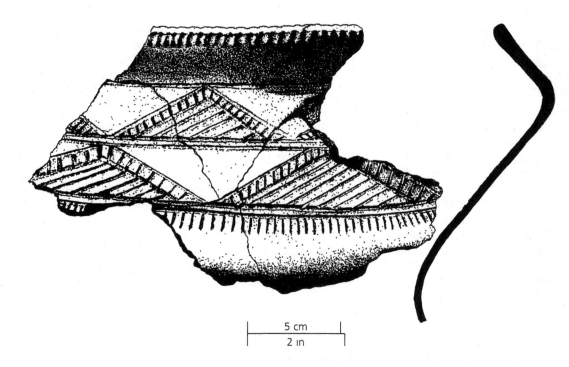

5 cm
2 in

Figure 48. *Mankato Incised, Mankato* vessel from the Cambria site (from Anfinson 1979, drawing by Lee Radzak).

mer-stones, 11 pitted hammer-stones, 2 grinding stones, and 36 sandstone abraders. No catlinite objects were recovered by Wilford or Nickerson.

At the Price site, 134 small chipped stone tools were recovered, along with 75 worked/utilized flakes and 30 cores/core tools (Scullin 1979). The small chipped stone tools include 49 projectile points, 27 end scrapers, 20 side scrapers, 18 knives, 8 spoke-shaves, 3 drills, and 2 gravers. This indicates a higher percentage of projectile points and a lower percentage of scrapers at the Price site as opposed to the Cambria site. The Price projectile points are predominantly

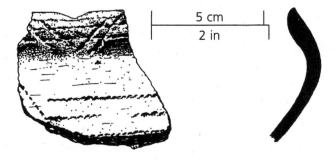

5 cm
2 in

Figure 49. *Judson Composite, Judson* rim sherd from the type site (from Anfinson 1979, drawing by Lee Radzak).

side-notched varieties and usually made of oolitic chert. Scullin (1979) noted that the scrapers at Price frequently are made of "exotic" materials (non-oolitic chert?), but he stated that Knife River Flint is uncommon. The Price site also yielded 2 incomplete ground stone celts, 4 stone "hoes", 3 anvils, 3 manos, and 20 sandstone abraders.

The Gillingham site, which also has a major Woodland component, yielded 14 relatively complete projectile points in Wilford's 1946 and 1948 excavations. Five are triangular unnotched; 5 are stemmed; and 4 are side-notched. There are also 3 knives, 13 end scrapers, and 2 side scrapers. Of the chipped stone tools recovered in 1948, 22 are of chert (only 2 oolitic), 6 are Knife River Flint, 2 others are chalcedony, and 5 are quartzite. A catlinite pipe, a catlinite plaque, and a milling stone also were recovered, but no sandstone abraders were found. The Cambria and Gillingham sites each produced a copper awl.

Bone and Shell Artifacts The Cambria site yielded a large quantity of worked bone. Watrall (1967, 1974:139) divided bone objects into three categories, based on inferred function: horticultural implements, miscellaneous implements, and decorational implements. Of the 203 worked bone objects at the Cambria site, 158 (78 percent) fit into the miscellaneous category which includes awls (54), punches (50), quill flatteners (19), beamers (8), projectile points (3), and fishhooks (2). There are 35 (17 percent) horticultural tools; 21 scapula hoes, 11 picks, and 3 bone sickles. Watrall (1967:48) initially described the sickles as squash knives. The 10 (6 percent) decorative objects include 5 pendants, 2 bone tubes, and a bone bead.

At the Price site, Scullin (1979) reported bison scapula hoes and knives, but there was a notable scarcity of other worked bone. Only two spatulas, two beads, and a piece of turtle carapace with a "three horned figure flanked by rectangles" carved into it were recovered. At the Gillingham site, only a bone awl and bead were found.

Worked shell was relatively scarce at the Cambria site. Recovered were three shell pendants, three notched river mussels, and a shell spoon (Watrall 1967:50). At the Price site, two mussel shell beads and a notched *Prunum apicinum* were found. The latter shell is an import from the Gulf Coast. No worked shell objects were noted by Wilford (1951) at the Gillingham site.

Subsistence

Watrall's (1967, 1974) analysis of the Cambria site faunal remains identified 746 elements from 14 mammal species. The identified elements are dominated by deer (276), followed by bison (197), *Canis sp.* (107), beaver (102), and raccoon (31). A number of other mammal species are represented by only a few or single elements. These include elk, muskrat, badger, skunk, otter, gopher, fox, mink, and woodchuck. If we look at minimum number of individual animals, there are 15 deer, followed by 8 *Canis sp.*, 7 raccoon, 6 beaver, 4 bison, 3 muskrat, 3 gopher, 3 woodchuck, 2 elk, 2 skunk, 2 otter, and 1 each of the other species listed above. Bison easily dominates the potential edible meat with 1,800 kg, followed by deer (675 kg), elk (350 kg), beaver (90 kg), *Canis sp.* (80 kg), raccoon (55 kg), and otter (12 kg).

The non-mammalian remains include 646 fish bones, 504 turtle bones, and 79 bird bones. These elements, however, were not subjected to detailed analysis. Watrall (1967:67) noted that some of the fish remains are from very large fish. At least two species of turtle are present, based on element size. Most of the bird bones are from very large species, probably waterfowl.

Eleven species of fresh-water mussel were recovered from the Cambria site (Watrall 1967:62). There are 131 identifiable valves and 283 unidentified fragments. The primary use of the mussels was probably for subsistence since there are so few worked shells and so little shell-tempered pottery. None of the shell shows any evidence of burning or heating.

Orrin Shane examined the faunal remains from the Price site (Scullin 1979) and identified 20 mammal species, 11 bird species, 13 fish species, and 4 reptile species. Beaver dominates the mammal elements with 66 (29 percent), followed by *Canis sp.* with 39 (17 percent), bison with 30 (13 percent), and deer with 29 (13 percent). Most of the bison elements are tools (i.e. scapula hoes, knives). Other mammal elements are from beaver, raccoon, and otter. Remains of at least 6 ducks were recovered from Price, along with those from a swan, a Canada goose, four hawks, an owl, and three songbirds. *Ictalurids* (catfish, bullheads) are the most common fish, with 34 individuals. Other fish species are buffalofish, redhorse, suckers, bass, pike, and panfish. Five painted turtles were evident, along with two snapping turtles and a softshelled turtle. Overall, the Price site is very similar to the Cambria site in its varied assemblage of upland and wetland fauna.

The Nickerson and Wilford excavations at the Cambria site made little attempt to recover floral remains, but Nickerson collected at least 1.5 liters of charred maize. This maize was identified later as Eastern or New England Flint (Watrall 1967:61). A more recent analysis of maize from the Cambria site identified it as Eastern 8 Row or Northern Flint dating from about A.D. 1200 (Scullin 1979).

Linda Shane analyzed Price site floral remains recovered from two storage pits by flotation and fine-mesh screening (Shane 1980). Recovered from these pits were seeds of maize, curcurbits, and sunflower. Wild plant seeds included chenopodium, walnut, rose, *Prunus,* and *Polygonum.* Scullin (1979) suggested earlier that beans and wild rice also might be at Price, but Shane found no evidence of these species.

Settlement Pattern

Elden Johnson (1986) grouped Cambria sites into four categories: 1) large villages on Minnesota River terraces; 2) small villages near the large villages on terraces of the Minnesota River or tributary rivers; 3) small habitations on lakes or interior rivers; and 4) burial sites. The only large villages noted by Johnson were the Cambria and Gillingham sites. He believed both to have been palisaded. While there is no evidence for fortifications at the Cambria site, Theodore Lewis mapped a ditch (Figure 50) at the Gillingham site (Winchell 1911:116). Smaller Cambria villages listed by Johnson are Owen Jones, Price, and Gautefald. Johnson believed that Cambria site inhabitants dominated the other Cambria peoples of the region through their role as principal agents in a Cahokia-based trade network.

While some of the sites shown on Figure 45 ultimately may be classified under other Plains Village phases (e.g., Big Stone), many of them, especially those in southwestern Minnesota, are no doubt Cambria Phase sites. They probably were occupied by the same people that occupied the Cambria type site. Clearly, the type site is the largest, the most intensively occupied, and the most artifactually diverse site in the phase. It deserves to be listed in a settlement class by itself. Smaller but important Cambria villages are Price, Gillingham, Jones, and perhaps Gautefald, Saienga (21CP2), and Harbo Hill (21BE10). All of these sites are on the Minnesota River, except Gautefald which is at the junction of Spring Creek and the Yellow Medicine River, 20 km southwest of the Minnesota River.

Cambria-like ceramics typically are found in small numbers in the upper levels at many of the major lake-related habitation sites in eastern South Dakota and southwestern Minnesota. None of these sites have yielded rolled rim ceramics or bison scapula hoes. Beyond the ceramics, there is little to differentiate the Cambria levels from earlier horizons at these sites. The similarity in subsistence remains and lithics, plus the fact that such sites were being used by Cambria peoples, seems to indicate a close relationship between Cambria and Woodland peoples.

Knudson (1967:250) believed that Nickerson's report suggested the possible presence of a long, rectangular house at the Cambria site. Nevertheless, no such features were found by subsequent excavations at the site or have been noted at other Cambria sites.

Trash/storage pits were common at the type site, Price, Owen Jones, and Gillingham.

Mortuary Practices

Elden Johnson (1961, 1986) attributed circular, flat-topped burial mounds and extended, primary burials to the Cambria Phase. At least 80 circular, flat-topped mounds were mapped by Lewis in southwestern Minnesota. Excavated mounds in the Prairie Lake Region with non-Great Oasis Plains Village affiliation include Judson (21BE3), Lewis (21BE6), Schoen #2 (21BS1), Schoen #1 (21BS2), Lindholm (21BS3), Miller (21BS4), Holtz (21BS5), Hartford Beach (39RO4), and Hiawatha Beach (39RO6). All but the first two sites are located on Big Stone Lake in western Minnesota. It is proposed here that the Big Stone Lake mounds with Plains Village affiliation now be considered as part of the Big Stone Phase and not Cambria.

Johnson's mortuary type site for Cambria, the Lewis site (21BE6), is located 3 km southeast of the Cambria site on a high Minnesota River terrace. Lewis Mound #1 contained shell-tempered ceramics, including a crude mortuary vessel decorated with a combination of trailed lines, punctates, and short dashed lines (Wilford [ca. 1956]). The mound contained five extended primary burials in a shallow subsoil pit. Lewis Mound #2 contained only a few fragmentary human remains along with some grit-tempered sherds, including several rolled rim sherds.

The fact that the ceramics in Lewis Mound #1 are shell tempered when shell tempering is rare at the Cambria site is somewhat disconcerting if Lewis is to

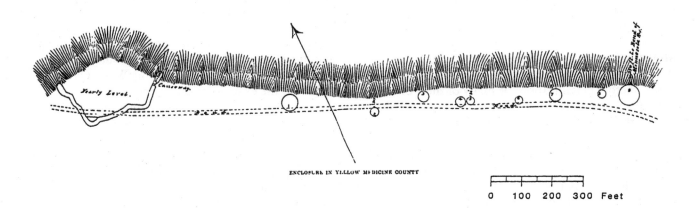

Figure 50. Lewis map of the Gillingham site (21YM3) surveyed in 1887 (from Winchell 1911:117).

be used as the mortuary type site. It appears, however, that a Cambria feature of burials is that they were accompanied by specialized ceramics, as indicated by the inclusion of miniature vessels. Plains Village-like mortuary vessels have been found in mounds at the High Island site (21SB1) and the Lake Shetek site (21MU3).

Mound groups are located near all of the major Cambria habitation sites except the Gautefald site. They, too, are associated directly with the Gillingham site (Figure 50) and the possible Cambria habitations at Saienga and Harbo Hill.

Dating

Five radiocarbon dates have been obtained from the Cambria and Price sites. The Cambria site dates are 815 ± 125 RCYBP (A.D. 1220) and 775 ± 130 RCYBP (A.D. 1260) (O. Shane 1981). The Price site dates are 845 ± 80 RCYBP (A.D. 1210), 885 ± 80 RCYBP (A.D. 1180), and 1000 ± 80 RCYBP (A.D. 1010) (Lass 1980b:30–31). The clustering of four of the five dates around A.D. 1200 may indicate that the temporal range of the Cambria Phase is quite limited. This is of special importance if the western non-Great Oasis sites are placed in the Big Stone Phase.

Big Stone Phase
(A.D. 1100–1300)

While the Cambria Phase was flourishing in the upper Minnesota River Valley, other Plains Village complexes were expanding in the northern northeastern Plains. Evidence for these complexes is largely in the form of small fortified villages. Such sites are especially common in the vicinity of Big Stone Lake and Lake Traverse at the northwestern end of the Prairie Lake Region (Winchell 1911:407).

Non-Great Oasis Plains Village sites in western Minnesota typically are classified as Cambria sites for lack of a better category. Yet, Cambria may be an unsatisfactory classification for many of the western sites. There are many differences from the Cambria sites in the central Minnesota River Valley. The Big Stone-Traverse sites yield ceramics that are somewhat similar to the *Linden* and *Mankato* types of the Cambria Phase, but no rolled rim or S-rim ceramics are evident. Lithic raw materials are dominated by Knife River Flint, not oolitic cherts. The artifact densities are relatively low within most of these sites, and most site sizes are fairly small. Subsistence differences are evident, with bison more important in the west. Most of

the major western sites are on lakes instead of rivers. More commonly, mounds are associated directly with western habitation sites.

At the Plains Anthropological Conference in 1983, James Haug of the South Dakota Archaeological Research Center proposed a Big Stone Phase, based on excavations at the Hartford Beach site (39RO5) on Big Stone Lake. The phase featured a more mixed Woodland-Plains Village way of life than that of the Cambria. Evidence for this can be found in the ceramics, lithics, and settlement pattern. Haug dated the Big Stone Phase to about A.D. 1100.

Because the Big Stone Phase appears to be a more satisfactory classification than Cambria to deal with the Plains Village sites of the northwestern Prairie Lake Region, Haug's (1983a) unpublished definition of the phase is refined and expanded here. Not all of the non-Great Oasis, non-Cambria Plains Village sites in the northwestern Prairie Lake Region are included in the Big Stone Phase. We find only those in a limited area around Big Stone and Traverse lakes which includes Traverse and Big Stone counties in Minnesota and Roberts County in South Dakota. Ultimately, additional Plains Village phases may be defined for western Minnesota and the adjacent eastern Dakotas.

Hartford Beach Site

The Hartford Beach site (39RO5) is located on a high terrace overlooking the west shore of Big Stone Lake (Figure 51). Big Stone Lake is immediately north of the Hartford Beach site; Spring Creek is immediately to the east. The site is protected by steep slopes on two sides, with the bluff descending steeply about 30 m to the lake and creek. The site contains an artificial ditch enclosing an area of about .4 ha (1 acre). A bastion projects from the southwest portion of the ditch. Cultural materials extend outside the enclosure. The total site area is perhaps 4 ha (Haug 1982). The enclosure has not been cultivated, but artifacts are present in rodent borrow mounds on the surface.

The site was originally tested by W. H. Over in 1922, but the exact location and extent of his excavations are not known. Over's field notes indicate five general excavation areas including tests in the trench and along the trench's inside ridge (Sigstad and Sigstad 1973a:226–29). Only a test near the site's southeastern edge found artifacts, a midden of clam shells. Over noted the similarity of Hartford Beach pottery to the ceramics found at another fortified village site (39MH1) near Brandon in southeastern South Dakota.

In 1981 the Hartford Beach site was tested by James Haug of the South Dakota Archaeological

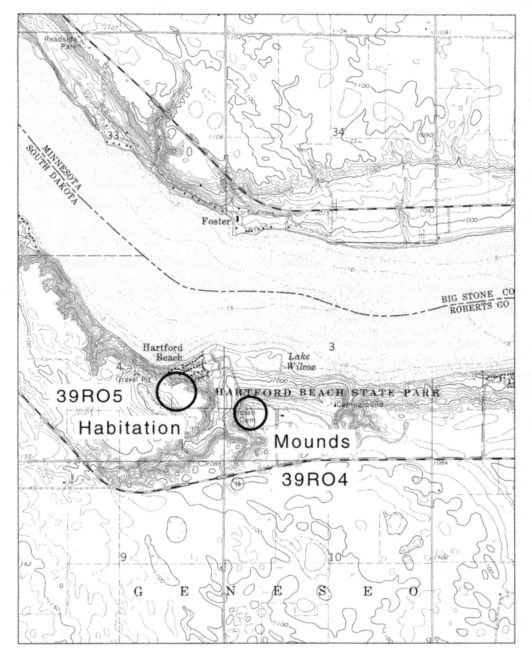

Figure 51. Locations of the Hartford Beach village (39RO5) and mound (39RO4) sites on the Big Stone Lake West USGS 7.5' map.

Research Center (Haug 1982). Four contiguous 1 x 2 m units were opened along the ditch north of the bastion. Four additional 1 x 2 m units and three 2 x 2 m units were opened in the enclosure interior. A 2 x 2 m unit also was excavated within the bastion. Two 2 x 2 m units were excavated outside of the enclosure to the south and west.

The trench across the ditch revealed seven post molds, indicating that a palisade had been placed within the ditch. Interior test units located a shallow, basin-shaped hearth with two post molds nearby. Another interior test unit area contained two cache pits. These contained charcoal, clam shells, ceramics, clay pipe fragments, bone debris, lithics tools, and debitage. Only a modest amount of artifacts were found by the 1981 excavations. Faunal remains were particularly scarce.

Browns Valley Site

The Browns Valley site (21TR5) was excavated by the University of Minnesota in the 1930s, but as described in Chapter 4, the excavations were so focused on the Paleoindian component that little attention was paid to the extensive Plains Village component. Figure 9 shows the well-defined enclosure at Browns Valley as mapped by Theodore Lewis in 1883. The Lewis map shows a 15 m diameter circular fortification only 45 m northwest of the Paleoindian burial.

> This earth work consists of an embankment 12 feet wide and 1 and one-half feet high, within which is a ditch 16 feet wide and 1 foot deep. The ends of the embankment, which is roughly circular, overlap, and the ditch at both ends extends beyond the ends of the embankment. At two places the ditch is crenulated by a succession of constrictions (Winchell 1911:309).

Just northwest of the fortification there was a flat-topped mound 17 m in diameter and 1.2 m high. About three-quarters of the fortification was destroyed by expansion of the Browns Valley gravel pit. The site's western quadrant may be largely undisturbed in a lightly developed residential area. The earthwork appeared to be faintly visible in this area in the summer of 1987.

The 1936 excavations at Browns Valley encountered numerous features associated with the Plains Village occupation of the site, although they did not penetrate the fortified area. The 1936 field director, James West, described the excavation as follows:

> This excavation was a continuation of that conducted in 1934 by Dr. Jenks and a seven foot vertical bank was maintained in front of us at all times. The gravel was gently scraped down this face to the bottom, from whence it was shoveled to the rear. This was done so as not to disturb any gravel overlying any deep find in the pit. . . . No additional traces of Browns Valley Man culture were found, but we did find many evidences of later Indian habitation as expressed in fire hearths, artifacts, and caches. Numerous small fire hearths were excavated. We inspected about fourteen of the larger hearths, sixty artifacts, and four caches. Animal bones were present in abundance, but no human bones were recovered. . . . The Browns Valley Man culture evidently is exceedingly rare as no more material was found within fifty feet of the original Browns Valley Man site. Later Indian material is common. . . . (Jenks 1937:11).

No mention was made as to whether or not the upper levels of the gravel pit soil were screened, although a photo of the 1936 excavation does show screening being performed.

The University of Minnesota collection from the Browns Valley site (excepting the Paleoindian materials) contains more than 400 sherds, 10 chipped stone tools, about 100 pieces of debitage, 4 ground stone tools, 7 bone tools, several large mussel shell fragments, and a handful of animal bone fragments. No doubt many artifacts, especially faunal remains, were not saved, particularly after West stopped supervising the excavation. West's report of the 1936 excavation has not been located.

Shady Dell Site

The Shady Dell site (21TR6) was mapped by Theodore Lewis in 1885. The map shows an enclosure with a large mound to the south and a small mound to the west (Winchell 1911:302–3). The enclosure was described by Lewis as an elevated area enclosed by a circular ditch. The ditch was 6 m across and .7 m deep. The site is on a point in a high bluff overlooking Lake Traverse. The site is 38 m above the lake with a wide terrace between the bluff bottom and the lake.

Lloyd Wilford tested the Shady Dell site in 1952 (Wilford [ca. 1958]a). He first mapped the site, noting it had changed very little since Lewis was there. He estimated the interior dimensions of the enclosure to be 30 x 18 m. Wilford excavated a 6 x 30-foot trench across the north side of the ditch and a 10 x 20-foot unit in a slight depression within the northwest quadrant of the enclosure. Sub-soil was present in the ditch bottom only 15 cm below the surface. No post molds were noted in the ditch. Several fragments of bison bone, a few shell fragments, and a few sherds were recovered from the trench.

The rectangular excavation unit was also shallow, encountering sub-soil at 30 cm. No post molds were encountered, but a circular pit, 85 cm across and 55 cm deep, was found. The pit contained some potsherds and bone, mainly fish bone. The excavation's artifact yield was relatively small with only 371 sherds, 7 chipped stone tools, a ground stone disk, and some animal bone and shell fragments.

Other Big Stone Phase Sites

In Minnesota there are at least six recorded small fortified sites along the east side of Lake Traverse: Browns Valley (21TR5), Shady Dell (21TR6), Tenney (21TR11), Bunker Hill (21TR12), and the unnamed 21TR14 and 21TR32 (Figure 52). A survey (C. Johnson 1991) found the Shady Dell and Bunker Hill sites

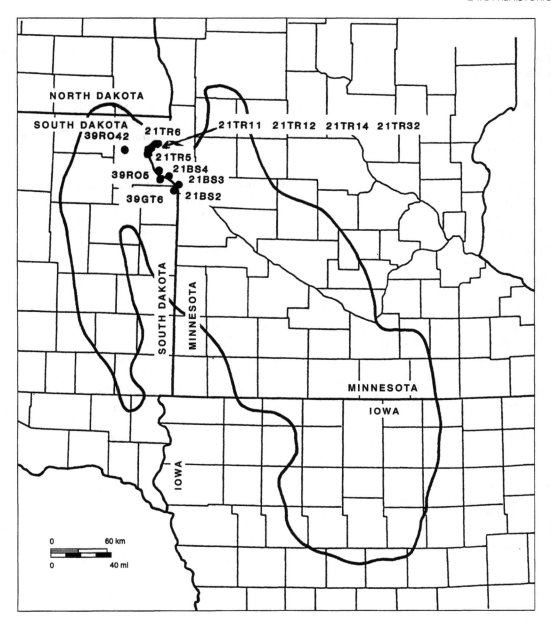

Figure 52. Locations of Big Stone Phase sites.

to be well preserved, but the other sites largely may be destroyed.

No enclosures are recorded along the east side of Big Stone Lake, but three are recorded on the west side of the lake: Hartford Beach, Linden, and 39GT6. Another enclosure site (39RO42) is located on the Coteau west of Big Stone Lake in Roberts County, South Dakota.

Non-fortified habitation sites yielding Plains Village ceramics in the Big Stone-Traverse vicinity include Artichoke Island (21BS23), Hanson (21BS22), Steilow (21BS14), Pomme de Terre (21SW5), and Strader

(21TR9) in Minnesota, and Jackson Island (39RO?) and Zacharias (39RO20) in South Dakota.

Of the non-fortified sites, only the Zacharias site has been tested extensively. It is located on the west side of Lake Traverse on a lower terrace. Wilford excavated a 10 x 10-foot unit at the site in 1953 (Wilford [ca. 1958]b). The site was dominated by Woodland materials, but Wilford also noted a small Cambria component. No stratigraphic differences were apparent, and no features were encountered. The site yielded clam shells, lithic tools and debitage, numerous sherds, and animal bone.

107

Technology

Ceramics Ceramics from the Hartford Beach site are of two basic forms: Woodland *Lake Benton Vertical Cordmarked* and Plains Village ceramics resembling *Anderson High Rims* of the Initial Middle Missouri Variant (Haug 1982:44–45). The Plains Village rims recovered by the 1981 excavation are generally of moderate height (25–35 mm), flare only slightly outward, and have flat lips. They have smooth surfaces and are undecorated. A high percentage of body sherds exhibit broad trailed decoration with both curvilinear and linear designs. A few shell-tempered sherds have been found in surface collections at the site. A tubular clay pipe fragment is decorated with fine trailed arrows and x's.

Most of the ceramics in the University of Minnesota collections from the 1936 excavations at the Browns Valley site have Plains Village affinities, although Woodland types also are present. Of the 190 body sherds with diameters greater than 2.5 cm and exterior surfaces intact, more than 90 percent have cordmarked surfaces and crushed granite temper and average about 6 mm in thickness. The cordmarking on most of the body sherds is non-oriented, suggesting indistinct fabric or cordwrapped paddle impressions. Most appear to be from globular vessels. No shell-tempered sherds are evident.

Six rims from three vessels are cordmarked. Tool-impressed lips are the only decoration. One of these vessels (Figure 53 bottom) exhibits an outwardly flared rim with a sharp-angled, thickened neck. The rim is .7 cm thick and 4.2 cm high. The cordmarking is vertically oriented but less distinct than most Woodland cordmarking in southwestern Minnesota. The closest description of these sherds in existing literature is *Lisbon Tool Impressed,* associated with the poorly defined Stutsman Focus of southeastern North Dakota (Wheeler 1963:201).

One cordmarked rim has a slight collar and possibly a castellation (Figure 54 lower left). It is sand tempered and .8 cm thick. The temper and distinct vertical cordmarking suggest Woodland affinities, but the upper rim form is Plains Village.

Six rim/near-rim sherds from five vessels have smooth surfaces with fine trailed-line decoration. They resemble the Great Oasis High Rim ware (Henning and Henning 1978), although the trailing is wider and somewhat cruder than most Great Oasis sherds. One vessel features a band of short, oblique lines below the lip followed by a band of horizontal lines (Figure 53, top left). Another has a similar pattern, but the lines are wider and the oblique band is made of tool impressions rather than trailed lines (Figure 53, top right).

One smooth-surfaced rim has a deeply tool-impressed lip (Figure 53, middle left). It is short and straight with thickening towards the neck. The temper is sand.

S-rims, rolled rims, and handles are lacking in the Browns Valley collection, as are wide trailed lines, single-twisted cord impressions, simple stamping, and check stamping. A ceramic elbow pipe was recovered in 1936. It closely resembles an example from the Gillingham site (21YM3).

The ceramics recovered from the Shady Dell site are mostly small crumbs. Of the 371 sherds, only 66 are larger than 25 mm in diameter. All of the sherds are grit tempered. Of the 297 body sherds, 266 (90 percent) are cordmarked and 31 (10 percent) are smooth.

There are 55 rim or near-rim sherds from Shady Dell. All of the rims and near-rims are decorated: 27 (49 percent) are single-twisted cord; 14 (26 percent) are cordwrapped stick; 9 (16 percent) have trailed lines; and 5 (9 percent) show dentate impressions. The cordwrapped stick and dentate sherds generally are Lake Benton types. The trailed-line and single-twisted cord rims are generally Plains Village types from globular vessels with low to medium height rims. The trailed lines are of narrow width and in simple horizontal bands. The single-twisted cord decorations are in oblique and horizontal bands.

The Zacharias site test unit yielded 1,726 sherds, of which most were small crumbs. The body sherds have surface treatments that are 70 percent cordmarked and 30 percent smoothed. Of the 88 large rims and near-rims, 29 percent are dentate, 27 percent cordwrapped stick, 11 percent trailed (only 4 percent broad trailed), 11 percent cordmarked, 8 percent single-twisted cord impressed, and 8 percent smoothed. Eleven sherds have punctates and 2 sherds have bosses. The ceramic assemblage is clearly dominated by Woodland attributes.

Three mound sites associated with the Big Stone Phase—the Schoen Mound #1 (21BS2), the Miller Mound (21BS4), and the Lindholm Mounds (21BS3)—have yielded Plains Village ceramics. The Schoen Mound #1 ceramics were classed as Cambria *Type A* by Elden Johnson (1961:70). The 15 sherds are from a single vessel that was grit tempered, smooth surfaced, and globular with moderately high straight rims. The decoration is narrow-trailed lined in horizontal bands with a single row of short, oblique tool impressions just below the flat lip (Figure 55).

The Miller Mound contained 22 grit-tempered sherds in the mound fill and one complete mortuary vessel (Figure 55). Fourteen of the body sherds are

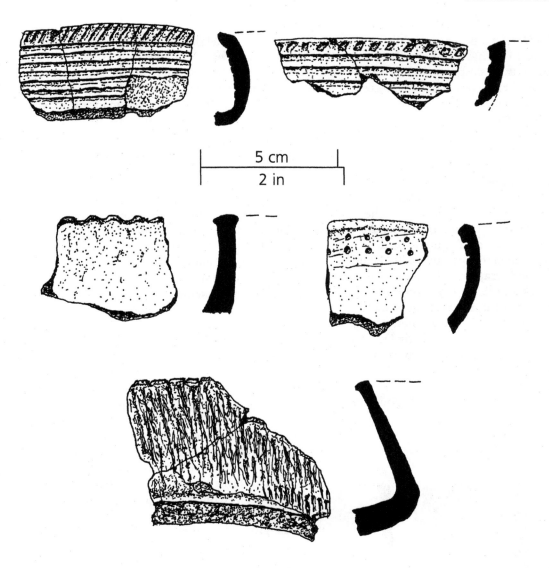

5 cm

2 in

Figure 53. Plains Village ceramics from the Browns Valley site (21TR5).

smooth surfaced. One is cordmarked. Of the seven decorated sherds, four have broad trailed lines and three have narrow trailed lines. The narrow trailed-line sherds are very similar to examples from Schoen Mound #1 and Browns Valley, resembling Great Oasis but somewhat cruder. Elden Johnson (1961:71) classified the Miller Mound sherds as Cambria *Type A*.

The mortuary vessel from the Miller Mound is globular, smooth surfaced, grit tempered, 96 mm high and 119 mm wide. It has an angular shoulder, a short, everted rim, and two opposing loop handles. The shoulders are decorated with trailed lines in the form of double-line sideways Vs with a horizontal jagged line inside the V. The lip is decorated with short trailed lines in a zig-zag pattern. The vessel is classified by Elden Johnson (1961:72) as Cambria *Type A*.

The Lindholm Mounds yielded a small mortuary vessel and three sherds from the mound fill (Wilford 1970:14). Two of the sherds are cordmarked bodies; the third is an undecorated rim with a smooth surface. The three sherds are all grit tempered. The globular mortuary vessel measures 71 mm high and 95 mm wide. The exterior surface is smooth, slightly polished, and undecorated. The low rounded rim is slightly outflaring with a flat, thickened lip.

Overall, the ceramics associated with the Big Stone Phase show much closer Woodland affiliations than do Cambria ceramics. However, there is considerable variety from site to site, and the mortuary vessels tend to be more Mississippian. An earlier Woodland component may be present at Browns Valley, but the other fortified village sites appear to be single component.

Smooth-surfaced, undecorated ceramics were the utilitarian ware at the Hartford Beach site while Browns Valley and Shady Dell have more cordmarked vessels. No check-stamping or simple stamping is present, and no S-rims, rolled rims, or collared rims are present at Big Stone Phase villages. Decoration is more common on the shoulders than the rims. Features are trailing and single-twisted cord. Handles are present only in some mortuary vessels.

Lithics The Hartford Beach site has yielded a considerable number of chipped stone tools, but a detailed analysis has yet to be completed. Three basic kinds of projectile points were found: corner-notched, triangular with deep side notches, and unnotched triangular. Most of the side-notched and unnotched points were found in the ditch or the cache pits (Haug 1982:47). A variety of end scrapers, side scrapers, and utilized flakes, as well as a drill, were recovered. Several raw material types were used, but there appears to be a fairly high percentage of Knife River Flint.

The single projectile point from the Shady Dell site was a small corner-notched point of white chert. All four end scrapers, the side scraper, and the knife are made of Knife River Flint. A circular schist disk, 80 mm in diameter and 8.5 mm thick, shows polish on both faces.

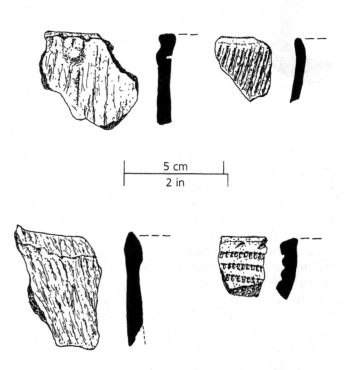

5 cm
2 in

Figure 54. Woodland ceramics from the Browns Valley site (21TR5).

The lithics from the Browns Valley site have not been analyzed in detail, but 57 percent of the flakes are Knife River Flint. Most flakes are small with no cortex evident. The other debitage is of locally available materials, including quartzite (37 percent) and chert (5 percent). Only one flake is made of Tongue River Silica. The chipped stone tools include 2 small side-notched projectile points (both white chert), 2 small end scrapers (both Knife River Flint), 4 small bifaces (1 Knife River Flint, 2 chert, 1 quartzite), and 2 large retouched Knife River Flint flakes. The ground stone tools recovered from Browns Valley are a large grooved maul, a large sandstone hoe, a large sandstone chopper, and a small nutting stone.

The Miller Mound contained two projectile points, one a fragment of Knife River Flint and the other a small corner-notched point made of gray chert. There is also a flake scraper of white chert. The Strader site yielded a high percentage of Knife River Flint lithics.

The one 10 x 10-foot unit at the multicomponent Zacharias site contained 57 projectile points, 61 end scrapers, 35 side scrapers, 17 bifaces, and 6 drills. Chert is the raw material for 44 percent of the chipped stone tools, with 42 percent Knife River Flint and 20 percent quartzite. Two are made of obsidian. The poorer materials generally were used for the projectile points. Most of the side scrapers are made of Knife River Flint. The projectile points are dominated by side-notched forms (23) with other points unnotched triangular (10), stemmed (8), corner-notched (6), and leaf-shaped with concave bases (3). Zacharias also yielded a grooved stone maul and a catlinite pipe fragment.

Bone and Shell Artifacts The Hartford Beach site yielded four bone tools—a bison scapula hoe, a metapodial flesher, and two bone awls. Extensive bone artifacts also were present at the Browns Valley site: four awls, a fragmentary bison scapula hoe, a spatula, and a polished antler tip. No bone or shell artifacts were recovered from the Shady Dell site. The Lindholm Mound contained a small, barrel-shaped shell bead.

Subsistence

Subsistence information is somewhat scarce for the Big Stone Phase. The Hartford Beach and Shady Dell sites yielded few animal remains. Hartford Beach contained some small fragments of bison and medium-sized mammal (dog or badger) bone. Fish bones were present in two of the pits, and Over noted a clam shell refuse heap in the ditch bottom on the southeast. Shady Dell also yielded fragmentary bison bone, clam shells, and fish bone. Few of the subsistence remains

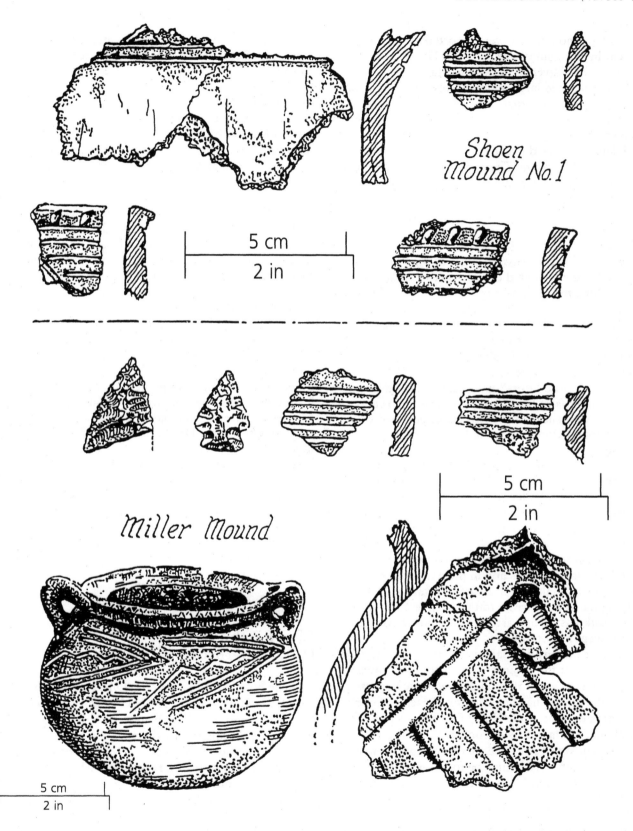

Figure 55. Artifacts from (top) Schoen Mound 1 (21BS2) and (bottom) Miller Mound (21BS4) sites (from E. Johnson 1961).

were saved from the 1936 excavations at the Browns Valley site, although they were reported to have been "present in abundance" (Jenks 1937:11). The handful of bone in the University of Minnesota's collection is primarily shattered large mammal (bison?) bone with a few turtle carapace fragments. Mussel shells also were present. Most of the bone at the Zacharias site was bison bone.

A few carbonized maize kernels were recovered at the Hartford Beach site. These, along with the scapula hoe, suggest that maize was both eaten and grown at the site. A bison scapula hoe also was present at Browns Valley.

Settlement

Surveys along the eastern edges of Big Stone and Traverse lakes have noted the presence of small lithic scatters along the bluff tops of Big Stone Lake. This is not true, however, along the bluff tops of Lake Traverse (C. Johnson 1991). Such sites are interpreted to be lookouts. Although stone artifacts have not been found along the bluffs of Lake Traverse, the lake's eastern bluffs contain several small fortified habitation sites; none of those "forts" have been recorded along the eastern bluffs of Big Stone Lake. The opposite is true of the west shore of the two lakes. Fortified villages are found along Big Stone Lake, but not Lake Traverse.

The fortified village sites tend to occupy promontories on high bluffs overlooking Big Stone or Traverse lakes. The Browns Valley site is not only the largest fortified site in the area, but is also somewhat of an exception with regard to its location. It occupies a high terrace between the two lakes. The strategic position of the Browns Valley site between two major continental drainage systems and in the narrow gap between the two lakes is of great importance. This location guards the narrow funnel between Minnesota and the Dakotas, sitting astride what must have been a major transportation route.

Most of the fortified habitation sites are relatively small, except for the Browns Valley site. The Browns Valley enclosure was 150 m in diameter encompassing an area of almost 2 ha. The Hartford Beach enclosure has an area of .4 ha while Shady Dell has an area of only .05 ha. Artifact density appears to be directly related to enclosure size. The smaller enclosures may not be village sites. They may be forts for refuge or even ceremonial sites. House forms have not been determined.

Most of the non-fortified Big Stone Phase habitation sites are located on lower terraces along Big Stone and Traverse lakes. Other smaller habitations are found on smaller lakes in the vicinity (e.g., the Hanson Island site). A few sites also are located on river terraces (e.g., 21SW5) or Lake Agassiz beaches (e.g., 21TR9).

Mortuary Treatment

Plains Village ceramics were recovered from Schoen Mound #1, Miller Mound, and Lindholm Mound. Flexed primary burials were found in these mounds, as well as in other vicinity mounds including the Schoen Mound #2 (21BS2), Hartford Beach Mound (39RO4), and Hiawatha Beach Mound (39RO6) (Table 6). Limited grave goods were included with the burials in Lindholm Mound #1, Miller Mound, Hartford Beach Mound, and Hiawatha Beach Mound. The grave goods include mortuary vessels, shell ornaments, and projectile points.

Flexed, primary burials seem to be typical of Big Stone Phase burials, while Cambria Phase burials feature non-flexed, extended primaries. Limited grave goods often accompany burials of both phases, with specialized mortuary vessels of particular interest. Elden Johnson (1961) noted that numerous low, flat-topped burial mounds were present in southwestern Minnesota. These were concentrated along the upper Minnesota River, around lakes Big Stone and Traverse, and along the upper Des Moines River. The distribution suggests an association with the Cambria, Great Oasis, and Big Stone complexes.

Dating

Two dates on the Plains Village component at the Hartford Beach site (39RO5) are 830 ± 70 RCYBP (A.D. 1220) and 650 + 70 RCYBP (A.D. 1290) (Haug 1983b). No other dates are currently available for the Big Stone Phase.

Blue Earth Phase
(A.D. 1000–1650)

The Blue Earth Phase of the Oneota Tradition is part of Henning's (1970, 1983b) Northwest Iowa "group continuity." This Oneota micro-tradition is identified in Minnesota by the presence of ceramics similar to the *Correctionville Trailed* type defined in northwestern Iowa (cf. Harvey 1979). The Northwest Iowa group continuity has major site concentrations on the Little Sioux River in northwestern Iowa and on the Blue Earth River in south-central Minnesota (Figure 56). At least three Oneota villages located along the St. Croix–Mississippi rivers in southeastern Min-

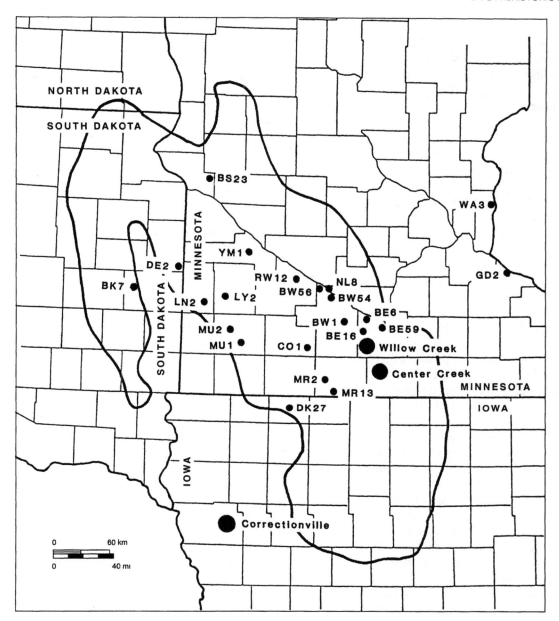

Figure 56.
Locations of Blue
Earth Oneota sites.

nesota and southwestern Wisconsin—Bartron (21GD2), Sheffield (21WA3), and Armstrong (47DE12)—also contain ceramics similar to Blue Earth and Correctionville (Gibbon 1983a). Some Blue Earth–Correctionville ceramics also are found in the Middle Mississippian villages at Silvernale (21GD3) and Bryan (21GD4).

Blue Earth and Correctionville are synonymous types and phases to some researchers (e.g., Henning 1983b, Gibbon 1983a), but Dobbs (1984:92) believed that Blue Earth and Correctionville ceramics are quite

different in form and decorational styles. There also appear to be subsistence-settlement differences between the two complexes. Dobbs (1984) tentatively suggested that Blue Earth–Correctionville is not a single phase, but perhaps four phases: Red Wing, Center Creek, Correctionville, and Fort Ridgely. Center Creek and Fort Ridgely are both Prairie Lake Region phases.

Dobbs differentiated the phases ceramically on the basis of vessel form, motifs, and, to some degree, manufacturing techniques. Unfortunately, most of the Oneota sherds from the Prairie Lake Region lake-

113

related sites are too small to determine vessel form and motifs. For the purposes of this study, all shell-tempered, smooth-surfaced sherds from the Prairie Lake Region (with the possible exception of those from the Cambria site, the Lewis Mound, and Fort Ridgely) are considered to be indicative of Blue Earth Phase components.

Dobbs (1984) divided the Oneota occupation of the Center Creek Locality into three stages: Emergent (A.D. 950–1150), Fluorescent (A.D. 1150–1400), and Terminal (A.D. 1400–1680). He believed that Center Creek Oneota may be ancestral to the ethnographically known Oto.

Center Creek Locality

The Center Creek Locality is in Faribault County, Minnesota, in the eastern part of the Prairie Lake Region near the confluence of Center Creek with the Blue Earth River (Figure 57). The Center Creek Locality contains more than 50 sites extending for several miles on either side of the confluence. Almost all of the sites are on the west side of the Blue Earth River. The middle portion of the locality is on the National Register of Historic Places as the Center Creek Archaeological District.

The Humphrey (21FA1) and Vosburg (21FA2) sites were the first investigated at Center Creek. These adjacent village sites were excavated by the University of Minnesota in 1938, 1947, and 1979 (Wilford 1945b; Gibbon 1983a; Dobbs 1984). At the Humphrey site, Wilford excavated a large, irregular unit of 2,400 square feet in 1938. It was on the north side of a gravel pit. In 1947, Wilford excavated a 20 x 15-foot unit at the Vosburg site, which is immediately east of the Humphrey site. In 1979 the University of Minnesota conducted additional excavation at the Vosburg site. A controlled surface collection of Vosburg was undertaken in 1981.

Surveys were conducted in the Center Creek area by the Minnesota Historical Society in 1979 and the University of Minnesota in 1980 and 1981. Many previously unrecorded sites were located. Most were affiliated with the Oneota occupation of the area. County highway construction in the area in the early 1980s also resulted in surveys and salvage excavations at two sites (Anfinson 1987a).

Willow Creek Locality

The Willow Creek Locality is in Blue Earth County, Minnesota, near the confluence of Willow Creek and the Blue Earth River (Figure 56). It is about 20 km north of the Center Creek Locality. Oneota sites at Willow Creek first were reported by a local collector (Kopischke 1962). The Science Museum of Minnesota conducted an extensive survey of the area in 1980, testing at least one site. At least 70 sites have been recorded in the Willow Creek Locality. Most have Oneota affiliations. No detailed reports on this work have been published, but it has been discussed briefly by Dobbs and Shane (1982).

Other Blue Earth Phase Sites

Small amounts of Oneota ceramics are found in the upper levels of many of the major Woodland lacustrine habitation sites in the Prairie Lake Region. These sites include Great Oasis (21MU2), Big Slough (21MU1), Pedersen (21LN2), Mountain Lake (21CO1), Fox Lake (21MR2), Synsteby (21BW1), Oakwood Lakes (39BK7), and Arthur (13DK27).

There is a major Oneota village at the Fort Ridgely site (21NL8) on the upper Minnesota River. The historic fort site was excavated by G. Hubert Smith in 1937. The Oneota component was encountered by accident during the excavation of Officers Quarters B (Smith 1938). Numerous shell-tempered sherds, chipped stone tools, a clay pipe, and bison bone were recovered. On the basis of the ceramics, Dobbs (1984) believed the Fort Ridgely Oneota component was not a Blue Earth Phase site. Rather, it may represent a previously undefined Oneota phase.

Technology

Ceramics The most recent description of *Blue Earth Trailed* ceramics is by Dobbs (1984:94–95). This is a refinement of descriptions presented by Wilford (1955:140–41) and Gibbon (1978). The ceramics used by Dobbs for the type definition were recovered largely from the Humphrey and the Vosburg sites in the Center Creek Locality. Dobbs' sample includes 82 sherds which extend from the lip to the shoulder, 207 other rim sherds, and 50 handles.

Blue Earth Trailed vessels are round bottomed, globular jars. They have rounded lips and straight to slightly outcurving rims that are slightly everted. Rim heights vary from 6 mm to 54 mm, with a mean of about 27 mm. The rim-shoulder junction (neck) is generally angular, but occasionally (14 percent) curved. Shoulders are broad and slightly curved. Short, double-strap handles, as well as some loop handles, are common. Handles are attached either at or below the rims. Wall thickness ranges from 2 mm to 13 mm, with a mean of about 4 mm for lips and 7 mm for rims. All of the type sample sherds are shell

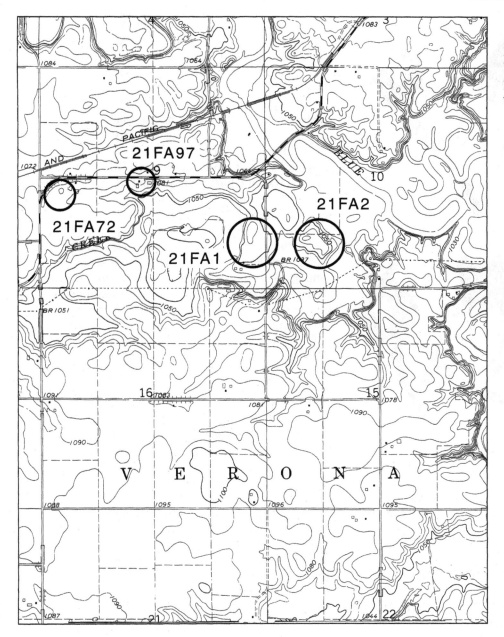

Figure 57. Locations of the Humphrey (21FA1), Vosburg (21FA2), Poole (21FA72), and Rynearson (21FA97) sites on the Huntley USGS 7.5' map.

tempered, although 2 percent of the body sherds from the Humphrey-Vosburg sites are grit tempered (these may be Woodland sherds). Vessel capacities range from 2 to 20 liters; orifice diameters range from 10 to 30 cm.

Interior and exterior surfaces are almost always smooth, with a few cordmarked-smoothed examples. Lips are usually undecorated, but shallow oblique or transverse tool impressions occasionally appear. About 60 percent of the rim interiors are decorated with tool impressions or trailed lines, but only 35 percent of the rim exteriors are decorated. Shoulders are almost always decorated with trailed lines, tool impressions, and occasional punctates. Trailed-line widths vary from 10 to 50 mm, but most are closer to the narrow end of the range.

Decorative designs are usually rectilinear, with concentric circles the only curvilinear motif (Figure 58). A common motif includes alternating panels of up- and-down oriented chevrons bordered by rows of punctates or short vertical lines (Figure 59). Small tabs or nodes occasionally appear in association with

115

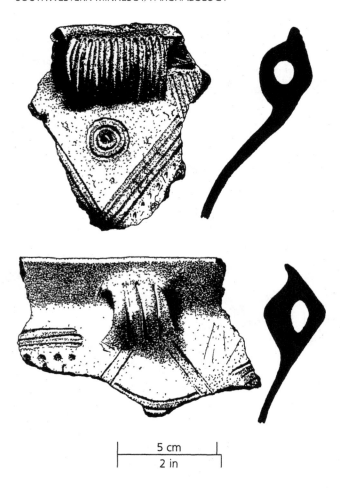

5 cm
2 in

Figure 58. Blue Earth rim sherds from the (top) Vosburg (21FA2) and (bottom) Bryan (21GD4) sites (from Anfinson 1979, drawing by Lee Radzak).

complex designs. Strap handles are decorated with vertical lines.

According to Dobbs (1984:92), *Blue Earth Trailed* vessels differ from *Correctionville Trailed;* the former are smaller and more globular. Other differences noted by Dobbs, but not described in detail, are in rim form and densities and styles of shoulder decoration. Temporal trends in Blue Earth ceramics also were suggested by Dobbs (1984:179–87). Emergent Stage vessels have more outflaring rims, less angular trailed-line shoulder chevrons, less geometric designs in general, and less use of discrete panels than Fluorescent Stage vessels. Fluorescent Stage vessels most closely match the type description of *Blue Earth Trailed.* Terminal Stage vessels tend to be more crudely made. They also have more lip notching, less interior and exterior rim decoration, less complex shoulder decoration, and less use of panels.

Dobbs (1984:107–16) defined nine provisional varieties of *Blue Earth Trailed,* based on cluster analysis. They are called *Center Creek Varieties 1–9.* Very little patterning of these varieties could be discerned by Dobbs with respect to horizontal distributions at the Humphrey-Vosburg sites, the association of one variety with another, or temporal placement.

Gibbon (1978) used cluster analysis to classify and then compare Blue Earth ceramics with Middle Mississippian ceramics from southeastern Minnesota. He defined six Blue Earth types called *Blue Earth Composite 1–6. Blue Earth Composite 6,* which lacks rim decoration, is closely related to Silvernale Phase ceramics.

Lithics Chipped stone tools associated with the Blue Earth Phase in the Prairie Lake Region are very similar to groups from other Oneota complexes (cf. Harvey 1979). The Center Creek area chipped stone tools are dominated by small unnotched projectile points and end scrapers (Dobbs 1984:79). Gibbon (1983a) noted both blade and non-blade technologies at the Vosburg site, but there are fewer blades in the Willow Creek Locality (Orrin Shane, personal communication 1987).

The projectile points are usually 15 to 20 mm in length and 10 to 15 mm in width. Only about 5 percent of the projectile points from the Center Creek area show any notching; these may be from pre-Blue Earth components. Over half the Blue Earth Phase points at Center Creek have straight bases. Concave and convex bases make up the remainder.

End scrapers are generally triangular in shape, have transverse working edges, and are usually retouched along two of the three edges. Side scrapers, knives, drills, wedges, gravers, gouges, choppers, flake tools, and blade tools also are found in the Center Creek assemblage. From 3 percent to 20 percent of the flakes appear to have been utilized (Dobbs 1984:80).

The Humphrey and Vosburg sites have yielded only modest amounts of non-chipped stone tools, including sandstone abraders, hammer-stones, anvil stones, celts, manos, and small geometrically shaped pieces of catlinite. At the Humphrey site, where Wilford excavated about 2,300 square feet, the ground stone tools recovered were 3 abraders, 4 hammerstones, 1 anvil, 4 celts, and 2 pieces of catlinite. Wilford excavated about 300 square feet at the Vosburg site and found 5 abraders, 1 hammer-stone, 1 mano, and 1 piece of catlinite.

Four basic types of raw material were used to create Center Creek chipped stone tools: oolitic chert, fine gray chert (Grand Meadow), white chert, and

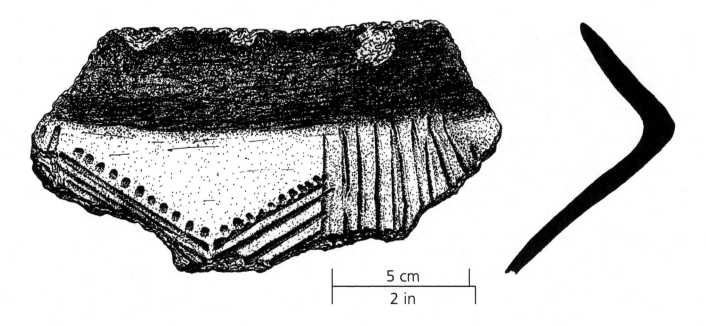

Figure 59. Blue Earth rim sherd from the Vosburg site (21FA2) (from Anfinson 1979, drawing by Lee Radzak).

quartzite (Dobbs 1984:77–78). No Knife River Flint or obsidian was reported. Oolitic chert appears to be the most common material. It accounts for 50 percent at most sites, with the gray chert next in importance with percentages varying from 15 to 40. White chert and quartzite usually account for less than 15 percent of the raw material at Center Creek sites. Small amounts of other cherts and chalcedonies also were found. The oolitic chert appears to come from local bedrock quarries 50 km down the Blue Earth River to the north or even nearby gravel deposits. The fine gray chert is found in outcrops at Grand Meadow, Minnesota, 130 km east of the Center Creek area (Trow 1981:102).

Center Creek projectile points generally are made of oolitic chert. Some examples are of gray or white chert. Over 90 percent of the end scrapers are of gray chert. Utilized flakes usually are made of oolitic or gray chert, with flake knives commonly made of gray chert, especially the blades. Five cores of gray chert with blade scars have been recovered (Dobbs 1984:82). Quartzite was used primarily for large tools like choppers.

Bone and Shell Artifacts Bone tools associated with the Blue Earth Phase in the Center Creek area include bison scapula hoes, picks of antler and bone,

and awls of bird and mammal bone. Miscellaneous bone objects from the Humphrey and Vosburg sites include split beaver incisors, a barbed harpoon, a bone tube, grooved and cut bone, a punch, and a pierced ornament (Gibbon 1983a). Almost all of the bison scapula hoes from the Center Creek area were found in the bottoms of pits. There, they often occurred in groups of three or more (Dobbs and Shane 1982:65). Shell tools and ornaments were rare at Center Creek, but a few were reported in local surface collections from the largest sites (Dobbs 1984:151).

Subsistence

A detailed analysis of Blue Earth Phase subsistence remains in the Prairie Lake Region is available only from the Vosburg site. Dobbs (1984) provided data on both the faunal and floral remains recovered by the 1979 site excavations. However, the fish, bird, and turtle remains in the faunal totals are from a single feature only. The 1979 excavations utilized some fine-mesh screening and flotation, but Dobbs did not discuss site sampling procedures in detail.

Fifteen mammal species were present, with the identifiable elements dominated by beaver (59) and *Canis sp.* (50). These were followed by deer (21) and elk (15). Mammals of minor economic importance were muskrat, raccoon, skunk, otter, mink, ground squirrel, woodchuck, and porcupine.

Besides the bison scapula hoes, only a single identifiable bison element was recovered. The fish-bone totals are no doubt under-represented because only the sample from one feature was included. The fish came from 11 species, with bullhead clearly the most important. Only a single turtle element was recovered. Bird bone was also uncommon, with only three elements from two species, cormorant and crane. Mussel shells were not mentioned by Dobbs, but mussel shells were recovered in the salvage excavation of a pit at the nearby Rynearson site (21FA97) in 1985 (Anfinson 1987a).

Carbonized plant remains of maize, common beans *(Phaseolus sp.)*, and sunflower were recovered by the 1979 excavations at the Vosburg site. Hazel, wild plum, and hawthorn were recovered. These remains were from the dry screens only; flotation remains have not yet been analyzed. The maize from Vosburg was highly variable, but four distinct types were present. These were Small Eastern Eight Row, Midwestern Twelve Row, North American Pop, and Oneota Type 3 (Bird and Dobbs 1986).

Settlement

Blue Earth Phase sites in the Prairie Lake Region are concentrated at the confluences of Willow Creek with the Blue Earth River and at Center Creek with the Blue Earth River (Dobbs and Shane 1982). Each location features perhaps 50 Blue Earth Phase sites. Other Blue Earth sites are scattered throughout the central portion of the Prairie Lake Region (Figure 56). As mentioned earlier, most of the interior sites are evidenced by small, shell-tempered sherds that are classified as Blue Earth because of a lack of associated historic materials and the lack of other well-defined Oneota phases in the region.

Dobbs (1984) defined six settlement types for the Center Creek area. These were based on site area, artifact density, and artifact types. This scheme has been applied to the Willow Creek Locality in a more limited manner (Dobbs and Shane 1982). The data used to develop the settlement model were obtained from surface collections. Settlement types 1 and 5 featured small site areas, low artifact densities, and high frequencies of scrapers. Hide processing was the inferred function for Type 1, while butchering and lithic work seem to have been a function of type 5 sites.

Type 2 sites have varying areas and densities but similar artifact densities. There are high numbers of ceramics and scrapers, inferring habitation sites where

hide processing was important. Type 3 sites have moderate-sized areas (1–3 ha), moderate amounts of lithic tools (except for projectile points and end scrapers, which are numerous), and high amounts of non-utilized flakes. Lithic workshop areas are inferred from these. Type 4 sites are moderate to large in area with low numbers of ceramics, projectile points, and scrapers, but high numbers of utilized flakes. This suggests butchering activities. Type 6 sites are very large and have dense artifact scatters high in ceramics, projectile points, and knives. This suggests large horticultural villages.

In general, the major habitation sites and cemeteries are located on elevated patches of outwash sediments in the Blue Earth River floodplain. Smaller habitation sites apparently involved in animal butchering and hide processing are just outside of the floodplain at slightly higher elevations. The highest sites farthest from the floodplain are small special-use sites where lithic reduction and animal processing took place (Dobbs 1984:163).

Very few Oneota habitation sites are reported in south-central Minnesota east of the Blue Earth River even in the Center Creek and Willow Creek localities. Woodland habitation sites on lakes east of the Blue Earth River do not seem to have Oneota components, while many such sites west of the river yield shell-tempered sherds.

Mortuary Treatment

Most burials attributable to the Blue Earth Phase in the Prairie Lake Region have been encountered accidentally during gravel removal operations in the Center Creek Locality. At the Vosburg site a few individual human elements and an infant burial were uncovered during archaeological excavations of pits. Graveling operations at the Humphrey and Vosburg sites also have encountered burials. The largest cemetery near Center Creek is 21FA84, located on the east side of the Blue Earth River. It contained perhaps 100 burials. Another cemetery also may be on the river's east side, about 6 km north of 21FA84 (Dobbs 1984:75).

In general, largely incomplete secondary burials have been found in small numbers in the major Blue Earth villages. Some of the remains are charred. Large cemeteries are located near these villages in settings similar to the villages, except on the opposite side of the river. Burials in the cemeteries appear to be extended primaries.

Outside of the Center Creek Locality, possible Blue Earth Phase burials have been excavated at the Camden (21LY2) and Great Oasis (21MU2) sites. The

Camden Mound, excavated by amateurs, yielded a shell-tempered vessel associated with what was probably a primary burial (Chamberlain 1936). At Great Oasis, a secondary bundle burial was found in a trash pit with shell-tempered sherds. Judson Mound #1 (21BE6) near the Cambria site yielded a shell-tempered mortuary vessel with five extended primary burials in a subsurface pit (Wilford [ca. 1956]). This last, however, is interpreted to be a Cambria burial.

Dating

The 33 radiocarbon dates for the Blue Earth Phase range between A.D. 1000 to 1510 (Dobbs 1982; Anfinson 1987a). Most of the dates from the Center Creek area fall between A.D. 1100–1400. Both the earliest (1035 ± 60 RCYBP [A.D. 1000]) and the latest (345 ± 140 RCYBP [A.D. 1510]) dates for Blue Earth are from the Center Creek Locality. The Center Creek area dates are the only dates available for Oneota in the Prairie Lake Region. No European trade goods have been found in association with Blue Earth materials.

Perspective on the Late Prehistoric Period

The transition to the Late Prehistoric in the northeastern Plains was marked by the appearance of horticultural villagers associated with the Plains Village Tradition about A.D. 900. The Plains Village Tradition appears to have developed out of a Woodland base in the eastern Plains. This development is the same age and somewhat related to the emergence of the Mississippian Tradition in the middle Mississippi River Valley centered at Cahokia, Illinois. Both traditions are related directly to the intensive use of maize. They are culminations of the Woodland trends towards intensive use of seeds as a food source, more sedentary lifestyles, and more complex social organization. Oneota is a recognizable entity in much of the upper Midwest, including the Prairie Lake Region, by about a hundred years later (ca. A.D. 1000). Oneota probably represents Mississippianized Midwest Woodland groups and also features intensive use of maize and permanent villages.

Plains Village complexes are present in the regions to the south, west, and northwest of the Prairie Lake Region; Middle Mississippian complexes are evident to the east. Oneota complexes are present in every region around the Prairie Lake Region, with intensive Oneota developments in the regions to the east and south. Despite the penetration of these horticultural village complexes into Prairie Lake Region, intensive maize horticulture and large villages were never extensive within the region. Essentially, these complexes were limited to the Minnesota and Blue Earth river valleys.

The presence of Plains Village and Oneota complexes within the Prairie Lake Region attests to the widespread cultural changes and population movements that occurred during the Late Prehistoric. The fate of the region's terminal Woodland peoples is still somewhat unclear, but they undoubtably were not all forced to leave immediately, killed-off, or transformed into horticultural villagers. While even the long-term cultural stability of the Prairie Lake Region was broached by population intrusions and cultural diffusion in the Late Prehistoric, Lake Benton peoples initially may have endured rather than embraced the strangeness and strangers. Some Lake Benton peoples may have survived relatively unchanged for several hundred years into the Late Prehistoric, occupying the geographically insulated Prairie Lake Region interior. Other Lake Benton peoples initially may have shared sites and resources with the horticultural villagers. Eventually, they adopted new lifestyles or abandoned all but the region's northwestern end (along with Great Oasis and Cambria) around A.D. 1200. The most plausible explanation for the abandonment is Oneota pressure from the east.

Much of the Prairie Lake Region was sparsely occupied during the latter half of the Late Prehistoric. Oneota settlements along the Blue Earth River lasted until at least A.D. 1500 and may have continued into the early period of contact with Europeans. However, Oneota use of the Prairie Lake interior was always marginal. There may have been some late Dakota intrusion into the northern border of the Prairie Lake Region before Europeans discovered the area. Nevertheless, Sandy Lake ceramics are found only in the Lake Traverse area at the region's far northwestern end. The Lake Traverse–Big Stone Lake area seems to have been a major interaction zone among native inhabitants during the period immediately before white contact.

No archaeological sites containing early French trade goods are known in the Prairie Lake Region. At the time of French contact, the Dakota appear to have controlled the region's western part, but control of the eastern part appears to be a matter of some dispute between the Dakota, the Oto, the Ioway, and perhaps even the Illinois. Other ethnographically known groups such as the Cheyenne and the Arapaho may have occupied the region's western area prior to French contact.

The Late Prehistoric Period is characterized as a period of change, but unlike the Early Prehistoric Period, the changes were as dependent on cultural factors as they were on environmental factors. The widespread intertribal warfare of the terminal Late Prehistoric continued on into the contact period, fueled further by the demands of foreign economies, technologies, and religions.

Chapter 7

Conclusions

The Prairie Lake Region is not just "peripherally" Plains. It is a Plains region environmentally and culturally. The dominant vegetation was grassland, and the dominant upland mammal was the bison. The cultures participated little in the "woodland"-oriented Midwestern Archaic, Middle Woodland, and Middle Mississippian influence spheres. The peoples of the Prairie Lake Region were partially dependent on bison hunting for at least 9,000 years, and there were two climaxes of focal bison hunting. One occurred about 5000 B.C. and the other in the Late Prehistoric Period (A.D. 900–1650). During the Late Prehistoric, the region contained Plains Village cultures closely related to the Middle Missouri Tradition of the Plains heartland. During the Euro-American contact period, the Prairie Lake Region was dominated by western and middle Dakota peoples (Teton, Yankton, Yanktonai) widely recognized as "classic" Plains groups.

The cited causes of cultural changes apparent in the eastern Plains and Midwest from the time of the recession of the Wisconsin glaciers to the appearance of Europeans usually fall into four categories: environmental change, diffusion of new ideas (mainly technological), population increase, and intrusions of new peoples. Of these, environmental change is the most popular because evidence for it can be documented by non-archaeological means, because there appears to be some chronological correspondence between major climatic and cultural events, and because significant and sustained environmental change forces cultural change in even the most resilient cultures.

Environmental change is widely accepted as the cause of the transition from Paleoindian to Archaic. Certainly, the climatic changes between 12,000 and 9,000 years ago are impressive and abrupt; transformation of the central Minnesota spruce forest into a pine forest may have taken place in only a century

(Anfinson and Wright 1990:226). The transition from Paleoindian to Archaic may partially result from the disappearance of Pleistocene megafauna, but much of the increasing sedentism of the Midwestern Archaic has been attributed to the deterioration of upland resources, along with the enrichment and stabilization of river-valley resources.

In the Prairie Lake Region, however, it was the upland resources that became the most important during the Archaic. Big game hunting remained the basic way of life throughout most of the Archaic, as bison populations expanded eastward with the post-glacial warming trend. While there were indeed shifts in the subsistence-settlement patterns in the Prairie Lake Region from the Paleoindian to the Archaic, these shifts were not as abrupt or as extensive as found in the eastern Midwest.

In the Prairie Lake Region, evidence for the earliest cultures is very scarce, and no Paleoindian sites have been subjected to controlled excavations. Therefore, documentation of this period is based largely on the presence of a few early projectile points held in local collections. The region's environment during this period, however, was considerably different than in later periods. Vegetation was forest. Topography was being shaped by glacial melt-water and ice-block collapse. Fauna included species that are now extinct and excluded forms that were later common.

While it is impossible to construct a detailed cultural history of the Early Prehistoric Period based on the sparse archaeological data available, early environmental history can be reconstructed with more detail. We can model cultural changes by interpolating resource availability and ethnographically and archaeologically known responses to similar environments.

The scarcity of archaeological remains in the Prairie Lake Region from the earliest part of the Early

Prehistoric Period, in part, may reflect resource-poor dense-forest vegetation, topographic and hydrological instability, and even regional isolation resulting from melt-water rivers. Bison would not have been widespread in the region at this time. Other large game animals may have been uncommon, and the diverse floral and faunal assemblage of the Middle Prehistoric had not yet developed. Better living may have been present in other regions, attracting more human activity. Human habitation of the Prairie Lake Region in Paleoindian times may have been largely seasonal or simply of a very low density.

With the appearance of grassland vegetation and topographical stability by 9,000 years ago, the subsistence resources of the Prairie Lake Region became more stable and more abundant. Bison and other animals rapidly colonized the region. Continued postglacial warming eventually led to an environment that was quite different from that of the Middle and Late Prehistoric. Water was scarce, wood was scarce, and the grassland vegetation would have been more typical of mixed-grass rather than tallgrass prairie. Late Early Prehistoric subsistence patterns were focused on upland resources. Most campsites would have been near the remaining water sources, not only to satisfy human needs, but because they attracted animals. Many warm-season campsites may have been located on the bottoms of largely dry lake basins or on the lowest terraces in the major river valleys. Water would have been present at these locations just below the surface or in small waterholes. Most of these sites are now covered with water or deeply buried in lacustrine or alluvial sediments.

The late Early Prehistoric culture of the Prairie Lake Region evidenced at the Granite Falls Bison site resembles the bison-oriented complexes at the Cherokee Sewer and Itasca sites in adjacent regions. The entire northeastern Plains at this time featured an environmental and perhaps cultural cohesiveness not seen in earlier or later periods. The necessities of a nomadic existence strongly differentiated the way of life on the northeastern Plains at this time from the more sedentary Archaic riverine hunter-gatherers of the eastern Midwest. If the environments and economies of the two areas were thus different, it is likely their social structures and ideologies were as well.

Despite some technological similarities, the term "Archaic Period" in the Plains can be confusing because there are significant temporal and cultural differences from the Eastern Woodlands Archaic. The Archaic Period in the western Plains is also somewhat different from the Archaic in the northeastern Plains. It is perhaps useful to refer to the Archaic of the west-

ern Plains as Plains Archaic and the initial Archaic of the northeastern Plains as Prairie Archaic. The terminal Archaic in the northeastern Plains exhibits strong regionalization, suggesting phases, such as the Mountain Lake Phase in the Prairie Lake Region.

While bison hunting continued to be important to Prairie Lake subsistence in the early Middle Prehistoric, the appearance of a cooler, wetter climate by 5,000 years ago fostered the development of a regionally adapted way of life. It promoted a stable cultural tradition that was to exist in the region for the next 4,000 years. With the multitudinous lake basins full of water most of the time, the wetlands of the Prairie Lake Region, coupled with the tallgrass uplands, offered a rich and diverse resource base that allowed a more sedentary existence and lessened the need for extraregional resources. The filled, interconnected lake basins also may have discouraged outside contact or at least outside intrusions since travel across the region would have been confusing and difficult. The only direct route would have been along the Minnesota River, which may explain later cultural developments centered there.

Beginning with the Mountain Lake Phase, the archaeological features of the Middle Prehistoric in the Prairie Lake Region include: major habitation sites on islands and peninsulas in the larger lakes; relatively diverse subsistence patterns utilizing upland and lowland species; dependence on local lithic resources; and resistance to outside influences involving changes in the basic way of life, social interaction, and ideological expressions. Middle Prehistoric changes largely are confined to technological improvements or stylistic forms. These markers differentiate phases but do not constitute significant cultural change with regard to ways of life.

The addition of pottery in the Fox Lake Phase links that phase to the Midwestern Woodland Tradition, but this relatively late addition is unaccompanied by the lithic assemblage, subsistence orientations, and mortuary practices of the Midwestern Early and Middle Woodland. The use of burial mounds probably appeared late in the Fox Lake Phase, but limited mortuary ritual is evident. Gardening and intensive seed gathering were not present in the Fox Lake Phase.

The Lake Benton Phase obviously had some initial cultural contacts to the northeast, as indicated by ceramic stylistic similarities to St. Croix–Onamia types. Other changes are evident in the widespread use of burial mounds, the use of the bow and arrow, and in ceramic manufacturing techniques such as crushed granite temper and thin vessel walls. There is no evidence, however, for significant changes in the way of life. Subsistence-settlement patterns remained the same, and no evidence exists for significant participation in interregional trade since raw material preferences remained unchanged. Exotic materials (e.g., marine shells) are rare. The use of horticulture or intensive wild rice harvesting, which was widespread in the Late Woodland complexes in adjacent regions, are not apparent in the terminal Woodland phase of the Prairie Lake Region. Changes from Fox Lake to Lake Benton are almost all of a technological nature, relating to a better way of performing existing tasks (e.g., hunting, cooking). Burial mounds are the major exception and suggest some ideological shifts.

The stability of the Middle Prehistoric culture of the Prairie Lake Region probably is best explained by a combination of factors. The most important are: lack of need for outside resources; difficulty of cross-country travel throughout much of the region; and environmental contrast to adjacent areas which made it less attractive to neighboring groups who had successfully adapted on their own. Other elements in the cultural stability of the Prairie Lake Region include the maintenance of stable population levels and the development of a subsistence economy that could adapt to short-term environmental changes equivalent to those caused by a 1930s-like drought.

The importance of economic resiliency to cultural stability cannot be overstated. Environmental change was a fact of life in the Prairie Lake Region. Seasonal changes caused drastic fluctuations in resource availability, and periodic droughts dried up many of the shallow lakes and rivers. At the heart of this successful adaptation was the abundance of naturally occurring food in the region, coupled with a diverse subsistence pattern that utilized upland, lowland, and aquatic resources. In times of drought when aquatic and lowland resources would have been less available, upland resources such as bison no doubt increased. The limited use of elk, waterfowl, mollusks, and seeds and the fact that horticulture was apparently never practiced by Woodland people in the Prairie Lake Region indicate that the region's full subsistence potential was used rarely because more preferred resources were usually available.

In the river bottom subsistence-settlement pattern of the Midwest, abundant localized resources led to an increasingly sedentary lifestyle, but many of the Prairie Lake Region resources required movement. Bison herds constantly moved; when they shifted outside the range of hunters from a particular camp, the camp moved. Unlike the complexes of the High Plains, however, Prairie Lake people were not dependent on the bison, and when other desirable resources (e.g., aquat-

ic tubers, muskrats) were seasonally available in locations inconvenient for bison hunting, camps may not have moved for many months or may have shifted to locations more convenient to exploit non-bison resources.

Even with the rich resources of the Prairie Lake Region, winter must have been a difficult time, especially when bison were scarce. Other faunal resources were available in winter, but they were more difficult to obtain. Muskrats could be dug out of frozen huts. Fish could be individually caught or speared through holes in the ice-covered lakes, and scattered deer could be hunted in the wooded river valleys. Major river valleys may have been preferred habitation locations in the winter, because they not only offered more varieties of mammals, but contained firewood and provided shelter from the bitter winds. Starvation probably was avoided except in the worst winters. The fact that storage pits are not a common feature at Prairie Lake Woodland sites may not indicate lack of knowledge of storage technology. Perhaps the people inhabiting these sites did not need such technology.

The "feast or famine" model often presented for the historic Dakota inhabitants of the Prairie Lake Region probably is not an accurate model of the region's Middle Prehistoric hunter-gatherer way of life. The ethnographically known nineteenth-century Dakota had changed greatly in their economic orientation after western contact. Advancement of the Euro-American frontier reduced game on which the Dakota depended. Bison herds were decimated by overhunting. At the same time, these peoples became increasingly dependent on traders and the American government. Moreover, archaeologists and historians generally believe that the eastern Dakota of the early 1800s were relatively recent immigrants into the Prairie Lake Region. Therefore, they may have not been familiar with the total spectrum of subsistence resources available or the most effective means for exploiting them. The aspect of early historic Dakota subsistence most important to understanding precontact exploitation patterns in the Prairie Lake Region is the Dakota's use of indigenous plant foods, especially legumes and tubers which would not have left easily recognizable or preservable archaeological remains.

The transition from the Middle Prehistoric to the Late Prehistoric in the Prairie Lake Region is denoted by the appearance of horticultural villages. These cultures brought not only a new way of life, but cultural diversity, cultural contacts, and population concentrations not previously seen. The initial horticultural village cultures appear to be migrants into the region since the indigenous terminal Woodland culture differs dramatically in key subsistence and artifactual aspects, especially ceramics.

The rise of Plains Village cultures in the eastern Plains has been associated with the onset of climatic conditions favorable to maize cultivation, while their eventual abandonment of large areas of the eastern Plains is often ascribed to the onset of drought conditions unfavorable to maize horticulture. This climatic model explaining Late Prehistoric cultural changes has been questioned, however (Anfinson and Wright 1990). The flowering of the Late Prehistoric village complexes occurs in the middle of what has been called (Barries et al. 1976) the Neo-Atlantic Climatic Episode, and the demise of most of them does not occur until well into the Pacific Episode (ca. A.D. 1150). Thus, changes in Late Prehistoric horticultural village cultures are not well tied to the standard climatic model.

The initial Late Prehistoric cultural changes in the Prairie Lake Region probably are explained best by migrations into the region caused by widespread population increases. It is unclear whether the increases were caused by the successful adaption of maize horticulture to the Midwest or by gradual population growth that increased dependence on horticulture. Whatever the reason, the coincidental appearance of a climate slightly more favorable to maize cultivation is most likely secondary to the development of varieties of maize well suited to northern environments and perhaps the complementary introduction of beans to fulfill nutritional needs not met by maize.

The effect of the intruding horticultural villagers on the indigenous Prairie Lake population is still not clear. The Great Oasis and Big Stone phases in the region appear to have the closest relationship in lifestyles with the terminal Woodland peoples, but Great Oasis is very limited in the region and Big Stone is poorly known. The fate of the terminal Woodland people has been one of the key research challenges of the Prairie Lake Region. Likely, the region was shared by Woodland, Plains Village, and Oneota peoples for several centuries. With the disappearance of Great Oasis and Cambria about A.D. 1200, evidences for terminal Woodland peoples are scarce. It is suggested here that at least some of the Lake Benton peoples became part of the Big Stone Phase, a terminal Late Prehistoric Plains Village complex present in the northwestern Prairie Lake Region. Additional Plains Village phases still may be defined in the northeastern Plains and perhaps even in the Prairie Lake Region.

The Prairie Lake Region appears to have been partitioned by the horticultural villagers. The eastern region was dominated by Oneota, the Minnesota River Valley by Cambria, the southwest by Great Oasis, and the northwest eventually by Big Stone. Incursions by eastern groups into the region's western parts, mainly to hunt bison, are evident at small campsites in southwestern Minnesota where mixed upper horizons contain terminal Woodland, Plains Village, and Oneota components. Large villages and mortuary sites for the horticultural villages, however, were confined to the home areas. This partitioning is especially apparent during the Blue Earth Oneota Phase. The use of elements of the late Middle Prehistoric subsistence-settlement pattern by these horticultural villagers may not reflect intensive contact or transformation of local populations, but simply the most efficient way to live in the region at certain times of the year.

The dominant element of the publications of Reid Bryson and his adherents regarding the interaction of climate and culture in the midwestern United States concerns the detrimental effect of the onset of the Pacific Episode. The recurring droughts supposedly associated with this period initially caused radical shifts in subsistence patterns in the western Midwest and eventually led to the demise of some cultures, the Mill Creek culture of northwestern Iowa being the most cited example.

Even with recurring droughts in parts of the Midwest in the Late Prehistoric, however, their cultural implications may be overemphasized or misinterpreted. In the northeastern Plains, where drought has a more severe impact than in the eastern Midwest, Mill Creek dates are concentrated between A.D. 1000 and 1300. If the Pacific Episode drought cycle began about A.D. 1150, Mill Creek persisted for at least another 150 years. If drought was the principal factor in Mill Creek's demise, the adverse effects of the drought were gradual, not sudden.

Indeed, there may have been sudden significant changes in the local Mill Creek environment, but those changes need not be a result of widespread climatic change. Increased bison exploitation suggests fewer deer and more bison in the Mill Creek area. The loss of deer habitat may have resulted from Mill Creek over-exploitation of the river-edge woodlands, rather than drought. Another explanation for decreased deer exploitation may not lie so much in a decrease of deer availability as in an increase in bison availability.

The increase in bison may not have happened because of local environmental changes. The well-documented increase in the Late Prehistoric Period throughout the eastern Plains may have been the result of increased dryness on the *western* Plains. No doubt, the presence of large bison herds near Mill Creek settlements would have brought about changes in hunting patterns regardless of fluctuations in the deer population. The increased availability of bison during the Pacific Episode made the eastern Plains a more attractive place to live than during previous periods, regardless of any decrease in the deer population or increased difficulties in practicing horticulture.

Maize horticulture was not abandoned in the northeastern Plains at this time. The ability to grow maize during the Pacific Episode has been demonstrated at a number of locations. In A.D. 1300, only one hundred miles to the northeast of the supposedly drought-stricken Mill Creek settlements, Blue Earth Oneota flourished in south-central Minnesota in a setting very similar to Mill Creek with villages concentrated in small river valleys. There is little evidence for a major shift in Blue Earth subsistence patterns at this time. The Vosburg site (21FA2), which was occupied between A.D. 1200 and 1500, has yielded very few bison bones. Subsistence appears to have relied on a mixture of horticulture and diverse hunting and gathering (Dobbs 1984).

Forty miles north of the Blue Earth heartland, Cambria peoples apparently abandoned their major villages in the Minnesota River Valley by A.D. 1300. Cambria subsistence patterns are very similar to Blue Earth with limited use of bison indicated in the major villages. Using the Mill Creek example, Watrall (1974) suggested that Cambria people abandoned their villages near the type site (21BE2) because of the adverse effects of climatic change on horticulture, woodland depletion, and soil-fertility depletion. Watrall predicted a Cambria subsistence shift to greater reliance on bison as drought and soil depletion made maize horticulture more difficult and woodland depletion reduced the local deer population.

The Minnesota River Valley, however, is an environmental setting very different from the Blue Earth River Valley or the small river valleys of northwestern Iowa. It is very broad and deep, with a dense river bottom forest. It would be difficult for the small Cambria population (perhaps several hundred people) to deplete the soil and wood even in a very restricted area. Numerous springs along the valley would have fostered low, wet areas with adequate moisture for horticulture even in times of severe drought.

Even in the northern section of the northeastern Plains, horticulture appears to have flourished in the late years of the Late Prehistoric. The Big Stone Phase in the northwestern Prairie Lake Region has clear evidence for horticulture. At the Shea site (39CS101) in eastern North Dakota the growing season was shorter than in the Prairie Lake Region. Yet, people utilizing maize were present in the mid-1440s (Michlovic and

Schneider 1988). Horticulture also flourished in the Middle Missouri trench at this time.

The demise of the Plains Village cultures of southwestern Minnesota cannot be attributed solely to climatic change, then, although a deteriorating climate may have contributed to other stresses on these cultures. The most telling argument against the climatic factor is the fact that Blue Earth Oneota was thriving when the eastern Plains Village cultures disappeared from the southern northeastern Plains. In this fact may lie the most important reason for the Plains Village changes.

As Oneota influences increased in the eastern Plains around A.D. 1200, Mill Creek and other eastern Plains Village groups began to add fortifications to their main villages and abandon outlying settlements (D. C. Anderson 1986, 1987). Southwestern Minnesota at this time appears to have been partitioned: Great Oasis was in the west; Cambria was in the north; and Blue Earth Oneota was in the east. The eastern Plains villages lasted only another century in southwestern Minnesota, but large Oneota villages did not extend into the western Prairie Lake Region, except, perhaps, for a minor incursion into the Minnesota River Valley.

It would appear that the best explanation for the cultural changes that occurred in the western Midwest at about A.D. 1200 is that Oneota expansion caused a great deal of friction in the area. The conflict between Oneota peoples and western Midwest groups has been suggested a number of times (e.g., Tiffany 1982a:98; Dobbs 1984:214; D. C. Anderson 1986:234; Anfinson 1987b:228). At the time the Plains Village Tradition was concentrating on the Middle Missouri and abandoning the southern part of the northeastern Plains, Oneota was experiencing its greatest expansion in the northeastern Plains and western Midwest. This expansion and the conflict it caused with other cultures is the most plausible explanation for the abandonment of the southern northeastern Plains by Plains Villagers. It also would explain the presence of fortified village sites in the northeastern Plains immediately prior to, during, and after this expansion as well as the restriction of major Oneota villages to more eastern localities. This conflict apparently lasted into early contact times, by then involving the Dakota. This is historically documented by the uneasiness of the various groups that visited Le Sueur at the mouth of the Blue Earth River in 1700 (cf. M. Wedel 1974), and it is archaeologically supported by the lack of early historic trade goods at precontact sites in the Prairie Lake Region.

Hickerson's (1970) study of the historic Ojibwe-Dakota conflict suggests that northern west-central Minnesota was virtually unoccupied in the last years of the Late Prehistoric because of intertribal resource competition. This may be a useful model to help explain the cultural situation in the Prairie Lake Region in Late Prehistoric and early contact times. With the increasing interest in bison hunting and maize cultivation, perhaps brought on by widespread population pressure, improved varieties of maize, and/or increased availability of bison in the eastern Plains, numerous groups expanded into the Prairie Lake Region. There, bison herds roamed and ideal maize growing areas existed. Initially, this expansion was relatively peaceful, but as resource competition and population pressure increased, so did hostility. Finally, around A.D. 1200, conflict was so intense that much of the Prairie Lake Region was abandoned for year-around settlement.

Directions for Future Research

The archaeological needs of the Prairie Lake Region are numerous, but concentrating work on a few specific problems could greatly increase understanding of the region. Certain geographic areas are virtually unknown. These include north-central Iowa and west-central Minnesota. While some reconnaissance surveys have been done, very little excavation has been undertaken. Major excavations at even a few multicomponent habitation sites in these areas would begin to fill gaps in the cultural history that are now only speculation. Excavations should include fine-scale recovery methods and intensive attempts at absolute dating.

A major survey effort also should be undertaken in the Minnesota River Valley. This should include specialized testing to locate deeply buried sites on alluvial fans and in the floodplain. If this survey was coupled with geomorphological and paleoenvironmental studies, site locations could be predicted more accurately and differences explained. Such a survey could locate Early Prehistoric sites and help investigate this poorly known period.

In order to better understand interregional relationships, a number of artifact attribute studies using existing collections would be very useful. Examples are careful comparisons of: 1) trailed-over-cordmarked ceramics in the western Midwest in order to under-stand the relationship between Fox Lake and such ill-defined complexes as Black Sand; 2) Lake Benton ceramics with St. Croix–Onamia ceramics to define the relationship between the Prairie Lake Region and central Minnesota in the late Middle Prehistoric; and 3) the numerous projectile points from the Pedersen site excavations, in order to produce a useful chronological sequence for the Prairie Lake Region points.

The ethnographic links to the archaeological cultures of the Prairie Lake Region also should be an important research focus. Many Plains groups have migration legends suggesting a Minnesota homeland in the Late Prehistoric. The Dakota clearly moved through western Minnesota on their way to the Plains, and this movement predates Ojibwe expansion into northern Minnesota. Yet, there is little evidence for the early presence of the Dakota in southwestern Minnesota. The Cheyenne apparently were once horticultural villagers in western Minnesota, and it is tempting to look for their origins in the Plains Village complexes of the Prairie Lake Region (perhaps in the Big Stone Phase).

One of the great needs of the Prairie Lake Region is an extensive radiocarbon chronology. We have only a limited idea about when the Woodland Tradition began, where the Fox Lake-Lake Benton transition was, when mound burial became widespread, and when the Woodland ended. The beginning of the Late Prehistoric Period is an especially interesting time that needs more absolute dating to understand better the development of the Plains Village way of life and the fate of the terminal Woodland people.

Overall, the Prairie Lake Region is an area of great frustration and great promise. The frustrations lie in the wealth of archaeological data that has been retrieved but not disseminated, the turbated and complex site stratigraphies that blend one cultural horizon into another in the deep prairie soils, and the portions of the region that are unknown archaeologically. The promises lie in the Prairie Lake Region's intermediate position with respect to other cultural and environmental regions, its long-term stability within a sea of change, and the development of cultures practicing a horticultural village way of life. Future archaeological research needs to focus on these particular problems and opportunities if we are to truly know the people of the region's past.

References Cited

Abbreviations

Ms   Manuscript
SHPO   State Historic Preservation Office, Minnesota
        Historical Society, St. Paul

Agogino, G. A., and W. D. Frankforter

1960   "A Paleo-Indian Bison Kill in Northwestern
        Iowa." *American Antiquity* 25:414–15.

Aldrich, C.

1884   "Antiquities of Hamilton County, Iowa." *Ameri-*
        can Antiquarian 6 (Jan.):42–43.

Alex, L. M.

1980   *Exploring Iowa's Past: A Guide to Prehistoric*
        Archaeology. Iowa City: University of Iowa Press.

1981   "Fish Bone Analysis: 39BK7." In "Archaeological
        Excavations," ed. Hannus, 289–301.

Alex, R. A.

1980   "Contents of a Soil Sample from the Great Oasis
        Site at Oakwood Lakes State Park." *Newsletter of*
        the South Dakota Archaeological Society, vol. 10,
        no. 1:1–3.

1981   "Village Sites off the Missouri River." In *The*
        Future of South Dakota's Past, ed. L. J. Zimmer-
        man and L. C. Stewart, 39–45. Special Publica-
        tion of the South Dakota Archaeological Society,
        no. 2. N.p.: University of South Dakota Archaeol-
        ogy Laboratory.

Anderson, D. C.

1977   *The Crim Site (13ET403).* Research Papers, vol.
        2, no. 9. Iowa City, Iowa: Office of the State
        Archaeologist, University of Iowa.

1980   "Stone Tool Assemblages from the Cherokee
        Sewer Site." In *Cherokee Excavations,* ed. D. C.
        Anderson and Semken, 197–238.

1986   "The Wittrock Excavations: Implications for the
        Study of Culture Process within the Initial Variant
        of the Middle Missouri Tradition." *North Ameri-*
        can Archaeologist, vol. 7, no. 3:215–41.

1987   "Toward a Processual Understanding of the Ini-
        tial Variant of the Middle Missouri Tradition:
        The Case of the Mill Creek Culture of Iowa."
        American Antiquity 52:522–37.

Anderson, D. C., and H. A. Semken Jr., eds.

1980   *The Cherokee Excavations: Holocene Ecology and*
        Human Adaptations in Northwestern Iowa. Stud-
        ies in Archaeology. New York: Academic Press.

Anderson, D. C., and M. L. Spriestersbach

1982   "The Stone Tool Assemblage." In *Preliminary*
        Report, ed. Tiffany, 86–118.

Anderson, D. L.

1979   "Laurel Ware." In *Handbook,* comp. and ed.
        Anfinson, 121–35.

Anderson, G. C.

1980   "Early Dakota Migration and Intertribal War: A
        Revision." *Western Historical Quarterly* 11
        (Jan.):17–36.

Anfinson, S. F.

1977   "An Analysis of the Big Slough Site (21MU1)
        with Particular Emphasis on the Ceramic Body
        Sherds." Master's thesis, University of Nebraska.

1979   *A Handbook of Minnesota Prehistoric Ceramics,*
        comp. and ed. Anfinson. Occasional Publications
        in Minnesota Anthropology, no. 5. St. Paul: Min-
        nesota Archaeological Society.

1982a   "Faunal Remains from the Big Slough Site
        (21MU1) and Woodland Cultural Stability in
        Southwestern Minnesota." *Minnesota Archaeolo-*
        gist, vol. 41, no. 1 (spring–summer):53–71.

1982b   "The Prehistoric Archaeology of the Prairie Lake
        Region: A Summary from a Minnesota Perspec-
        tive." *Journal of the North Dakota Archaeologi-*
        cal Association 1:65–90.

1984   "Cultural and Natural Aspects of Mound Distri-
        bution in Minnesota." *Minnesota Archaeologist,*
        vol. 43, no. 1 (spring–summer):3–30.

1986   "Prehistoric Subsistence-Settlement Patterns in the
        Prairie Lake Region." In *The Prairie: Past, Pres-
        ent and Future: Proceedings of the Ninth North
        American Prairie Conference: Held
        July 29–August 1, 1984, Moorhead, Minnesota,*
        ed. G. K. Clambey and R. H. Pemble, 8–15.
        Fargo, N.Dak.: Tri-College University Center for
        Environmental Studies.

1987a   "Investigations at Two Oneota Sites in the Center
        Creek Locality." *Minnesota Archaeologist,* vol.
        46, no. 1:31–45.

1987b "The Prehistory of the Prairie Lake Region in the Northeastern Plains." Ph.D. diss., University of Minnesota.

Anfinson, S. F., and R. J. Peterson

1988 "Minnesota Municipal and County Highway Archaeological Reconnaissance Study: 1988 Annual Report." St. Paul: Minnesota Historical Society, 1989. Copy in SHPO.

1989 "Minnesota Municipal and County Highway Archaeological Reconnaissance Study: 1989 Annual Report." St. Paul: Minnesota Historical Society, 1990. Copy in SHPO.

Anfinson, S. F., and H. E. Wright Jr.

1990 "Climatic Change and Culture in Prehistoric Minnesota." In *The Woodland Tradition in the Western Great Lakes: Papers Presented to Elden Johnson,* ed. G. E. Gibbon, 213–32. Publications in Anthropology, no. 4. Minneapolis: Department of Anthropology, University of Minnesota.

Angier, B.

1974 *Field Guide to Edible Wild Plants.* [Harrisburg, Pa.]: Stackpole Books.

Baerreis, D. A.

1970 "Environmental Archaeology in Western Iowa," ed. Baerreis. *Northwest Chapter of the Iowa Archaeological Society Newsletter,* vol. 18, no. 5 (Sept.):3–15.

Baerreis, D. A., R. A. Bryson, and J. E. Kutzbach

1976 "Climate and Culture in the Western Great Lakes Region." *Midcontinental Journal of Archaeology,* vol. 1, no. 1:39–57.

Bareis, C. J., and J. W. Porter, eds.

1984 *American Bottom Archaeology: A Summary of the FAI-270 Project Contribution to the Culture History of the Mississippi River Valley.* American Bottom Archaeology. Urbana: Published for the Illinois Department of Transportation by the University of Illinois Press.

Bartlein, P. J., and T. Webb III

1982 "Holocene Climatic Changes Estimated from Pollen Data from the Northern Midwest." In *Quaternary History of the Driftless Area: With Special Papers: Prepared for the 29th Annual Meeting, Midwest Friends of the Pleistocene,* 67–82. Field Trip Guide Book, no. 5. Madison: Geological and Natural History Survey, University of Wisconsin-Extension.

Baugh, T. G., ed.

1986 "Current Trends in Southern Plains Archaeology." *Plains Anthropologist,* Memoir 21, vol. 31, no. 114, pt. 2.

Beals, R. L., H. Hoijer, and A. R. Beals

1977 *An Introduction to Anthropology.* 5th ed. New York: Macmillan.

Beissel, D., K. L. Brown, M. E. Brown, and K. Zimmerman

1984 "Cultural Resources Investigations of the Upper Minnesota River (639) Project, Deuel and Grant Counties, South Dakota, and Lac Qui Parle and Yellow Medicine Counties, Minnesota." Submitted to the U.S. Army Corps of Engineers, St. Paul District; contract no. DACW37-82-M-1508. Vermillion: University of South Dakota Archaeology Laboratory. Copy in SHPO.

Benn, D. W.

1981a "Archaeological Investigations at the Rainbow Site, Plymouth County, Iowa," by Benn et al. Prepared for the U.S. Department of the Interior, National Park Service, Rocky Mountain Regional Office, under contract no. C3571 (78).

1981b "Ceramics from the MAD Sites and Other Prairie Peninsula and Plains Complexes." Ms. Copy in author's possession.

1982 "The Ceramic Assemblage." In *Preliminary Report,* ed. Tiffany, 38–86.

1983 "Diffusion and Acculturation in Woodland Cultures on the Western Prairie Peninsula." In *Prairie Archaeology,* ed. Gibbon, 75–86.

1988 National Register of Historic Places, Multiple Property Documentation Form for Big Sioux Prehistoric Prairie Procurement System Archaeological District, prepared by Benn for the State Historic Preservation Office, State Historical Society of Iowa.

Bennett, H. A.

1934 "The Mystery of the Iowa Buffalo." *Iowa Journal of History and Politics* 32:60–73.

Bernabo, J. C., and T. Webb III

1977 "Changing Patterns in the Holocene Pollen Record of Northeastern North America: A Mapped Summary." *Quaternary Research* 8:64–96.

Bird, R. M., and C. A. Dobbs

1986 "Archaeological Maize from the Vosburg Site (21FA2), Faribault County, Minnesota." *Missouri Archaeologist* 47 (Dec.):85–105.

Birk, D. A.

1986 "In Search of the Mound Builders: A Phase III Cultural Resources Investigation of the Black Bear Site (21CW96), Crow Wing County, Minnesota." Submitted to the U.S. Army Corps of Engineers, St. Paul District; contract no. DACW 37-86-M-0068. Reports of Investigations, no. 6.

Minneapolis: Institute for Minnesota Archaeology. Copy in SHPO.

Bleed, P.

1969   *The Archaeology of Petaga Point: The Preceramic Component*. Minnesota Prehistoric Archaeology Series, [no. 2]. St. Paul: Minnesota Historical Society.

Blitz, J. H.

1988   "Adoption of the Bow in Prehistoric North America." *North American Archaeologist*, vol. 9, no. 2:123–45.

Bonney, R. A.

1962   "A Chronological Analysis of Southern Minnesota Woodland." Master's thesis, University of Minnesota.

1965   "Evidence for Early Woodland Occupations in Southwestern Minnesota." *Minnesota Archaeologist*, vol. 27, no. 1:2–48.

Bonnichsen, R., D. Stanford, and J. L. Fastook

1987   "Environmental Change and Developmental History of Human Adaptive Patterns; The Paleoindian Case." In *North America and Adjacent Oceans during the Last Deglaciation*, ed. W. F. Ruddiman and H. E. Wright Jr., 403–24. The Geology of North America, vol. K-3. Boulder, Colo.: Geological Society of America.

Borchert, J. R.

1950   "The Climate of the Central North American Grassland." *Annals of the Association of American Geographers* 40:1–39.

Borchert, J. R., and D. P. Yaeger

1969   *Atlas of Minnesota Resources and Settlement*. Prepared for the Minnesota State Planning Agency. Rev. ed. [Minneapolis]: Department of Geography, University of Minnesota.

Bradley, L. E., and W. Ranney

1985   "Archaeological Survey and Testing of a Proposed Construction Site at Waubay Wildlife Refuge, Waubay, South Dakota." Prepared for the [U.S. Department of the Interior], Fish and Wildlife Service. Vermillion, S.Dak.: DIS Inc.

Breckenridge, W. J.

1944   *Reptiles and Amphibians of Minnesota*. Minneapolis: University of Minnesota Press.

Brown, J. [A.], and C. Cleland

1968   "The Late Glacial and Early Postglacial Faunal Resources in Midwestern Biomes Newly Opened to Human Adaption." In *The Quaternary of Illinois: A Symposium in Observance of the Centennial of the University of Illinois*, ed. R. E. Bergstrom, 114–22. Special Publication, no. 14. [Urbana: College of Agriculture, University of Illinois].

Brown, J. A., and R. K. Vierra

1983   "What Happened in the Middle Archaic? Introduction to an Ecological Approach to Koster Site Archaeology." In *Archaic Hunters and Gatherers*, ed. Phillips and Brown, 165–95.

Brown, K. L., M. E. Brown, and N. H. Hanenberger

1982   *Prehistoric Stone Tools of South Dakota: A Guide*. Special Publication of the South Dakota Archaeological Society, no. 6. Vermillion: University of South Dakota Archaeology Laboratory.

Bryson, R. A.

1966   "Air Masses, Streamlines, and the Boreal Forest." *Geographical Bulletin*, vol. 8, no. 3:228–69.

Bryson, R. A., D. A. Baerreis, and W. M. Wendland

1970   "The Character of Late-Glacial and Post-Glacial Climatic Changes." In Symposium on Pleistocene and Recent Environments of the Central Plains (1968: University of Kansas), *Pleistocene and Recent Environments of the Central Great Plains*, ed. W. Dort Jr. and J. K. Jones Jr., 53–74. Lawrence: University Press of Kansas.

Bryson, R. A., and W. M. Wendland

1969   "Tentative Climatic Patterns for Some Late Glacial and Post-Glacial Episodes in Central North America." In *Life, Land and Water*, ed. Mayer-Oakes, 271–98.

Buchner, A. P.

1980   "An Update on the Larter Site (EaLg-1)." In *Studies in Eastern Manitoba Archaeology*, 37–70. Papers in Manitoba Archaeology, Miscellaneous Papers, no. 10. [Winnipeg]: Manitoba Department of Cultural Affairs and Historical Resources, Historic Resources Branch.

Buechler, J.

1982   "Test Excavations at the Volunteer Site (39BK8)." *South Dakota Archaeology* 6:1–31.

Caine, C. A. H. (C. A. Caine-Hohman)

1969   "The Archaeology of the Snake River Valley." Master's thesis, University of Minnesota.

1983   "Normative Typological and Systemic Approaches to the Analysis of North-Central Minnesota Ceramics." Ph.D. diss., University of Minnesota.

Caldwell, W. W., and D. R. Henning

1978   "North American Plains." In *Chronologies in New World Archaeology*, ed. R. E. Taylor and C. W. Meighan, 113–45. Studies in Archeology. New York: Academic Press.

Carver, Jonathan

1976   *The Journals of Jonathan Carver and Related Documents, 1766–1770*, ed. J. Parker. Bicentennial ed. St. Paul: Minnesota Historical Society Press.

Chamberlain, G. H.

1936   "The Story of the Camden Vase: Made at a Time When the Sioux Indians Were Mound Builders." *Club Dial* (Contemporary Club, White Plains, N.Y.), vol. 9, no. 6 (Mar.):15–16, 37–38.

Christiansen, G. W., III

[1990]   "A Preliminary Report on the 1990 Test Excavations at the Peterson Site (21YM47): Yellow Medicine County, Minnesota." Minneapolis: Institute for Minnesota Archaeology. Copy in SHPO.

Clayton, L., and S. R. Moran

1982   "Chronology of Late Wisconsin Glaciation in Middle North America." *Quaternary Science Reviews* 1:55–82.

Clements, F. E., and V. E. Shelford

1939   *Bio-Ecology.* New York: J. Wiley & Sons.

Comfort, A. I.

1978   "Indian Mounds Near Fort Wadsworth, Dakota Territory." In *Annual Report of the Board of Regents of the Smithsonian Institution*, 1871, p. 389–402. Washington, D.C.: GPO, 1873. Reprint. *Minnesota Archaeologist*, vol. 37, no. 1 (Feb.):2–15.

Cook, T. G.

1976   *Koster: An Artifact Analysis of Two Archaic Phases in Westcentral Illinois.* Koster Research Reports, no. 3. Evanston, Ill.: Northwestern University Archeological Program.

Dallman, J. E.

1970   "Dietary Study." In "Environmental Archaeology," ed. Baerreis, 13.

Deetz, J.

1967   *Invitation to Archaeology.* Garden City, N.Y.: Published for the American Museum of Natural History by the Natural History Press.

Diedrick, R. T., and R. H. Rust

1979   "Glacial Lake Evidence in Western Minnesota as Interpreted from the Soil Survey." In *Swift County, Minnesota: A Collection of Historical Sketches and Family Histories*, 7–9. Benson, Minn.: Swift County Historical Society.

Dobbs, C. A.

1979   "Archaic Subsistence in Southwestern Minnesota: The View from Granite Falls." Master's thesis, University of Minnesota.

1982   "Oneota Origins and Development: The Radiocarbon Evidence." In *Oneota Studies*, ed. Gibbon, 91–105.

1984   "Oneota Settlement Patterns in the Blue Earth River Valley, Minnesota." Ph.D. diss., University of Minnesota.

1989   "A Phase One Archaeological Survey of the Cottonwood, Redwood, and Yellow Medicine Drainages in Southwestern Minnesota." Submitted to the U.S. Army Corps of Engineers, St. Paul District; contract no. DACW 37-85-M-1113. Reports of Investigations, no. 15. Minneapolis: Institute for Minnesota Archaeology.

1990   Letter to Scott [F.] Anfinson, SHPO, Sept. 11, regarding investigations by the Institute for Minnesota Archaeology at the Granite Falls Bison Kill Site (21YM47). Copy in SHPO.

Dobbs, C. A., and O. C. Shane III

1982   "Oneota Settlement Patterns in the Blue Earth River Valley, Minnesota." In *Oneota Studies*, ed. Gibbon, 55–68.

Eddy, S., and T. Surber

1947   *Northern Fishes: With Special Reference to the Upper Mississippi Valley.* Rev. ed. Minneapolis: University of Minnesota Press.

Edman, F. R.

1969   *A Study of Wild Rice in Minnesota: A Staff Report.* Minnesota Resources Commission Staff Report, no. 14. [St. Paul]: The Commission.

Eggers, A. V.

1985   "Final Report: Historical and Archaeological Survey of the Big Stone National Wildlife Refuge," by Eggers et al. Prepared for the U.S. Department of the Interior, Fish and Wildlife Service; contract no. 14-16-0003-83-125. Playa del Rey, Calif.: Geoscientific Systems and Consulting.

Ernst, C. H., and L. French

1977   "Mammals of Southwestern Minnesota." *Journal* (Minnesota Academy of Science), vol. 43, no. 1:28–31.

Featherstonhaugh, G. W.

1970   *A Canoe Voyage Up the Minnay Sotor, with an Account of the Lead and Copper Deposits in Wisconsin; of the Gold Region in the Cherokee Country; and Sketches of Popular Manners.* 2 vols. London: Richard Bentley, 1847. Reprint. St. Paul: Minnesota Historical Society.

Felch, R. E.

1978   "Drought: Characteristics and Assessment." In *North American Droughts*, ed. N. J. Rosenberg, 25–42. American Association for the Advancement of Science; AAAS Selected Symposium, 15. Boulder, Colo.: Westview Press.

Fenton, M. M., S. R. Moran, J. T. Teller, and L. Clayton

1983 "Quaternary Stratigraphy and History in the Southern Part of the Lake Agassiz Basin." In *Glacial Lake Agassiz,* ed. Teller and Clayton, 49–74.

Fisher, A. K., W. D. Frankforter, J. A. Tiffany, S. J. Schermer, and D. C. Anderson

1985 "Turin: A Middle Archaic Burial Site in Western Iowa." *Plains Anthropologist,* vol. 30, no. 109:195–218.

Fitting, J. E.

1978 "Regional Cultural Development, 300 B.C. to A.D. 1000." In *Northeast,* ed. B. G. Trigger, 44–57. *Handbook of North American Indians,* vol. 15. Washington, D.C.: Smithsonian Institution.

Flanders, R. E.

1977 "The Soldow Site, 13BH1: An Archaic Component from North Central Iowa." *Journal of the Iowa Archeological Society* 24:125–47.

Flanders, R. E., and R. Hansman

1961 "A Woodland Mound Complex in Webster County, Iowa." *Journal of the Iowa Archeological Society,* vol. 11, no. 1 (July):1–12.

Fortier, A. C., T. E. Emerson, and F. A. Finney

1984 "Early Woodland and Middle Woodland Periods." In *American Bottom Archaeology,* ed. Bareis and Porter, 59–103.

Fowler, M. L.

1955 "Ware Groupings and Decorations of Woodland Ceramics in Illinois." *American Antiquity* 20:213–25.

Frison, G. C.

1978 *Prehistoric Hunters of the High Plains.* New World Archaeological Record. New York: Academic Press.

Fryklund, P. O.

1941 "Fellow Members of the Minnesota Archaeological Society"; "A Catalog of Copper from Roseau County, Minnesota." *Minnesota Archaeologist,* vol. 7, no. 3 (July):4; 5–16.

Geier, C. R.

1978 "An Analysis of the Pottery Assemblage from the Hog Hollow Site: A Transitional Middle\Late Woodland Habitation in the Mississippi River Valley." *Wisconsin Archeologist,* n.s., 59:151–245.

Geyer, Karl A. (Charles A. Geyer)

1838 Botanical journal. Photocopy in Minnesota Historical Society Collections, St. Paul.

Gibbon, G. E.

1978 "A Simplified Algorithm Model for the Classification of Silvernale and Blue Earth Phase Ceramic Vessels." In *Some Studies,* ed. A. Woolworth and Hall, 3–11.

1982 *Oneota Studies,* ed. Gibbon. University of Minnesota Publications in Anthropology, no. 1. Minneapolis: University of Minnesota, Department of Anthropology.

1983a "The Blue Earth Phase in Southern Minnesota." *Journal of the Iowa Archeological Society* 30:1–84.

1983b *Prairie Archaeology: Papers in Honor of David A. Baerreis,* ed. Gibbon. Publications in Anthropology, no. 3. Minneapolis: Department of Anthropology, University of Minnesota.

1986 "Does Minnesota Have an Early Woodland?" In *Early Woodland Archeology,* ed. K. B. Farnsworth and T. E. Emerson, 84–91. Kampsville Seminars in Archeology, vol. 2. Kampsville, Ill.: Center for American Archeology Press.

Gilmore, M. R.

1977 *Uses of Plants by the Indians of the Missouri River Region.* Ph.D. diss., University of Nebraska, 1914. In *Thirty-Third Annual Report of the Bureau of American Ethnology,* 1911–12 (Washington, D.C.: GPO, 1919), 43–154. Reprint. Enlarged ed. Lincoln: University of Nebraska Press, Bison Books.

Green, J. C., and R. B. Janssen

1975 *Minnesota Birds: Where, When, and How Many.* Minneapolis: Published by the University of Minnesota Press for the James Ford Bell Museum of Natural History.

Gregg, M. L.

1987 "Archeological Excavation at the Naze Site (32SN246)," ed. Gregg. Prepared for the U.S. Department of the Interior, Bureau of Reclamation, Missouri Basin Region, Billings, Mont., in partial fulfillment of contract 4-CS-60-00630, work order no. 5 between the Bureau and the University of North Dakota.

1990 "An Early Plains Woodland Structure in the Northeastern Plains." *Plains Anthropologist,* vol. 35, no. 127:29–44.

Gregg, M. L., and P. R. Picha

1989 "Early Plains Woodland and Middle Plains Woodland Occupation of the James River Region in Southeastern North Dakota." *Midcontinental Journal of Archaeology*, vol. 14, no. 1:38–61.

Greiser, S. T.

1985 "Predictive Models of Hunter-Gatherer Subsistence and Settlement Strategies on the Central High Plains." *Plains Anthropologist*, Memoir 20, vol. 30, no. 110, pt. 2.

Griffin, J. B.

1952 "Some Early and Middle Woodland Pottery Types in Illinois." In *Hopewellian Communities in Illinois*, ed. T. Deuel, 93–128. Scientific Papers, vol. 5, no. 3. Springfield: Illinois State Museum.

1960 "Climatic Change: A Contributory Cause of the Growth and Decline of Northern Hopewellian Culture." *Wisconsin Archeologist*, n.s., 41:21–33.

Grimm, E. C.

1984 "Fire and Other Factors Controlling the Big Woods Vegetation of Minnesota in the Mid-Nineteenth Century." *Ecological Monographs* (Ecological Society of America), vol. 54, no. 3:291–311.

1985 "Vegetation History along the Prairie-Forest Border in Minnesota." In *Archaeology*, ed. Spector and Johnson, 9–30.

Haberman, T. W.

1981 "Floral Remains." In "Archaeological Excavations," ed. Hannus, 203–26.

Hannus, L. A.

1981 "Archaeological Excavations at 39BK7: Oakwood Lakes Bank/Shoreline Protection Project: Area 1: #S 804714-01-3: Brookings County, South Dakota: Fall 1979," ed. Hannus. Submitted to the South Dakota Department of Water and Natural Resources. Contract Investigations Series, no. 33. N.p.: South Dakota Archaeological Research Center.

1982 "Cultural Resource Investigations of the South Dakota Segment of the Northern Border Pipeline Project: Intensive Archaeological Survey, Testing and Mitigation in McPherson, Edmunds, Brown, Spink, Clark, Codington, Hamlin, Deuel and Brookings Counties, South Dakota," by Hannus et al. South Dakota State University, principal contractor. Prepared for the Northern Plains Natural Gas Company; contract agreement dated Sept. 4, 1979.

1985 "An Overview and Summary of the Archeology of the Northern Border Pipeline Project in Montana, North Dakota, South Dakota, Minnesota and Iowa." Prepared for the Northern Border Pipeline Company, Omaha, Nebraska.

Hannus, L. A., R. P. Winham, and E. J. Lueck

1986 "Cultural Resource Reconnaissance Survey of Portions of Moody, Lincoln and Union Counties, South Dakota [within the Upper and Lower Big Sioux and Yankton Study Units] with Reports on the Heath Site (39LN15) and the Blood Run/Rock Island Site (13LO2/39LN2)." Submitted to the Historical Preservation Center, Vermillion, S.Dak. Archeological Contract Series, no. 26. Sioux Falls, S.Dak.: Archeology Laboratory of the Center for Western Studies, Augustana College.

Harlan, J. R., and E. B. Speaker

1969 *Iowa Fish and Fishing*. 4th ed. [Des Moines]: Iowa State Conservation Commission.

Harrison, C.

1985 *The Archaeology of Two Lakes in Minnesota*. Cultural Resource Series, no. 2. [Alexandria, Va.]: U.S. Bureau of Land Management, Eastern States Office.

Harvey, A. E.

1979 *Oneota Culture in Northwestern Iowa*. Report, 12. Iowa City: Office of the State Archaeologist, University of Iowa.

Haug, J. K.

1977 "A Great Oasis Site in Marshall County." *Newsletter of the South Dakota Archaeological Society*, vol. 7, no. 2:5.

1979 "An Archaeological Test Excavation at the Garden Site, 39DE6." *Newsletter of the South Dakota Archaeological Society*, vol. 9, no. 4:1–7.

1982 "Excavations at the Winter Site and at Hartford Beach Village: 1980–1981." Fort Meade: South Dakota Archaeological Research Center, Office of Cultural Preservation, Department of Education and Cultural Affairs.

1983a "Early Plains Village Sites in Northeastern South Dakota." Paper presented at the 41st annual Plains Conference, Rapid City, S.Dak., Nov. 2–5.

1983b "Winter and Hartford Beach Site Carbon Dates Received." *Newsletter of the South Dakota Archaeological Society*, vol. 13, no. 1 (Apr.):4.

Haug, J. K., and B. Sterner

1978 "Projectile Points from the Ries Site." *Newsletter of the South Dakota Archaeological Society*, vol. 8, no. 4:1–2.

Haworth, E. Y.

1972 "Diatom Succession in a Core from Pickerel Lake, Northeastern South Dakota." *Geological Society of America Bulletin* 83 (Jan.):157–72.

Henning, D. R.

1967 "Mississippian Influences on the Eastern Plains Border: An Evaluation." *Plains Anthropologist,* vol. 12, no. 36:184–94.

1970 "Development and Interrelationships of Oneota Culture in the Lower Missouri River Valley." *Missouri Archaeologist* 32 (Dec.):3–180.

1971 "Great Oasis Culture Distributions." In *Prehistoric Investigations,* ed. M. McKusick, 125–33. Report, 3. Iowa City, Iowa: Office of the State Archaeologist, University of Iowa.

1973 "Plains Villages: Eastern Periphery of the Plains." Ms. Copy in author's possession.

1983a "The Initial Variant of the Middle Missouri Tradition." In "Archaeological Reconnaissance Survey," by Hudak, 1:4.42–4.65.

1983b "The Oneota Cultural Tradition." In "Archaeological Reconnaissance Survey," by Hudak, 1: 4.66–4.79.

Henning, D. R., and E. R. Henning

1978 "Great Oasis Ceramics." In *Some Studies,* ed. A. Woolworth and Hall, 12–26.

Hickerson, H.

1970 *The Chippewa and Their Neighbors: A Study in Ethnohistory.* New York: Holt, Rinehart & Winston.

Hodge, W. T.

1974 "The Climate of South Dakota." In *Climates of the States,* by the U.S. National Oceanic and Atmospheric Administration, 2:861–76.

Howard, J. H.

1968 "Archeological Investigations at the Spawn Mound, 39LK201, Lake County, South Dakota." *Plains Anthropologist,* vol. 13, no. 40:132–45.

Hudak, G. J.

1971 "Archaeological Site Survey: Southwestern Minnesota, 1971." Copy in SHPO.

1972a "Boulder Outlines in Southwestern Minnesota." *Plains Anthropologist,* vol. 17, no. 58, pt. 1:345–46.

1972b "Excavations at the Thompson Site (21MU17)." Copy in SHPO.

1974 "The Pedersen Site (21LN2), Lincoln County, Minnesota." Master's thesis, University of Nebraska.

1976 *Woodland Ceramics from the Pedersen Site.* Scientific Publications of the Science Museum of Minnesota, n.s., vol. 3, no. 2. St. Paul: The Museum.

1978 "Archaeological Survey and Mitigation of Sites Near Granite Falls, Minnesota: S.P. 8701-25 (TH 23), Minn. Proj. F23-2 (37), Approximately 1.5 Miles South of Granite Falls, Yellow Medicine County, Minnesota"; Hudak, project director. [St. Paul: Science Museum of Minnesota.]

1983 "An Archaeological Reconnaissance Survey of the Northern Border Pipeline for the Northern Plains Natural Gas Company: Minnesota Segment," by Hudak et al. 3 vols. [Stillwater, Minn.]: Archaeological Field Services, Inc. Copy in SHPO.

Hudak, G. J., and E. Johnson

1975 *An Early Woodland Pottery Vessel from Minnesota.* Scientific Publications of the Science Museum of Minnesota, n.s., vol. 2, no. 4. St. Paul: The Museum.

Hudson, L.

1979 "State's Oldest Human Dwelling Believed Found Near Mt. Lake." *Minnesota Archaeologist,* vol. 38, no. 1:26–31.

Hurley, W. M.

1966 "The Silver Creek Sites (47-Mo-1 to Mo-5): A Complex of Five Woodland Site Locations in Monroe County, Wisconsin." Master's thesis, University of Wisconsin, Madison.

1975 *An Analysis of Effigy Mound Complexes in Wisconsin.* Anthropological Papers, no. 59. Ann Arbor: Museum of Anthropology, University of Michigan.

Irwin-Williams, C., H. Irwin, G. Agogino, and C. V. Haynes

1973 "Hell Gap: Paleo-Indian Occupation on the High Plains." *Plains Anthropologist,* vol. 18, no. 59:40–53.

Ives, J. C.

1962 "Mill Creek Pottery." *Journal of the Iowa Archeological Society,* vol. 11, no. 3 (Mar.):1–59.

Jelgersma, S.

1962 "A Late-Glacial Pollen Diagram from Madelia, South-Central Minnesota." *American Journal of Science* 260 (summer):522–29.

Jenks, A. E.

1897–98 "The Wild Rice Gatherers of the Upper Lakes: A Study in American Primitive Economics." In *Nineteenth Annual Report of the Bureau of American Ethnology,* 1897–98, pt. 2:1013–1137. Washington, D.C.: GPO, 1900.

1935 "Recent Discoveries in Minnesota Prehistory." *Minnesota History* 16 (Mar.):1–21.

1936 *Pleistocene Man in Minnesota: A Fossil Homo Sapiens.* Minneapolis: University of Minnesota Press.

1937   "Minnesota's Browns Valley Man and Associated
            Burial Artifacts." *Memoirs* (American Anthropo-
            logical Association), no. 49.

Johnson, A. E., and W. R. Wood

1980   "Prehistoric Studies on the Plains." In *Anthropol-
            ogy on the Great Plains,* ed. W. R. Wood and
            M. Liberty, 35–51. Lincoln: University of
            Nebraska Press.

Johnson, C. M.

1973   "House Four at Broken Kettle West." Ms. on file,
            Department of Anthropology, University of
            Nebraska, Lincoln.

1991   "Archaeological Reconnaissance Investigations in
            Traverse County, Minnesota." Prepared for the
            Minnesota Historical Society. Reports of
            Investigations, no. 150. Minneapolis: Institute for
            Minnesota Archaeology. Copy in SHPO.

Johnson, E.

1959   "An Archaic Horizon Cache from Southern Min-
            nesota." *Proceedings* (Minnesota Academy of
            Science) 27:3–5.

1961   "Cambria Burial Mounds in Big Stone County."
            Minnesota Archaeologist, vol. 23, no. 3
            (July):53–81.

1964a   *An Archaeology Program for Minnesota, Pre-
            pared by MORRC in Cooperation with Elden
            Johnson and the Minnesota Historical Society.*
            Minnesota, Legislature, Minnesota Outdoor
            Recreation Resources Commission report, no. 5.
            St. Paul: The Commission.

1964b   "Twenty New Radiocarbon Dates from Minne-
            sota Archeological Sites." *Minnesota Archaeolo-
            gist,* vol. 26, no. 2 (Apr.):34–49.

1969   "Decorative Motifs on Great Oasis Pottery."
            Plains Anthropologist, vol. 14, no. 46:272–76.

1973   *The Arvilla Complex.* Based on field notes by
            L. A. Wilford. Minnesota Prehistoric Archaeology
            Series, no. 9. St. Paul: Minnesota Historical
            Society.

1974   "Lloyd A. Wilford and Minnesota Archaeology."
            In *Aspects of Upper Great Lakes Anthropology:
            Papers in Honor of Lloyd A. Wilford,* ed. E.
            Johnson, 1–7. Minnesota Prehistoric Archaeology
            Series, no. 11. St. Paul: Minnesota Historical
            Society.

1986   "Cambria and Cahokia's Northwestern Periph-
            ery." Paper presented at the 51st annual meeting
            of the Society for American Archaeology, New
            Orleans, La., Apr. 23–26. Copy in author's
            possession.

1988   *The Prehistoric Peoples of Minnesota.* Rev. 3d ed.
            Minnesota Prehistoric Archaeology Series, no. 3.
            St. Paul: Minnesota Historical Society Press.

Johnson, W. C.

1971   "Noteworthy Plants of the North Dakota Prairie
            Coteau Forest." *Prairie Naturalist,* vol. 3, no. 1
            (Mar.):31–32.

Justin, M.

1991   "Final Archaeological Survey and Site Assessment
            Report and Cultural Resource Management Rec-
            ommendations: Proposed Minnesota Department
            of Transportation S. P. 2102-19 for Reconstruc-
            tion of T. H. 27 from 0.2 Miles West CSAH 4 at
            Holmes City to 1.0 Mile West of T. H. 2 in
            Alexandria, Douglas County." Minnesota Trunk
            Highway Archaeological Reconnaissance Survey.
            St. Paul: Minnesota Historical Society. Copy in
            SHPO.

Keating, W. H.

1959   *Narrative of an Expedition to the Source of
            St. Peter's River, Lake Winnepeek, Lake of the
            Woods, &c. Performed in the Year 1823, by
            Order of the Hon. J. C. Calhoun, Secretary of
            War, under the Command of Stephen H. Long.* 2
            vols. Philadelphia: H. C. Carey & I. Lea, 1824.
            London: G. B. Whittaker, 1825. Reprint of 1825
            ed. 2 vols. in 1. Minneapolis: Ross & Haines.

Kehoe, T. F.

1966   "The Small Side-Notched Point System of the
            Northern Plains." *American Antiquity*
            31:827–41.

1974   "The Large Corner-Notched Point System of the
            Northern Plains and Adjacent Woodlands." In
            Aspects, ed. E. Johnson, 103–14.

Keller, R.

1982   "Literature Search." In "Cultural Resource Inves-
            tigations," by Hannus et al., 5.1–5.17.

Keslin, R. O.

1958   "A Preliminary Report on the Hahn (Dg 1 and
            Dg 2) and Horicon (Dg 5) Sites, Dodge County,
            Wisconsin." *Wisconsin Archeologist,* n.s.,
            39:191–273.

Keyes, C. R.

1928   "The Hill-Lewis Archeological Survey." *Minne-
            sota History* 9 (June):96–108.

1940   "Report on the Work of the Iowa Archaeological
            Survey." *Iowa Journal of History and Politics*
            38:94–96.

Knauth, O.

1963   "The Mystery of the Crosses." *Annals of Iowa,*
            3d ser., 37:81–91.

Knudson, R. (R. K. Shay)

1966   "Cambria Village Ceramics." Master's thesis, University of Minnesota.

1967   "Cambria Village Ceramics." *Plains Anthropologist,* vol. 12, no. 37:247–99.

Kopischke, E. D.

1962   "A Blue Earth River Village Site in Minnesota." *Minnesota Archaeologist,* vol. 24, no. 3 (July):74–82.

Küchler, A. W.

1964   *Potential Natural Vegetation of the Conterminous United States.* Map and accompanying manual. Special Publication, no. 36. New York: American Geographical Society.

Kuehnast, E. L.

1974   "The Climate of Minnesota." In *Climates of the States,* by the U.S. National Oceanic and Atmospheric Administration, 2:706–24.

Landes, R.

1968   *The Mystic Lake Sioux: Sociology of the Mdewakantonwan Santee.* Madison: University of Wisconsin Press.

Lane, R. B.

1974   "An Archaeological Surface Survey of Dome Pipeline Corporation's Proposed Pipeline Right-of-Way across the State of Minnesota: May–September 1974." Prepared for the Corporation; contract dated Apr. 19, 1974. Copy in SHPO.

Lass, B. M.

1980a   "Prehistoric Habitation in Northeastern South Dakota: Glimpses from Deuel and Hamlim Counties." Master's thesis, University of Minnesota.

1980b   "Radiocarbon Dates from Minnesota Archaeological Sites to 1979." *Minnesota Archaeologist,* vol. 39, no. 1:29–39.

Lehmer, D. J.

1954a   *Archeological Investigations in the Oahe Dam Area, South Dakota, 1950–51.* In *River Basin Surveys Papers,* no. 7. Smithsonian Institution, Bureau of American Ethnology, Bulletin 158. Washington, D.C.: GPO.

1954b   "The Sedentary Horizon of the Northern Plains." *Southwestern Journal of Anthropology* 10 (summer):139–59.

1971   *Introduction to Middle Missouri Archeology.* Anthropological Papers, 1. Washington, D.C.: U.S. Department of the Interior, National Park Service.

Lensink, S. C.

1981a   "Archaeological Investigations in the Prairie Pothole Region of Northcentral Iowa." Ms. Copy in author's possession.

1981b   "Modeling Prehistoric Population Density Using Projectile Point Data." Paper presented at the Midwestern Archaeological Conference, University of Wisconsin-Madison, Oct. 16–18. Copy in author's possession.

1984   "A Quantitative Model of Central-Place Foraging among Prehistoric Hunter-Gatherers." Ph.D. diss., University of Iowa.

Lewis, S. E., and P. M. Heikes

1990   "A Preliminary Report on a Paleo-Indian Bison Kill Site (21YM47) Near Granite Falls, Minnesota." *IMA Quarterly Newsletter* (Institute for Minnesota Archaeology), vol. 5, no. 3 (June):[4]–[5].

Lewis, T. H.

1886   "Mounds on the Red River of the North." *American Antiquarian* 8 (Nov.):369–71.

1889   "Stone Monuments in Southern Dakota." *American Anthropologist* 2:159–65.

1890   "Effigy-Mound in the Valley of the Big Sioux River, Iowa." *Science,* o.s., vol. 15, no. 378, May 2, p. 275.

1891   "Bowlder *[sic]* Outline Figures in the Dakotas, Surveyed in the Summer of 1890." *American Anthropologist* 4:19–24.

Lofstrom, T.

1988   "A Possible Altithermal Habitation Site in Faribault County." *Minnesota Archaeologist,* vol. 47, no. 2:51–58.

Logan, W. D.

1976   *Woodland Complexes in Northeastern Iowa.* Publications in Archeology, 15. Washington, D.C.: U.S. Department of the Interior, National Park Service.

Long, Stephen H.

1978   *The Northern Expeditions of Stephen H. Long: The Journals of 1817 and 1823 and Related Documents,* ed. L. M. Kane, J. D. Holmquist, and C. Gilman. St. Paul: Minnesota Historical Society Press.

Lothson, G. A.

1976   *The Jeffers Petroglyphs Site: A Survey and Analysis of the Carvings.* Minnesota Prehistoric Archaeology Series, no. 12. St. Paul: Minnesota Historical Society.

1983   *The Alton Anderson Site (21WW4), Watonwan County, Minnesota.* Occasional Publications in

Minnesota Anthropology, no. 4. St. Paul: Minnesota Archaeological Society.

Lucking, L.

[1977]   "The Prehistoric and Protohistoric Peoples of Otter Tail County." Ms. Copy in SHPO.

Ludwickson, J., D. Blakeslee, and J. O'Shea

1981   "Missouri National Recreational River: Native American Cultural Resources." Prepared for the Heritage Conservation and Recreation Service, Interagency Archeological Services-Denver, under contract no. C53011 (80).

Lueck, E. J., R. P. Winham, and L. A. Hannus

1987   "Cultural Resource Reconnaissance Survey of Portions of Lake County, South Dakota within the Vermillion Basin and Upper Big Sioux Archeological Regions of South Dakota: With Reports on the Hilde Mound Site (39LK7), Christiansen's Point Site (39LK18), Site 39LK15, and Site 39LK16." Submitted to the Historical Preservation Center, Vermillion, S.Dak. Archeological Contract Series, no. 32. Sioux Falls, S.Dak.: Archeology Laboratory of the Center for Western Studies, Augustana College.

Lugenbeal, E. N.

1982   "The Ceramics of the White Oak Point Site." Minnesota Archaeologist, vol. 41, no. 2 (fall–winter):5–33.

Lukens, P. W.

1963   "Some Ethnozoological Implications of Mammalian Faunas from Minnesota Archeological Sites." Ph.D. diss., University of Minnesota.

Lynch, T. F.

1988   "Current Research," ed. Lynch. American Antiquity 53:627–51.

1990   "Glacial-Age Man in South America? A Critical Review." American Antiquity 55:12–36.

McNerney, M. J.

1970   "A Description of Chipped Stone Artifacts from Northeastern South Dakota." Plains Anthropologist, vol. 15, no. 50, pt. 1:291–96.

Mallam, R. C., and E. A. Bettis III

[1979?]   "The Iowa Northern Tier Archaeological Project." Ms. Copy in author's possession.

1981   "The E. B. Stillman Site: Archaeological Investigations in Hungry Hollow." Ms. Copy in author's possession.

Manson, P. W., G. M. Schwartz, and E. R. Allred

1968   Some Aspects of the Hydrology of Ponds and Small Lakes. Technical Bulletin 257. [St. Anthony Park]: Agricultural Experiment Station, University of Minnesota.

Martin, L. D., R. A. Rogers, and A. M. Neuner

1985   "The Effect of the End of the Pleistocene on Man in North America." In Environments and Extinctions: Man in Late Glacial North America, ed. J. I. Mead and D. J. Meltzer, 15–30. Peopling of the Americas; Edited Volume Series. Orono, Maine: Center for the Study of Early Man, University of Maine at Orono.

Martin, P. S., and H. E. Wright Jr., eds.

1967   Pleistocene Extinctions: The Search for a Cause, by the International Association for Quaternary Research. New Haven: Yale University Press.

Mason, C.

1964   "An Early Woodland Vessel from Wisconsin." Wisconsin Archeologist, n.s., 45:158–60.

Mason, R. J.

1981   Great Lakes Archaeology. New York: Academic Press.

Matsch, C. L.

1972   "Quaternary Geology of Southwestern Minnesota." In Geology of Minnesota: A Centennial Volume in Honor of George M. Schwartz, ed. P. K. Sims and G. B. Morey, 548–60. [St. Paul]: Minnesota Geological Survey.

Matsch, C. L., R. H. Rutford, and M. J. Tipton

1972   "Quaternary Geology of Northeastern South Dakota and Southwestern Minnesota." In Field Trip Guide Book, by the Minnesota Geological Survey, 1–34.

Matsch, C. L., and H. E. Wright Jr.

1969   "The Southern Outlet of Lake Agassiz." In Life, ed. Mayer-Oakes, 121–40.

Mayer-Oakes, W. J., ed.

1969   Life, Land and Water: Proceedings, by the Conference on Environmental Studies of the Glacial Lake Agassiz Region (1966: University of Manitoba). University of Manitoba, Department of Anthropology, Occasional Papers, no. 1. Winnipeg: University of Manitoba Press.

Meltzer, D. J.

1989   "Why Don't We Know When the First People Came to North America?" American Antiquity 54:471–90.

Meyer, R. W.

1967   History of the Santee Sioux: United States Indian Policy on Trial. Lincoln: University of Nebraska Press.

Michlovic, M. G.

1979   *The Dead River Site (21 OT 51).* Occasional Publications in Minnesota Anthropology, no. 6. St. Paul: Minnesota Archaeological Society.

1980   "Ecotonal Settlement and Subsistence in the Northern Midwest." *Midcontinental Journal of Archaeology,* vol. 5, no. 2:151–67.

1983   "The Red River Valley in the Prehistory of the Northern Plains." *Plains Anthropologist,* vol. 28, no. 99:23–31.

1985   "The Problem of the Teton Migration." In *Archaeology,* ed. Spector and Johnson, 131–45.

1986   "Cultural Evolutionism and Plains Archaeology." *Plains Anthropologist,* vol. 31, no. 113:207–18.

Michlovic, M. G., and F. Schneider

1988   "The Archaeology of the Shea Site (32 CS 101)." Submitted to the State Historical Society of North Dakota.

Miller, M. E., M. D. Stafford, and G. W. Brox

1991   "The John Gale Site Biface Cache." *Plains Anthropologist,* vol. 36, no. 133:43–56.

Miller, P.

1980   "Dig Unearths Clues to Vanished Prairie Tribe." *Midland Cooperator* (Midland Cooperatives, Inc., Superior, Wis.), Mar. 24, p. 6.

Miller, P. A.

1980   "Archaic Lithics from the Coffey Site." In *Archaic Prehistory on the Prairie-Plains Border,* ed. A. E. Johnson, 107–11. Publications in Anthropology, no. 12. Lawrence: University of Kansas.

Minnesota, Waters Section

1968   *An Inventory of Minnesota Lakes.* Bulletin, no. 25. St. Paul: The Section, Division of Waters, Soils, and Minerals, Minnesota Conservation Department.

Minnesota Geological Survey

1972   *Field Trip Guide Book for Geomorphology and Quaternary Stratigraphy of Western Minnesota and Eastern South Dakota.* Guidebook Series, no. 7. St. Paul: Minnesota Geological Survey, University of Minnesota.

Minnesota Historical Records Survey Project

1941   *Report of the Chippewa Mission Archaeological Investigation.* St. Paul: The Project, Division of Community Service Programs, Work Projects Administration.

Minnesota Historical Society

1979   *Historic Resources in Minnesota: A Report on Their Extent, Location, and Need for Preservation: Submitted to the Minnesota Legislature.* St. Paul: The Society.

1981   *Minnesota Statewide Archaeological Survey Summary, 1977–1980: Submitted to the Minnesota Legislature.* St. Paul: The Society.

Minnesota State Planning Agency, Water Resources Coordinating Committee

1970   *Minnesota Water and Related Land Resources, First Assessment.* St. Paul.

Montet-White, A.

1968   *The Lithic Industries of the Illinois Valley in the Early and Middle Woodland Period.* Museum of Anthropology, Anthropological Papers, no. 35. Ann Arbor: University of Michigan.

Morey, G. B.

1981   *Geologic Map of Minnesota: Bedrock Outcrops.* State Map Series, vol. S-10. [St. Paul]: Minnesota Geological Survey, University of Minnesota.

Morrow, T.

1984   *Iowa Projectile Points.* Special Publication. Iowa City: Office of the State Archaeologist, University of Iowa.

Moyer, L. R.

1906–10a "The Prairie Flora of Southwestern Minnesota." *Bulletin* (Minnesota Academy of Science) 4:357–72.

1906–10b "The Prairie Legumes of Western Minnesota." *Bulletin* 4:373–78.

Moyle, J. B.

1945   "Classification of Lake Waters upon the Basis of Hardness." *Proceedings* (Minnesota Academy of Science) 13:8–12.

1965   *Big Game in Minnesota,* ed. Moyle. Technical Bulletin, no. 9. [St. Paul?]: Minnesota Department of Conservation, Division of Game and Fish, Section of Research and Planning.

Munson, P. J.

1982   "Marion, Black Sand, and Havana Relationships: An Illinois Valley Perspective." *Wisconsin Archeologist,* n.s., 63:1–17.

Nelson, L. S.

1973   "The Results of the Archaeological Survey in Portions of Southeastern North Dakota, Northeastern South Dakota, and West-Central Minnesota." Copy in SHPO.

Neuman, R. W.

1975   *The Sonota Complex and Associated Sites on the Northern Great Plains.* Publications in Anthropology, no. 6. Lincoln: Nebraska State Historical Society.

Nicholson, B. A.

1989 "Modeling a Horticultural Complex in South-Central Manitoba during the Late Prehistoric Period—The Pelican Lake Focus." Paper presented at the 47th annual Plains Conference, Sioux Falls, S.Dak., Oct. 18–21.

Nickerson, W. B.

1988 "Archaeological Evidences in Minnesota." *Minnesota Archaeologist,* vol. 47, no. 2:4–40.

Nicollet, J. N.

1976 *Joseph N. Nicollet on the Plains and Prairies: The Expeditions of 1838–39 with Journals, Letters, and Notes on the Dakota Indians,* trans. and ed. E. C. Bray and M. C. Bray. St. Paul: Minnesota Historical Society Press.

Norquist, C. L.

1967a "Albert Lea Lake Salvage Project." *Minnesota Archaeological Newsletter* (Department of Anthropology, University of Minnesota), no. 12 (fall):1–4.

1967b "An Historic Indian Burial in Southwestern Renville County (21 RN 14)." *Minnesota Archaeologist,* vol. 29, no. 1:18–19.

Nowak, T. R.

1981 "Lithic Analysis of the Oakwood Lakes Site (39BK7), Brookings County, South Dakota: A Woodland Period Stone Tool Assemblage of the Northeastern Prairie Periphery." In "Archaeological Excavations," ed. Hannus, 51–152.

Nowak, T. R., and L. A. Hannus

1982 "Lithic Analysis: Part IV: Projectile Point Analysis." In "Cultural Resource Investigations," by Hannus, 18.1–18.73.

Nystuen, D. W., and C. G. Lindeman

1969 *The Excavation of Fort Renville: An Archaeological Report.* Minnesota Historical Archaeology Series, no. 2. St. Paul: Minnesota Historical Society.

Orr, E.

1914 "Indian Pottery of the Oneota or Upper Iowa River Valley in Northeastern Iowa." *Proceedings* (Iowa Academy of Science) 21:231–39.

Peterson, L. D., T. A. Olmanson, and W. W. Radford, eds.

[1990] "The Minnesota Trunk Highway Archaeological Reconnaissance Study: Annual Report 1989." Submitted in accordance with agreement 73877. A cooperative program of the Minnesota Department of Transportation; the U.S. Department of Transportation, Federal Highway Administration; and the Minnesota Historical Society. Copy in SHPO.

Phillips, J. L., and J. A. Brown, eds.

1983 *Archaic Hunters and Gatherers in the American Midwest.* New World Archaeological Record. New York: Academic Press.

Pond, S. W.

1986 *The Dakota or Sioux in Minnesota As They Were in 1834.* Reprint of "The Dakotas or Sioux in Minnesota As They Were in 1834," *Minnesota Historical Society Collections* 12 (1908):319–501. St. Paul: Minnesota Historical Society Press, Borealis Books.

Pratt, D.

1989 "New Occupation Level Found at Granite Falls Bison Kill Site." *IMA Quarterly Newsletter* (Institute for Minnesota Archaeology), vol. 4, no. 4 (Dec.):[2].

Radiocarbon

1986 Radiocarbon correction tables. Vol. 28, passim.

Radle, N. J.

1981 "Vegetation History and Lake-level Changes at a Saline Lake in Northeastern South Dakota." Master's thesis, University of Minnesota.

Radle, N. J., C. E. Keister, and R. W. Battarbee

1989 "Diatom, Pollen, and Geochemical Evidence for the Paleosalinity of Medicine Lake, S. Dakota, during the Late Wisconsin and Early Holocene." *Journal of Paleolimnology* 2:159–72.

Ready, T.

1979 "Cambria Phase." In *Handbook,* comp. and ed. Anfinson, 51–65.

Reeder, R. L.

1980 "The Sohn Site: A Lowland Nebo Hill Complex Campsite." In *Archaic Prehistory on the Prairie-Plains Border,* ed. A. E. Johnson, 55–66. Publications in Anthropology, no. 12. Lawrence: University of Kansas.

Reeves, B.

1973 "The Concept of an Altithermal Cultural Hiatus in Northern Plains Prehistory." *American Anthropologist* 75:1221–53.

Risser, P. G., E. C. Birney, H. D. Blocker, S. W. May, W. J. Parton, and J. A. Wiens

1981 *The True Prairie Ecosystem.* US/IBP Synthesis Series, vol. 16. Stroudsburg, Pa.: Hutchinson Ross Publishing Co.; [New York]: distributed by Academic Press.

Ritzenthaler, R. E.

1967 *A Guide to Wisconsin Indian Projectile Point Types.* Popular Science Series, vol. 11. Milwaukee, Wis.: Milwaukee Public Museum.

Roe, F. G.

1970   *The North American Buffalo: A Critical Study of the Species in its Wild State.* 2d ed. Toronto: University of Toronto Press.

Rood, R. J., and V. O. Rood

1984–85   "Archeological Resources along the Coteau des Prairies in Roberts and Marshall Counties, South Dakota." *South Dakota Archaeology* 8–9:53–79.

Rothrock, E. P., and D. Ullery

1938   *Ground Water Fluctuations in Eastern South Dakota.* South Dakota State Geological Survey; Report of Investigations, no. 30. Vermillion: University of South Dakota.

Ruhe, R. V.

1969   *Quaternary Landscapes in Iowa.* Ames: Iowa State University Press.

Salzer, R. J.

1974   "The Wisconsin North Lakes Project: A Preliminary Report." In *Aspects,* ed. E. Johnson, 40–54.

Scaglion, R.

1980   "The Plains Culture Area Concept." In *Anthropology on the Great Plains,* ed. W. R. Wood and M. Liberty, 23–34. Lincoln: University of Nebraska Press.

Scullin, M.

1979   "Price Site (21BE25) [21BE36]: Preliminary Notes on a Previously Unidentified Site of the Cambria Focus." Ms. Copy in author's possession.

1981   "Minnesota's First Farmers? Late Woodland Ceramics and Maize on the Blue Earth River (The Nelson Site: 21BE24)." Ms. Copy in author's possession.

Sellards, E. H.

1952   *Early Man in America.* Austin: University of Texas Press.

Semken, H. A., Jr.

1982   "Mammalian Remains." In *Preliminary Report,* ed. Tiffany, 119–32.

Shane, L. C. K.

1980   "Seed Analyses: Price Site (21BE25), Blue Earth County, MN." Ms. Copy in author's possession.

Shane, O. C., III

1978   *The Vertebrate Fauna of the Mountain Lake Site, Cottonwood County, Minnesota.* Scientific Publications of the Science Museum of Minnesota, n.s., vol. 4, no. 2. St. Paul: The Museum.

1981   "Radiocarbon Chronology for the Late Prehistoric Period in Southern Minnesota." Report on grant no. 8576. *Year Book 1980,* 409–10. Philadelphia: American Philosophical Society.

1982   "Fox Lake Subsistence and Settlement: New Evidence from Southwestern Minnesota." *Minnesota Archaeologist,* vol. 41, no. 1 (spring–summer):45–52.

1989   "Ice Age Hunters in Minnesota." *IMA Quarterly Newsletter* (Institute for Minnesota Archaeology), vol. 4, no. 3 (Sept.):[4]–[5].

1991   "Final Report to the Minnesota Historical Society for Contract 90-C2443: Radiocarbon Assays of Bone from the Browns Valley Skeleton." St. Paul: Science Museum of Minnesota. Copy in SHPO.

Shay, C. T.

1971   *The Itasca Bison Kill Site: An Ecological Analysis.* Minnesota Prehistoric Archaeology Series, [no. 6]. St. Paul: Minnesota Historical Society.

1978   "Late Prehistoric Bison and Deer Use in the Eastern Prairie-Forest Border." *Plains Anthropologist,* Memoir 14, vol. 23, no. 82, pt. 2:194–212.

Shay, R. K., see Knudson, R.

Sibley, H. H.

1950   *Iron Face: The Adventures of Jack Frazer, Frontier Warrior, Scout, and Hunter. A Narrative Recorded by "Walker-in-the-Pines" (Henry Hastings Sibley),* ed. T. C. Blegen and S. A. Davidson. Chicago: Caxton Club.

Sigstad, J. S.

1970   "A Report of the Archeological Investigations, Pipestone National Monument, 1965–1966." *Journal of the Iowa Archeological Society* 17 (Dec.):[i]–[51].

Sigstad, J. S., and J. K. Sigstad

1973a   *Archaeological Field Notes of W. H. Over,* ed. Sigstad and Sigstad. Research Bulletin, no. 1. [Vermillion]: South Dakota State Archaeologist, Department of Education and Cultural Affairs.

1973b   *The Sisseton Mound: A Tribal Project.* Archaeological Studies Circular, no. 14. Vermillion: W. H. Over Dakota Museum, University of South Dakota.

Skaar, K.

1991   "Field Completion Report: Heyman's Creek Archaeological Data Recovery Project: Minnesota Department of Transportation: S. P. 5202-37: For Reconstruction of T. H. 14 from T. H. 15 at New Ulm to T. H. 99 at Nicollet, Nicollet County." St. Paul: Minnesota Historical Society. Copy in SHPO.

Smith, G. H.

1938 "Archaeological Work at Ft. Ridgely, Minnesota, 1936–1937." *Minnesota Archaeologist,* vol. 4, no. 2 (Feb.):13–16.

1941 *Archaeological Report on Big Stone Lake Burial Mound,* by Smith and the Minnesota State-wide Archaeological and Historical Survey Project. [St. Paul]. Copy in MHS.

Snortland-Coles, S.

1983 "A Reassessment of Northern Plains Woodland Burial Complexes." Paper presented at the 41st annual Plains Conference, Rapid City, S.Dak., Nov. 2–5. Copy in author's possession.

[South Dakota], State Lakes Preservation Committee

1977 "A Plan for the Classification, Preservation, and Restoration of Lakes in Northeastern South Dakota." Sponsored by the State of South Dakota and the Old West Regional Commission.

Spector, J., and E. Johnson, eds.

1985 *Archaeology, Ecology and Ethnohistory of the Prairie-Forest Border Zone of Minnesota and Manitoba.* Reprints in Anthropology, vol. 31. Lincoln, Nebr.: J & L Reprint Co.

Springer, J. W., and S. R. Witkowski

1982 "Siouan Historical Linguistics and Oneota Archaeology." In *Oneota Studies,* ed. Gibbon, 69–83.

Stanley, V.

1980 "Paleoecology of the Arctic-Steppe Mammoth Biome." *Current Anthropology* 21 (Oct.):663–66.

Steece, F. V.

1972 "Ice-Stagnation Drift, Coteau des Prairies, South Dakota." In *Field Trip Guide Book,* by the Minnesota Geological Survey, 35–47.

Stevens, J. H.

1890 *Personal Recollections of Minnesota and Its People, and Early History of Minneapolis.* Minneapolis: Privately published.

Stewart, K. W., and C. C. Lindsay

1983 "Postglacial Dispersal of Lower Invertebrates in the Lake Agassiz Region." In *Glacial Lake Agassiz,* ed. Teller and Clayton, 391–419.

Stewart, R. E., and H. A. Kantrud

1971 *Classification of Natural Ponds and Lakes in the Glaciated Prairie Region.* Resource Publication, 92. Washington, D.C.: Bureau of Sport Fisheries and Wildlife.

Struever, S.

1968 "A Re-Examination of Hopewell in Eastern North America." Ph.D. diss., University of Chicago.

Syms, E. L.

1977 "Cultural Ecology and Ecological Dynamics of the Ceramic Period in Southwestern Manitoba." *Plains Anthropologist,* Memoir 12, vol. 22, no. 76, pt. 2.

Tatum, L. S., and R. Shutler Jr.

1980 "Bone Tool Technology and Subsistence Activity at the Cherokee Sewer Site." In *Cherokee Excavations,* ed. D. C. Anderson and Semken, 239–55.

Teller, J. T., and L. Clayton, eds.

1983 *Glacial Lake Agassiz.* Geological Association of Canada Special Paper, 26. St. John's, Nfld.: The Association.

Tiffany, J. A.

1981 "A Compendium of Radiocarbon Dates for Iowa Archaeological Sites." *Plains Anthropologist,* vol. 26, no. 91:55–73.

1982a *Chan-ya-ta: A Mill Creek Village.* Report, 15. Iowa City: Office of the State Archaeologist, University of Iowa.

1982b *A Preliminary Report on the Arthur Site, East Okoboji Lake, Iowa,* ed. Tiffany. Research Papers, vol. 7, no. 1. Iowa City: Office of the State Archaeologist, University of Iowa.

1983 "An Overview of the Middle Missouri Tradition." In *Prairie Archaeology,* ed. Gibbon, 87–108.

Transeau, E. N.

1935 "The Prairie Peninsula." *Ecology* 16 (July):423–37.

Trow, T. L.

1979 "The Prehistory of Brown and Redwood Counties: An Archaeological Survey of the Cottonwood River Watershed." St. Paul: Minnesota Statewide Archaeological Survey, SHPO. Copy in SHPO.

1981 "Surveying the Route of the Root: An Archaeological Reconnaissance in Southeastern Minnesota." In *Current Directions in Midwestern Archaeology: Selected Papers from the Mankato Conference,* comp. and ed. S. F. Anfinson, 91–107. Occasional Publications in Minnesota Anthropology, no. 9. St. Paul: Minnesota Archaeological Society.

Trygg, J. W.

1964 *Composite Map of the United States Land Surveyors' Original Plats and Field Notes.* Minnesota Series, Sheet 3. Ely, Minn.: J. Wm. Trygg.

U.S. National Oceanic and Atmospheric Administration

1974 *Climates of the States: A Practical Reference Containing Basic Climatological Data of the United*

States. 2 vols. [Port Washington, N.Y.: Water Information Center].

Valentine, J. H.

1969 "An Archaic Burial and a Workshop Site Near New Ulm." *Minnesota Archaeologist*, vol. 30, no. 3:72–75.

Van der Zee, J.

1913 "Captain James Allen's Dragoon Expedition from Fort Des Moines, Territory of Iowa, in 1844." *Iowa Journal of History and Politics* 11:68–108.

Van Zant, K. L.

1976 "Late- and Postglacial Vegetational History of Northern Iowa." Ph.D. diss., University of Iowa.

1979 "Late Glacial and Postglacial Pollen and Plant Macrofossils from Lake West Okoboji, Northwestern Iowa." *Quaternary Research* 12:358–80.

Vondracek, B., and K. W. Gobalet

1982 "Fish Remains." In *Preliminary Report*, ed. Tiffany, 133–39.

Waite, P. J.

1974 "The Climate of Iowa." In *Climates of the States*, by the U.S. National Oceanic and Atmospheric Administration, 2:657–75.

Walker, P. H.

1966 *Postglacial Environments in Relation to Landscape and Soils on the Cary Drift, Iowa.* Research Bulletin 549. Ames: Agriculture and Home Economics Experiment Station, Iowa State University.

Ward, D. J. H.

1905 "The Investigation of the Okoboji Mounds and the Finds." *Iowa Journal of History and Politics* 3:427–35.

Waters, T. F.

1977 *The Streams and Rivers of Minnesota.* Minneapolis: University of Minnesota Press.

Watrall, C.

1967 "An Analysis of the Bone, Stone and Shell Materials from the Cambria Focus." Master's thesis, University of Minnesota.

1968 "Analysis of Unmodified Stone Material from the Cambria Site." *Journal* (Minnesota Academy of Science) 35:4–8.

1974 "Subsistence Pattern Change at the Cambria Site: A Review and Hypothesis." In *Aspects*, ed. E. Johnson, 138–42.

1976 "Ecotones and Environmental Adaption Strategies in the Prehistory of Northwestern Minnesota." Ph.D. diss., University of Minnesota.

Watson, P. J.

1976 "In Pursuit of Prehistoric Subsistence: A Comparative Account of Some Contemporary Flotation Techniques." *Midcontinental Journal of Archaeology*, vol. 1, no. 1:77–100.

Watts, W. A., and R. C. Bright

1968 "Pollen, Seed, and Mollusk Analysis of a Sediment Core from Pickerel Lake, Northeastern South Dakota." *Geological Society of America Bulletin* 79 (July):855–76.

Webster, C. L.

1887 "Ancient Mounds and Earth-works in Floyd and Cerro Gordo Counties, Iowa." In *Annual Report of the Board of Regents of the Smithsonian Institution, 1887*, pt. 1:575–89. Washington, D.C.: GPO, 1889.

Wedel, M. M.

1974 "Le Sueur and the Dakota Sioux." In *Aspects*, ed. E. Johnson, 157–71.

Wedel, W. R.

1961 *Prehistoric Man on the Great Plains.* Norman: University of Oklahoma Press.

1964 "The Great Plains." In *Prehistoric Man in the New World*, ed. J. D. Jennings and E. Norbeck, 193–220. Chicago: University of Chicago Press.

Wegner, S. A.

1979 "Analysis of Seed Remains from the Chan-Ya-Ta Site (13BV1), A Mill Creek Village in N.W. Iowa." *South Dakota Archaeology* 3:1–80.

Wheeler, R. P.

1963 "The Stutsman Focus: An Aboriginal Culture Complex in the Jamestown Reservoir Area, North Dakota." In *River Basin Surveys Papers*, ed. F. H. H. Roberts Jr., no. 30, p. 167–233. Smithsonian Institution, Bureau of American Ethnology, Bulletin 185. Washington, D.C.: GPO.

White, R.

1978 "The Winning of the West: The Expansion of the Western Sioux in the Eighteenth and Nineteenth Centuries." *Journal of American History* 65 (Sept.):319–43.

Wilford, L. A.

1937 "Minnesota Archaeology: With Special Reference to the Mound Area." Ph.D. diss., Harvard University.

1941 "A Tentative Classification of the Prehistoric Cultures of Minnesota." *American Antiquity* 6:231–49.

1945a "The Cambria Village Site [1941]." Ms. Copy in SHPO.

1945b   "Three Village Sites of the Mississippi Pattern in Minnesota." *American Antiquity* 11:32–40.

1946a   "Owen D. Jones Village Site." Ms. Copy in SHPO.

[ca. 1946]b   "The Fox Lake Village Site." Ms. Copy in SHPO.

1951   "The Gillingham Site." Ms. Copy in SHPO.

[ca. 1954]a   "The Big Slough Village Site." Ms. Copy in SHPO.

[ca. 1954]b   "The Great Oasis Village Site." Ms. Copy in SHPO.

1954c   "The LaMoille Rock Shelter." *Minnesota Archaeologist,* vol. 19, no. 2 (Apr.):17–24.

1955   "A Revised Classification of the Prehistoric Cultures of Minnesota." *American Antiquity* 21:130–42.

[ca. 1956]   "The Lewis Mounds." Ms. Copy in SHPO.

[ca. 1958]a   "The Shady Dell Enclosure." Ms. Copy in SHPO.

[ca. 1958]b   "Zacharias Village Site." Ms. Copy in author's possession.

1960a   "The First Minnesotans." In *Minnesota Heritage: A Panoramic Narrative of the Historical Development of the North Star State,* ed. L. M. Brings, 40–79. Minneapolis: T. S. Denison.

1960b   "A Sickle from the Great Oasis Site in Minnesota." *Plains Anthropologist,* vol. 5, no. 9:28–29.

1961   "The Pedersen Site at Lake Benton." Ms. Copy in SHPO.

1962   "The Village Site at Mountain Lake." Ms. Copy in SHPO.

1970   *Burial Mounds of the Red River Headwaters.* Minnesota Prehistoric Archaeology Series, [no. 5]. St. Paul: Minnesota Historical Society.

Wilford, L. A., E. Johnson, and J. Vicinus

1969   *Burial Mounds of Central Minnesota: Excavation Reports.* Minnesota Prehistoric Archaeology Series, [no. 1]. St. Paul: Minnesota Historical Society.

Willey, G. R., and P. Phillips

1958   *Method and Theory in American Archaeology.* Chicago: University of Chicago Press.

Williams, P. M.

1975   "The Williams Site (13 PM 50): A Great Oasis Component in Northwest Iowa." *Journal of the Iowa Archeological Society* 22 (Dec.):1–33.

Williams, W., Sr.

1869   "History of Webster County, Iowa." *Annals of Iowa,* 1st ser., 7:282–93, 327–46.

Wilson, J. N.

1958   "The Limnology of Certain Prairie Lakes in Minnesota." *American Midland Naturalist,* vol. 59, no. 2:418–37.

Winchell, N. H.

1911   *The Aborigines of Minnesota: A Report on the Collections of Jacob V. Brower, and on the Field Surveys and Notes of Alfred J. Hill and Theodore H. Lewis,* by the Minnesota Historical Society, collated by Winchell. St. Paul: The Society.

Winchell, N. H., and W. Upham

1884–88   *The Geology of Minnesota,* by the Geological and Natural History Survey of Minnesota. 6 vols. in 7. Vols. 1 (1884) and 2 (1888) by Winchell, assisted by Upham. Minneapolis: Johnson, Smith & Harrison, State Printers, 1884–1901.

Winham, R. P., E. J. Lueck, and L. A. Hannus

1985   "Cultural Resource Reconnaissance Survey of Minnehaha County, South Dakota [Within the Lower Big Sioux Study Unit and a Small Portion of the Vermillion Basin Study Unit]." Submitted to the Historical Preservation Center, Office of Cultural Preservation, Vermillion, S.Dak. Archeological Contract Series, no. 17. Sioux Falls, S.Dak.: Archeology Laboratory of the Center for Western Studies, Augustana College.

Wittry, W. L.

1959   "Archeological Studies of Four Wisconsin Rockshelters." *Wisconsin Archeologist,* n.s., 40:137–267.

Wood, W. R.

1971   *Biesterfeldt: A Post-Contact Coalescent Site on the Northeastern Plains.* Smithsonian Contributions to Anthropology, no. 15. Washington, D.C.: Smithsonian Institution Press.

1985   "The Plains-Lakes Connection: Reflections from a Western Perspective." In *Archaeology,* ed. Spector and Johnson, 1–8.

Woolworth, A. R., and M. A. Hall, eds.

1978   *Some Studies of Minnesota Prehistoric Ceramics: Papers Presented at the First Council for Minnesota Archeology Symposium, 1976.* Occasional Publications in Minnesota Anthropology, no. 2. St. Paul: Minnesota Archaeological Society.

Woolworth, A. R., and N. L. Woolworth

1980   "Eastern Dakota Settlement and Subsistence Patterns Prior to 1851." *Minnesota Archaeologist,* vol. 39, no. 2:70–89.

Wormington, H. M.

1957   *Ancient Man in North America.* Popular Series, no. 4. Denver: Denver Museum of Natural History.

Wright, H. E., Jr.

1972   "Quaternary History of Minnesota." In *Geology of Minnesota: A Centennial Volume in Honor of George M. Schwartz,* ed. P. K. Sims and G. B. Morey, 515–47. [St. Paul]: Minnesota Geological Survey.

1974   "The Environment of Early Man in the Great Lakes Region." In *Aspects,* ed. E. Johnson, 8–14.

1987   "Synthesis; The Land South of the Ice Sheets." In *North America and Adjacent Oceans during the Last Deglaciation,* ed. W. F. Ruddiman and Wright, 479–88. The Geology of North America, vol. K-3. Boulder, Colo.: Geological Society of America.

Wright, H. E., Jr., C. L. Matsch, and E. J. Cushing

1973   "Superior and Des Moines Lobes." In *The Wisconsinan Stage,* ed. R. F. Black, R. P. Goldthwait, and H. B. Willman, 153–85. Memoir 136. [Boulder, Colo.]: Geological Society of America.

Wright, H. E., Jr., T. C. Winter, and H. L. Patten

1963   "Two Pollen Diagrams from Southeastern Minnesota: Problems in the Regional Late-Glacial and Postglacial Vegetational History." *Geological Society of America Bulletin* 74 (Nov.):1371–96.

Yarnell, R. A.

1964   *Aboriginal Relationships between Culture and Plant Life in the Upper Great Lakes Region.* Museum of Anthropology, Anthropological Papers, no. 23. Ann Arbor: University of Michigan.

Young, D., S. Patrick, and D. G. Steele

1987   "An Analysis of the Paleoindian Double Burial from Horn Shelter No. 2, in Central Texas." *Plains Anthropologist,* vol. 32, no. 117:275–98.

Zimmerman, L. J.

1985   *Peoples of Prehistoric South Dakota.* Lincoln: University of Nebraska Press.

Zumberge, J. H.

1952   *The Lakes of Minnesota: Their Origin and Classification.* Minnesota Geological Survey, Bulletin 35. Minneapolis: University of Minnesota Press.

Glossary

alluvial soils deposited by moving water, such as those found in stream beds or floodplains

Archaic an archaeological tradition that follows the Paleoindian and lasts until about 500 B.C., when people began exhibiting more regionally based hunting-and-gathering economics and used ground stone tools as well as spear points with notched or stemmed bases.

artifacts objects altered or manufactured by humans

biface a stone tool with flake scars on both faces

BP Before Present (set at 1950)

burial forms *Primary* burials contain remains that were deposited when the body was intact, usually shortly after the time of death; they can be either *flexed* or *extended*. *Secondary* burials contain remains that were deposited when the body was not fully intact; they are often missing some elements and can be assembled like a *bundle.*

ceramics pottery artifacts

chalcedony an opaque, silicate mineral preferred for making stone tools because of its ease of flaking and resulting sharp edges; chalcedony is often called flint in Europe.

chert a very fine-grained rock that can be shaped by removing flakes or chips

colluvial soils deposited by the movement of sediments down hill slopes

conoidal conelike in shape

dendro-correction a dating technique that utilizes the patterns and spacing of annual tree rings preserved in wood samples to verify the accuracy of radiocarbon dating

fauna refers to animals; faunal remains usually consist of bone, teeth, shell, or scales

flaking process of removing small pieces of stone from a larger piece by the application of pressure or percussion

flora refers to plants; floral remains usually consist of pollen, charred seeds and wood, or phytoliths (fossilized plants)

fluted points spear points thinned by the removal of large, longitudinal flakes to aid in binding the point to the spear shaft

in situ a Latin term meaning "in place," referring to archaeological remains that were discovered or remain in their original depositional context

lithics stone artifacts, including tools and discarded chips

lacustrine relating to or formed in lakes

lanceolate narrow and tapering in shape

Mississippian an archaeological tradition centered along the Mississippi River from A.D. 900 to 1300, when people made shell-tempered ceramics, lived in permanent villages, and intensively cultivated corn and other crops.

Oneota an archaeological tradition of the Midwest dating from A.D. 900 to 1700; it is characterized by semi-permanent villages, maize horticulture, shell-tempered globular ceramics with high rims, and small, triangular arrowheads.

ovate oval or egglike in shape

Paleoindian an archaeological tradition in North America dating from 11,500 to 9,000 years ago, when humans hunted large mammals and made specialized stone tools including large lanceolate spear points

period a stage of cultural development given chronological limits

phase a cultural unit exhibiting artifactual similarity during a limited period of time and generally occupying a single region

Plains Village an archaeological tradition of the Plains culture area dating from A.D. 900 to 1700; it is characterized by semi-permanent villages, maize horticulture, grit-tempered globular ceramics, and small, triangular arrowheads.

points weapon tips attached to wooden shafts to form spears, lances, or arrows

preform the initial sizing and shaping of an artifact

punctates   decorative impressions in the surface of ceramic vessels made by simple pointed implements

radiocarbon dating   method for determining the approximate age (from 50,000 to 1,000 years old) of organic remains; it is based on the known rate of decay of radioactive carbon that begins when a plant or animal dies. Radiocarbon dates usually are prefaced by the name of the laboratory (e.g., Beta) that conducted the testing.

RCYBP   Radio Carbon Years Before Present (set at 1950)

sherds   pieces of broken pottery vessels

site   any location that shows evidences of human occupation

stratigraphy   the successive layers of natural and cultural levels at a site

taiga   moist subarctic forest dominated by spruces and firs

temper   use of sand, grit, or rock to bring clay to a workable state and reduce shrinkage upon drying

till   nonstratified sediment deposited by a glacier

tradition   a major cultural unit exhibiting long-term continuity of artifact styles and subsistence patterns, represented by large groups of sites in multiple regions

type   a basic unit of archaeological analysis referring to a group of artifacts which share stylistic attributes

typesite   any site regarded as the first or most typical example of a particular culture or tradition

uniface   a stone tool with flakes removed from only one face

ware   a group of ceramic types that are similar because of the same manufacturing techniques, shapes, and surface finishes

Woodland   an archaeological tradition dating from 500 B.C. to A.D. 1200, when people practiced horticulture, made pottery, used the bow and arrow, buried their dead in cemeteries marked by mounds of earth, and lived in semipermanent villages

Minnesota Prehistoric Archaeology Series

*1. *Burial Mounds of Central Minnesota: Excavation Reports* (1969) by Lloyd A. Wilford, Elden Johnson, and Joan Vicinus

*2. *The Archaeology of Petaga Point: The Preceramic Component* (1969) by Peter Bleed

*3. *The Prehistoric Peoples of Minnesota* (1988) by Elden Johnson

5. *Burial Mounds of the Red River Headwaters* (1970) by Lloyd A. Wilford

6. *The Itasca Bison Kill Site: An Ecological Analysis* (1971) by C. Thomas Shay

7. *Roster of Excavated Prehistoric Sites in Minnesota to 1972* (1972) by Jan E. Streiff

8. *The Laurel Culture in Minnesota* (1973) by James B. Stoltman

*9. *The Arvilla Complex* (1973) by Elden Johnson

*10. *The Sheffield Site: An Oneota Site on the St. Croix River* (1973) by Guy E. Gibbon

11. *Aspects of Upper Great Lakes Anthropology: Papers in Honor of Lloyd A. Wilford* (1974) edited by Elden Johnson

12. *The Jeffers Petroglyphs Site: A Survey and Analysis of the Carvings* (1976) by Gordon A. Lothson

*13. *The Mississippian Occupation of the Red Wing Area* (1979) (microfiche) by Guy E. Gibbon

*14. *Southwestern Minnesota Archaeology: 12,000 Years in the Prairie Lake Region* (1997) by Scott F. Anfinson

*Available for sale from the Minnesota Historical Society Press